Cack-Handed

Cack-Handed

A MEMOIR

Gina Yashere

AMISTAD
— 35 —

An Imprint of HarperCollinsPublishers

CACK-HANDED. Copyright © 2022 by Gina Yashere. All rights reserved.
Printed in the United States of America. No part of this book may be used
or reproduced in any manner whatsoever without written permission
except in the case of brief quotations embodied in critical articles and
reviews. For information, address HarperCollins Publishers, 195 Broadway,
New York, NY 10007.

HarperCollins books may be purchased for educational, business, or
sales promotional use. For information, please email the Special Markets
Department at SPsales@harpercollins.com.

FIRST HARPERCOLLINS PAPERBACK PUBLISHED IN 2022

Designed by SBI Book Arts, LLC

All photographs courtesy of the author

Library of Congress Cataloging-in-Publication Data is available upon request.

ISBN 978-0-06-296172-3

22 23 24 25 26 LSC 10 9 8 7 6 5 4 3 2 1

To my mum. Who else.
This book is about me,
but really about her.

*The moment anyone tries to demean or degrade
you in any way, you have to know how
great you are. Nobody would bother to beat
you down if you were not a threat.*

—CICELY TYSON

When I was a kid, my mum would speak in proverbs. She had one for every occasion without fail. EVERY. SINGLE. OCCASION. A proverb was used to make a point, prove a point, illustrate a point, and sometimes didn't seem to have a point, but Mum always had one ready to whip out like a Nigerian gunslinger. I could have sworn she made some of them up! Having grown up and discussed at length with other children of Africans, it seems that my siblings and I were not alone, and African parents all over the globe were bombarding their kids with these sayings. Looking back and deciphering these proverbs, there are some wise ones, some hilarious ones, and straight-up crazy ones. As an ode to all those African parents, each chapter of the book is headed by some of mine and my mum's favorites.

The definition of cack-handed is left-handed, which I am, and also clumsy and awkward, which I am. It also represents the unconventional track my life and career have taken.

This is a book about following your dreams.

It's not one of those self-help ladi-dadi, anything is possible if you just believe, and eat nothing but almonds and kale–type books.

This is a book about wanting something and going for it, despite how ridiculous, impossible, and stupid it sounds to other people.

This book is about trying. Whether you succeed or not.

You can judge at the end of the book whether or not you think I've succeeded, but you better believe I've given it a go. (Or given it a shot, for Americans who prefer everything to have a gun reference.)

Enjoy.

Contents

CONTENTS

Cack-Handed

1

Man Is like Pepper— You Only Know Him When You've Ground Him

My grandmother Patience Ebuwa Obaseki died under suspicious circumstances. My mother believes that her father's other wives finally succeeded in getting rid of her, by poisoning her food. When she died, she had a large mysterious mark on her throat, from either the poison or the injuries sustained during the poisoning.

I don't know much about her, and I never saw her, not even in a picture, but my mother tells me that she was a lively and humorous character, and when my mother was a little girl in Nigeria, she would entertain my mother with vividly funny stories and made-up songs. My grandmother was the mother of six children and the first of several wives of a wealthy chief and businessman, Samson Okankan Obaseki, in Benin City, in southern Nigeria. My grandfather was a member of a family that had links to the ruling echelons of the Benin Empire.

Polygamy was widely practiced in Nigeria before British Christian missionaries came along and told them that the shit was barbaric and sinful. It didn't dawn on or even seem to matter to the missionaries that polygamy was about survival—more wives meant more on your team! The wealthier a man was, the bigger the compound he could own and the more wives he could take care of. Many wives meant many children, and in Nigeria, having many children is highly respected and greatly envied. Kind of like in the US, where the bigger the garage, the more cars you put in it. My grandfather was the Nigerian Jay Leno. And for many of his wives, depending on how many sons they produced, this also meant more power.

My mother had thirteen brothers and sisters from the other wives of her father, but her mother was the first wife and had produced the most children, which made her the most powerful within the compound among the other wives. It also made her a target.

My grandmother actually gave birth to ten children, but mysteriously, all five boys she birthed died before they were three from mysterious illnesses, and one, even, to a dog attack. This prompted my grandmother to believe that the other, less-favored wives of her husband were practicing juju on her to undermine her standing, by casting spells and killing all her male children, which in Nigerian society, as well as the rest of patriarchy, is the more desired gender. As a result of this, my mother, Grace Nekpen-Nekpen Obaseki—the first of the surviving girls—had five younger sisters born from her mother but no living brothers.

Despite my grandmother's lack of living male children, my grandfather still adored his first wife and their girl children, and my mother was his favorite. My mother showed a keen intelligence from early childhood, and in an era when daughters were often not educated and only groomed for wifedom and motherhood, she was sent to the best private and convent boarding schools, and she traveled with her dad on many of his business trips abroad. My mum thrived in school and her further studies, qualifying as an English teacher by the time she was twenty and becoming an assistant school principal by age twenty-four. Her mother became afraid that she, as the favorite and most accomplished child of her father, would also be a target of the other wives, as had been her sons, so she begged my grandfather to send my mum out of Nigeria, to further her studies in England and get her away from the jealous other wives. Eventually, after my grandmother's death, my distraught grandfather sent Mum to London and told her never to return.

You may not have heard of the Kingdom of Benin—not to be confused with the country Benin. However, if you've ever been to a museum anywhere in the world and seen any cool as hell Edo bronze sculptures and masks, then you have. To cut a long story short, Benin was a powerful forest kingdom within what is now Nigeria. The Edo people of the kingdom were ruled by an oba, whose ultimate power was basically his ability to determine life and death for those within the confines of his multiethnic empire. The area was rich in natural resources, and from the 1400s to the mid-1500s, the Edo traded with the Portuguese, who were the first Europeans to arrive there, and then the Dutch, swapping their rubber, palm oil, pepper, and ivory for copper and brass, which Edo artists cast into various elaborate works of art. Basically, the Kingdom of Benin was the real Wakanda. (If you don't get this reference, then you have been truly living under a Jupiter-size rock.) The kingdom was an extremely advanced society, and Europeans described Benin City as one of the most beautiful and well-planned cities in the world.

Don't believe me? This is from *The Guardian*:

In 1691, the Portuguese ship captain Lourenco Pinto observed: "Great Benin, where the king resides, is larger than Lisbon; all the streets run straight and as far as the eye can see. The houses are large, especially that of the king, which is richly decorated and has fine columns. The city is wealthy and industrious. It is so well governed that theft is unknown and the people live in such security that they have no doors to their houses.

In contrast, London at the same time is described by Bruce Holsinger, professor of English at the University of Virginia, as being a city where "thievery, prostitution, murder, bribery and a thriving black market made the medieval city ripe for exploitation by those with a skill for the quick blade or picking a pocket."[1]

Most Westerners assume that it was Europeans who brought civilization to Africa and that Africans should be grateful, but in London, they were still throwing their piss out their windows and having sex in shit-filled alleys while the area now known as Nigeria had a thriving, advanced social network. This is true of many other civilizations throughout Africa and the world before European contact.

The Edo, also called the Bini, are originally from what is now known as southern Nigeria. Benin City was the center of the Kingdom of Benin, which had its heyday from the fourteenth to the seventeenth centuries. Their territory is west of the Niger River and extends from the northern hills down to the swamps of the Niger Delta. The Edo people were very advanced and controlled most of the trade happening in this area. The Brits wanted a piece of this action, but the oba put certain restrictions on what the Edo were or were not allowed to trade. The Brits wanted to just take all the Edo people's shit, using Benin's wealth and re-sources to expand and enrich the British Empire. They tried to do a sneaky invasion of Benin in 1896, but they had their asses handed to them by the Edo warriors. The Brits got their revenge a year later, returning to Benin with a huge army to undertake one of their infamous "punitive" expeditions—capturing the oba, exiling him, and then burning Benin City to the ground. The Brits looted all of the bronze, ivory, and other artifacts, and loaded it up on their warships to take back to London, selling it to British and European museums. The money raised through the sale of these precious goods helped pay for the looting army. Ahhh, the circle of life . . . A recent *Guardian* article declared the "British museum is the world's largest receiver of stolen goods."[2]

If only the Edo people had had vibranium (another *Black Panther* reference for the ignorant amongst you) . . . The Brits continued their stranglehold on Nigeria through slavery and co-lonialism, as did other European countries throughout Africa, eventually slicing up the continent and sharing it amongst them-selves like a huge pie. My parents are descendants of those proud Edo people.

Love, like rain, does not choose the grass on which it falls.

It was in England that my mum met my dad, who was also from Benin City. She went all the way to London to meet the boy next door. From the 1950s through the 1970s, England was not the most welcoming place for Black people, in that it wasn't wel-coming at all. As well as the Nigerian influx, due to the Brits' aforementioned meddling in Nigerian geographical boundaries, there was an influx of East Indians, for pretty much the same reasons. This was coupled with the fact that the British government had invited a ton of people from the Caribbean, which was part of the Commonwealth—or should I say, from their former plantations—to help rebuild the country after World War II, to do a lot of the jobs that white English people didn't want to do, like nursing, driving buses, and sorting and delivering the mail. The problem was that the British hadn't really prepared the English natives for this influx of color, the actual results of British colonialism.

It was like a father left his family, started another elsewhere, then suddenly brought all his new kids home to live with his original family, to help with the housework and share the resources. Instead of him starting a family elsewhere, a closer analogy would be more like he went to another country, tied up a bunch of women in a basement, and then brought over the resulting offspring. The image of England of the '50s and '60s was all bowler hats, canes, tea and crumpets, the genteel cry of "Tally-ho!" It was also a time when people had no problem with posting signs on their doors that said, NO BLACKS, NO DOGS, NO IRISH, so, unsurprisingly, adequate accommodations were hard to come by, even when you had more than sufficient means, as my mum did.

This is why a lot of the neighborhoods Black people found themselves living in—raising their families, working, creating additional markets (as my mum did by selling African goods)— didn't have the best living conditions. Notting Hill and Brixton were such neighborhoods, and that explains why Black people hated the movie *Notting Hill*. Who would have known, watching that film, that it was once a Black area and the location of one of England's worst race riots? Or that from the '50s to the '70s its houses were managed by slumlords? It was one of the few places in London where Black people were able to rent rooms, due to the xenophobia and suspicion Brits had for us. Black people stayed regardless, made the area cool, and started a yearly Notting Hill street carnival (similar to New York's Labor Day Parade) that put London on the map, but then they were driven out by gentrification, so by the time the movie came out, Hugh Grant was the face of the area, and the only Black person with a speaking part was a security guard. That would have been like shooting a remake of Spike Lee's *Do the Right Thing* but with Radio Raheem played by Justin Timberlake.

There was a small, thriving Nigerian social scene in London in the '60s, and that is where my mum and dad met. There were many Nigerians studying in the UK, as a result of the British interference in Nigeria, and the fact Nigerians had been taught that the British education system was superior to their own.

To cut a long story short, after slavery was outlawed in England, the Brits colonized Nigeria in order to keep control of both its resources and its people. They decided to teach Nigerian children to read (in English), write, and do arithmetic. Sounds very generous of them. They convinced Nigerians that this was a superior style of learning to their current system of orally passing down to the younger generation skills that benefited the community as a whole, such as farming, fishing, traditional medicine, and blacksmithing. Kids were taken from their families and put in boarding schools to be fully immersed in the Western values system. Nothing wrong with a bit of literacy and maths, I hear you thinking. But in so doing, the Brits convinced Nigerian families to place more importance on individual enrichment via examinations, rankings, and performance statistics than on traditional cultural upbringing. Basically, they swapped out community spirit for good old individualistic capitalism.

When Nigeria finally gained independence from the Brits in 1960, the country was left in some disarray due to tribal conflicts, for the most part caused by the arbitrary borders the Brits had drawn up, and because the Brits had installed puppet leaders to continue managing their colonial interests, even though they were supposed to have withdrawn. This led to various coups and infighting. After an initial economic boom due to how much oil and natural resources Nigeria had, a mixture of mismanagement, corruption, and greed among some top members of government led to a recession, a devaluation of Nigeria's currency, and massive unemployment. The government's inability to afford the high wages of its civil servants and teachers led to strikes and a general collapse of Nigerian infrastructure, including the education system. Nigerians who could afford to focused on getting their children educated outside the country, in order to give them a better chance of gainful employment later.

Cue Mum and Dad ending up in Europe to study.

My dad, Yusuf Kumbi Iyasere, came from Nigeria to study for his master's degree in Prague, capital of what was then Czechoslovakia, in central Europe. (Side note: you might have noticed my dad's last name has no *h*. The *s* is pronounced "ssh," but apparently Europeans couldn't get their heads round that, so my dad added an *h* to appease them. Either that or my parents told me that story to cover the evidence of a mistake on my birth certificate. I would later drop the *I* when embarking on my comedy career because it's essentially silent and people kept mispronouncing my name as "Ayesha." I'm the only person in the family to spell my name Y-a-s-h-e-r-e.) Like my mother, Dad came from a well-connected Benin City family. His brother lived in South London with a friend, who was my mum's distant cousin. One day when my dad visited his brother, my mum's cousin suggested they all go over to visit my mum in North London. Mum was quite eligible at the time, with her background and accomplishments; there were many men interested in her, including my father's brother.

When the men arrived in North London, my mother invited them in for tea. They sat and chatted—probably about the goings-on in Nigeria, the challenges of immigrant living, probably with Elvis or Jim Reeves playing in the background, because for some reason Africans loved those white crooners. After it got late, the men left for the long Tube ride back to South London, after which my father told the other two men that he was going to pop out for a cigarette. But that's not what he did. He hopped right back on the Tube and took that hour-long journey all the way back to North London. He found a phone box near my mum's house and dialed her number, which he had memorized while visiting earlier by making sure he sat next to the phone labeled with its number (as they were in the olden days).

My mum answered, "Hello?"

"Do you know who this is? I was sitting in your house not long ago."

"Why are you calling me?"

"Because I'm near your house. I would like to come back."

Apparently, stalking was an effective wooing technique in the late '60s, as my mum didn't call the police but instead allowed him in, and they talked into the early hours. They soon became an item, the "it" couple on London's Nigerian social scene, like a Kanye and Kim but without the butt implants and MAGA hats. My dad's brother was furious, since my dad had snagged her right out from under his nose. Despite reservations from both their families—Mum's side because although he was from a well-known family, his family was not wealthy, and Dad's side because he was a Muslim and would convert to Christianity to marry my mum in a church—he put a ring on her finger, and they decided to make a life in England together. Well, not quite together. While my mother stayed in London, my dad went back and forth to Prague to finish his master's. My mother was obviously charmed by his "Go get 'em" attitude.

Unable to get work as a teacher, due to the attitudes evident in the previously mentioned rental signs, Mum enrolled in a secretarial course and did various admin jobs way below her skill set while also financially supporting my dad with his studies. My mother paid for his accommodations, clothes, and even his food. She saw this as an investment in her future family and figured that once he had more qualifications, he'd be in a better position for both himself and the family when he returned to London. In the meantime, he'd pop over to London whenever school was on hiatus, and despite them living in two different countries, they got busy and started their new family.

Both of my parents had a child each from previous relationships. My dad, a son, whom I found out about many years later because Nigerians are the Ray Donovans of Africa and love to keep family secrets, and my mum, a daughter, from a short-lived relationship when she first arrived in London. This was Taiwo, who Mum sent back to Nigeria temporarily, to stay with her extended family, while she and her new husband set up a family unit long distance. Taiwo's name in Yoruba roughly means "First to taste the world," because she is the first of twins. Her twin brother would have been called Kehinde, which means "One after Taiwo," but he didn't make it out of the womb alive, a fact I didn't work out till I was sixteen. Nigerians don't tend to talk about death, and coupled with their love of secrets, that meant that through most of my childhood I assumed I had an older brother living in Nigeria.

The first new Iyashere was me. I was born eight years after my sister Taiwo.

My full name is Regina Obedapo Ebuwa Iyashere. For most of my childhood I was called by the shortened version of my middle name, Dapo. At the time of my birth, Mum lived in a house in North London on Regina Road, which had been turned into ten one-room flats, each occupied by families from different parts of Nigeria. Yep, my first name is after the road my mum lived on—so my mother actually started the naming-your-kid-after-a-location trend waaaay before David and Victoria Beckham named their kid Brooklyn. I'm just glad I wasn't born on Fanny Hands Lane (that's a real London street).

I was born with a large birthmark in the same spot as my grandmother's mark on her neck, the one that appeared when she was poisoned to death. This brought great joy to my mum, as her mother had been returned to her. Nigerians are huge believers in reincarnation, and Mum has often told me that when she and her sisters were young, they'd often laugh as my grandmother regaled them with stories of who she would come back as in her next life. My grandmother had said she would return as the exact opposite of who she actually was, one of many wives of a Nigerian chief. She said she would return speaking perfect English, unfettered by any man, unburdened by children; she was going to see the world, work a man's job if she wanted, and be a much freer spirit, doing whatever she wanted. Sound familiar?

Being a reincarnation got me the second middle name of Ebuwa, after my grandma, and also the family nickname "Granny," which my mum still calls me to this day. I would have preferred a better nickname, like "Throat Ninja," but whatever. "Granny" is what I got, and my mum takes great pleasure in dragging out those two syllables. "Grrrannnyyy!!" This also meant that I could never get rid of this birthmark, as it is essential to who I am in the family. Not that I have ever wanted to. I enjoy the story of where it came from, the link it gives me to the grandmother I never saw or knew, and it makes me feel special. No superpowers unfortunately, but hey, at least I can boast that I've lived once already.

One time I did one of those call-in psychic sessions that were big back in the day. I thought it would be fun. The psychic told me there was an older woman guiding me through life, who I assumed was my grandmother. And the way my life has gone, I do feel as though I have a guardian angel, if you will.

When I look in the mirror, I'm reminded that my life and character traits seem to have exactly matched my grandmother's next-life predictions, and I wonder if she enjoys how she turned out this time around. Most of the time, though, I don't notice my birthmark. It's just part of my body, like my eyes, or my small ears, which got me the less endearing nickname "Pigeon Head" from my brothers, though that doesn't even make sense! Pigeons don't have visible ears. But then again, my ears were pretty small, so it kind of does make sense. Kids are assholes. Anyway, the only times my birthmark comes to my attention is when people stare at it on public transport, when people ask me if it's a tattoo of a heart, when my doctor periodically asks me if it has changed shape, bled, or behaved in an otherwise sinister manner, when makeup artists ask me if I want to cover it for TV (nope), or when in the odd photo the angles are off and I look like I'm sporting a goatee. I *really* notice it then.

I'm not the only reincarnation in my family. When my mother was pregnant with my brother Dele, who came eighteen months after me, my mother's dead father visited my father in a dream. My father woke up to see the father-in-law he had never met standing by his bed in Prague. My grandfather grilled him on his family name, education, and background. He told my father that he was coming back as their next child, who would be a son, and to call him Bamidele, which means "Follow me home." It's a name often given to children born abroad or outside the father's home state or town. My father then ran to a phone box to call my mother to tell her the news. As a testament to Nigerians' belief in reincarnation, my mother didn't ask my dad why his must-be-drunk ass was calling her at 3 a.m. but rejoiced in the news of her father's imminent return . . . In a time before a baby's gender could be identified prebirth, this visit came in handy, as my mother did indeed give birth to a son—and Bamidele became his name.

2

Languages Differ, but Coughs Are the Same

My brother Dele arrived eighteen months after I did, but by the time I was born, my dad had finished his master's and decided he wanted to continue studying to gain a PhD. My mum's family was furious, wanting him to return to England, get a job, and begin supporting his growing family. My mum, who had been attracted by my dad's fierce intelligence as well as his good looks, agreed to continue the long-distance marriage and keep financing his academic dreams. Again, this support was in part love and in part an investment in the future of their new family. Another eighteen months after Dele came along, my youngest brother, Sheyi, arrived (as I said, my parents had been getting busy). But somewhere along the line, around Sheyi's conception, my parents' marriage began to break down.

When my dad finished his PhD, he was unhappy with the lack of opportunity in England. He was also under increasing pressure from his family to return to Nigeria, where he was reminded he would actually be able to use his prestigious academic qualifications, rather than collect fares on London double-decker buses or sort mail, which were the only jobs available to many Black people, particularly Black men, in England at the time.

As I have heard the story, he received a call from his sister, who told him their mother was ill and he had to come back to Nigeria to look after her, as he was the only son. Apparently, my dad had wanted his new family—Mum, me, Dele, and Sheyi (still floating in a sac of amniotic fluid at that time)—to return to Nigeria as a family unit at some point, though he as yet had no means to support us, or even get us there, and my mum was too heavily pregnant to travel anyway. My mum refused, as this diverged from their initial plan to set up home in England, where her children, who were British, were entitled to all the opportunities the UK had to offer.

My mother implored my father not to leave her alone in England with two toddlers and heavily pregnant with another child. She reasoned that my father's sister could easily take on the role of looking after his mother. Her pleas seemed to fall on deaf ears, though. My dad probably had it in his head already that his prospects would be much better in Nigeria than in England. He left when I was about two and a half years old, to care for his mother, who didn't die till ten years later.

Mum never forgave my father for leaving. She gave birth to Sheyi in a hospital, alone, in a foreign country, while all the other mothers had husbands arriving with flowers and gifts for their new babies. It didn't help that she also began to hear rumors about my father and other women in Nigeria. She closed her heart to him, although she never went through a divorce, as my father still harbored hopes of her returning to Nigeria and refused to give her one. She concentrated on her family and getting by. While I was growing up, she would often rant about how useless he was and how he'd abandoned us. Her anger and feelings of betrayal never abated. I knew not to bring him up for fear of souring her mood on any given day, so I was forced to bury my curiosity. Almost forty years would pass before I saw him again.

. . .

In London, my mum had no extended family anymore and no money, as her wealthy father had died before I was born. He'd had a car accident, and a car door had badly damaged his arm. His doctors told him that he needed to have it amputated, as the arm had an infection that would soon spread throughout his body and kill him. My grandfather basically pulled a Bob Marley: "No, I'm going to heaven with all the limbs I was born with." He refused to have the arm amputated, the infection spread, and he died. While he was sick, he told my mother's siblings not to tell her, because he didn't want her to risk returning to Nigeria, placing herself in danger from his other, still-prone-to-poisoning wives. My mum didn't find out what had happened to him until after he died. As is the patriarchy in Nigeria, my grandfather's eldest son from one of his other wives (who had also been sent to England to study but had done nothing of the sort and had only managed to impregnate an English aristocrat's daughter) returned to Nigeria under a cloud of scandal and took control of their father's land, property, and money. Although he was feckless, he still had a penis. He squandered the inheritance and left my mum with nothing.

Mum's bond with her father had been particularly strong and had defied any of the sexist stereotypes many associate with Africa. Throughout the years, her father visited her in London, but by the time of his death, it had been seven years since she'd last seen him, and her final memory of him was weighed down with a bitter load of regret.

I know that behind my mum's stoic front there is a complex array of emotions that she, like so many of us, processes through seemingly unrelated acts. I've rarely seen my mum cry, but I have seen her eat a lot of sweets. When my mum came to England, she partook of all the sugar that was available. She has never been one of those mothers who tell their children they love them, but when I was growing up, sweets were one of the ways she showed us her love. When we were good, or when she felt especially loving towards us, she'd give us sweets. She always carried goodies in her handbag, and whenever we'd hear her purse rustle, we kids became Pavlovian dogs. Our mouths would instantly start to water, and we'd strain our necks towards the rustling sound in anticipation of getting lucky and receiving her handout of treats. Her favorite sweets were once Polo mints—round white mints with a hole in the middle, like Life Savers in the US. My mum became addicted to those. She loved them. While others resort to alcohol or drugs to self-soothe, my mum's crutch, and now mine, is sugar.

The last time Mum saw her father was at Heathrow Airport. He was on his way back to Nigeria after visiting her, and she was at the airport along with her uncle to see him off. He had stepped away briefly, to get his boarding pass, and while he was gone, my mum thought she'd use the opportunity to find her favorite mints, as she had run out. She told her uncle that she would be right back.

Her uncle tried to reason with her. "Listen, your father's about to get on a flight, and he'll be back in a minute—why don't you wait, say your goodbyes to him, and then you can go get your mints?"

"I'll be back before," she promised, and off she went.

Heathrow Airport at the time was not the monolithic shopping mall it is today; it took some time to find a shop that sold the mints she wanted. And as fate would have it, her dad returned before she got back.

"Where's my daughter?"

"She's gone to get sweets," her uncle informed him.

"Well, I have to go. My flight is taking off."

By the time my mum returned, her father was already in the air. Her uncle also let her know that her father had been annoyed that he didn't get to see her again before he left. That was the last time she saw him alive. She has been unable to eat those mints ever since.

If life has beaten you severely in the face and your face is swollen, smile and act like a fat man.

After my dad went back to Nigeria, Dele and I were fostered by an old white woman while Mum reorganized her situation and prepared to have her fourth child, again alone and in a strange country. Although I use the word "fostered," no governmental entities were involved in this arrangement. This was not a case of a negligent mother having her child removed from her by some sort of child protection agency. This was a private arrangement between my mum and this woman in Devon, some 180 miles from London.

To summarize a *Guardian* article on the subject, when the British departed Nigeria in the '50s and '60s, they left behind a foreign political and economic system that they didn't really bother to teach Nigerians how to run. To put it in Gina's no-bullshit terms: the Brits came to Nigeria, raped it of all its resources, and, when they'd finished screwing it up, left the country in such a state that a lot of Nigerians chose to follow the Brits back to the UK in order to get access to the education and opportunities no longer available in their own country, with hopes of either staying to raise their families there or returning to Nigeria with newly acquired skills to help fix their country.

But being far from home meant that Nigerians were also far

removed from their own social, familial networks, which are often relied upon when raising children. For many Nigerians, the act of raising a child is seen as a collective endeavor—it takes a village. And in placing their children with British families, they reasoned they would ensure their children learned a bit of British culture.

Imagine Nigerians coming to the UK and employing British nannies! Yup, Black kids had white nannies. Let that sink in. Nigerian parents had actual Mary Poppinses . . . I don't know if you can pluralize Poppins. Okay, they weren't actual Poppinses, as they didn't live in stately homes, use umbrellas to fly, or speak like they had just swallowed Richard E. Grant while having crumpets with the queen.

This process of fostering was called "farming," and while there were some horror stories to come out of it—as in Adewale Akinnouye-Agbaje's film of the same name—luckily for me and my brother, the experience was way more like a non-magical Disney version.

In general, the nannies hired to look after Nigerian kids tended to be poorer working-class white folks, taking anywhere from one to seven kids from various families and getting paid cash under the table. The time the children spent with these foster families varied, from weeks to months to sometimes years and the children never fully returning to their Nigerian families. The singer Seal was one of these Nigerian children fostered by English parents, as was the aforementioned actor-director Adewale. It was less a spoonful of sugar and more cigarette ash in your cornflakes. But for some Nigerian parents, so inculcated by British colonialism, it was a status symbol to have their child taken care of by a white nanny. For most, like my mum, it was a pragmatic solution. They might enter into these private financial arrangements with white families in order to work or study, to get a piece of the colonial pie.

The details of a white fosterer would pass between Nigerians like a good Yelp review, while another fosterer would be found via a discreet newspaper advert. This was like a pre-internet Craigslist but without the stolen bikes. My mum found her woman via the newspaper. They met, cash was exchanged, and Dele and I went to live in a large house in the Devon countryside with an old lady who had white hair and a piano and liked to take us to car washes, where we'd sit inside her car wondrously trying to lick the soapsuds dripping down the car windows. Toddlers are so easy to entertain.

When Mum came to bring us home, I was around three years old and ran towards her excitedly, preceded by my eighteen-month-old brother, Dele. Why he was faster than me, when at that point I was twice his age, is a mystery, but as justice will have it, he fell over and began to cry. I managed to catch up, and my mother attempted to scoop us both up while she held another human in her arms, who turned out to be my newly born youngest brother, Sheyi.

I don't even know if we turned back to say goodbye to car-wash lady, such was our excitement at being reunited, but I'm sure she understood. The reason for our joy was not the new human but the fact that we had at that point not seen our mum for what felt like years, though it was probably no more than a few months. Before my mum came back for us, the lady in Devon had asked to adopt us permanently, but my mum refused, and back to London we went.

Mum had initially made her living and supported my dad doing office work at an accountancy firm, having taken courses at the Institute of Chartered Secretaries and Administrators, but finding suitable work became challenging being the sole caretaker of three young children. Mum became somewhat of an entrepreneur, selling goods that her friends would bring her from Nigeria, like leather bags and colorful traditional cloth that she would tailor into clothing on her trusty sewing machine. I remember Mum saving for over a year to buy the first computerized sewing machine that could change the type of stitch at the touch of a button. My childhood was full of colorful dresses, wraps, scarves, and meters of material. She allowed her customers to pay for the items on a hire-purchase basis, so they got the goods but were able to pay for them in installments. She kept a ledger with the names of all her customers and their payments, and every weekend she would dress us and we would do the rounds, visiting each of her customers to collect the money owed. We loved those trips. These were the times as kids we got to go to other people's homes on the estate. The distance was short. None of my mother's customers was more than a fifteen-minute walk from where we lived. But as sheltered East End kids, that short distance felt like the world. We imagined we were visiting friends, especially since a large part of my out-of-school socializing was playing with the kids of my mum's debtors while our mothers did business in the kitchen.

Later, Regina Road was no longer a suitable place to live, as our family now also included my twelve-year-old sister, Taiwo, whom my mum had sent for from Nigeria. My mother moved us all to Bethnal Green, East London, which is part of the borough of Tower Hamlets, the poorest borough in London at the time. In the 1970s, Bethnal Green was an area of street markets, drab postwar buildings, and cheap rent. It is the site of the world's first-ever council housing estate (the Boundary Estate) and was also Jack the Ripper's old haunt. But as a single mother, an immigrant, with no family or community and with a determination that her children would grow up in England, this is where our family spent the next few years.

The East End of London in the 1970s was not a nice place

to live as a white person, let alone a dark-skinned foreign family, and it was certainly far from the gentrified neighborhood it is now, with its high-end boutiques and cereal café charging the equivalent of eight dollars for a bowl of Cheerios. There was a lot of suspicion among the white working-class residents of the wave of people of color moving into the neighborhood, thus fueling racial tensions. The National Front, a Far-Right "political party," was very active in the area, preying on the xenophobia of the native white residents. NF graffiti was pretty ubiquitous on East End walls around that time. It was not uncommon to find signs that read KEEP BRITAIN WHITE, WOGS OUT, and PAKIS OUT.

The population of Bethnal Green was mainly poor working-class white people, immigrants from Bangladesh, and a sprinkling of African and Caribbean immigrant families. The community was a reflection of all the places England had gone and "civilized." My mother was one of these people. My mum's friend Mary, who was from Mauritius, was another. She and Mum would chat in the kitchen, where Mum would spread out her wares for Mary to peruse them, while we enjoyed a rare instance of being allowed to play with Mary's sons, Roger and Ronny, in another room.

We lived in Colville House, a postwar-built block of brown council flats, which in the US would be called low-income housing, or "the projects." The flat was a three-bedroom with one separate toilet and bathroom. I remember distinctly the dampness of that apartment. The walls were slimy and wet all year round and had green spots all over them from the damp, which my mum often tried to protect us from by stuffing old newspapers between the walls and the beds. But that damp often managed to transfer itself like alien spore, and we'd wake to find mold spots on our blankets and clothes. Thank goodness none of us developed any serious respiratory illnesses. I've never seen that kind of damp since, and I don't know whether it's because I've moved up in life or it's just gone the way of most phenomena of the '70s, like the Farrah Fawcett haircut and white dog shit. But that damp is why, to this day, I cannot stand blankets anywhere near me and would rather sleep in the middle of a blizzard with nothing but a scarf covering my genitalia than let a blanket touch my skin.

My mum had one bedroom, and my brothers shared the second. The third I shared with my sister Taiwo, who is eight years older than me. This was not fun for either of us. She had spent several years in Nigeria living with my mum's sister while Mum was setting up in the UK, so she came into our lives when I was a toddler.

This is a common phenomenon among African, Latin, and Caribbean communities. When parents decide to travel to another country to look for better work opportunities, they usually leave existing kids behind with their grandparents or other family members, with a view to bringing them over at a later date. In the Caribbean, the term for those kids left behind is "barrel children," a phrase coined by Dr. Claudette Crawford-Brown of the University of the West Indies, after the containers these parents regularly use to send supplies back to their children. Dr. Crawford-Brown has spent over thirty years studying the psychological effects on these kids. Often they never make it to the new country, and the ones that do may arrive years later, only to find themselves transplanted into a situation in which the parents have other children, and if the parents are working hard to make ends meet, these older "barrel" kids are typically expected to pitch in with house duties and help care for the younger children. Their feelings of abandonment, confusion, and resentment may never be acknowledged.

This is exactly the situation twelve-year-old Taiwo found herself in. I was by then four, Dele was around two and a half, and Sheyi was a year old when Taiwo came back from Nigeria. She was thrown straight into babysitting, cleaning, cooking, and all the other household chores while Mum went out to work to provide for four children alone. In a new household with three small children she had no sibling attachment to, she was expected to help look after them after school and on weekends while still a child herself, and this was compounded by the fact that she considered me and Dele spoiled. Apparently at that time she was already aware that Dele and I were the reincarnations of my mother's parents, and were therefore more loved, and even though we *all* had been born in England, she was the one who had been sent to Nigeria, where she'd had terrible experiences. Her aunt had treated her as free household help rather than a beloved niece, and from the beginning, Taiwo had felt like a second-class citizen in her own family.

I was a precocious four-year-old and spoke exactly what came to my mind, as toddlers tend to do. Not understanding where this extra adult had come from, I innocently asked my mum if she'd brought a servant over from Nigeria. I knew my mum had come from wealth, and at four, I didn't understand that we were now poor. I had no concept of class, and I made a natural four-year-old's deduction. Big stranger. Cleaning house and cooking. Equals servant. I truly believe Taiwo hated me from that day. She was stuck wiping our asses every time we did a poo, and I don't know what they put in those potato chips in the East End back then, but our assholes were like those never-ending squeezy cake decorators, and she got no respite. Her resentment at her situation needed a release, and unfortunately Dele and I were those perfect punching bags. She slapped us, pinched us, used painfully hot water when bathing us. Whatever she could do to cause us pain without leaving marks, she did. She then threatened us to keep our mouths shut.

Sheyi was not a special reincarnation child, and he was a baby, so he was spared her fury, but Dele and I from a young age lived in fear of our mum leaving the house to go to work or go shopping. We'd cling to her legs, begging her to take us with, or not to go at all, but we couldn't tell her why so instead begged her with our eyes, as we knew that if we opened our mouths, the retribution would be severe the moment that front door closed. Mum never understood. She was simply leaving her babies with her trusted older daughter.

From a young age we were taught to respect Taiwo as an adult because of the age gap, and anyway, to us, she *was* an adult. We had never seen her play, have fun, be a child! And so we never saw her as a sister or compatriot in that sense. We knew she was our sister in the literal sense, and she was still a young child forced into a situation above her control, but to us, she was just an extension of our mother's harsh discipline.

Her having to share a room with me, and trying to protect her belongings and anything vaguely shiny from this noisy destructive dwarf, couldn't have been fun for her either. She had a record player and a wonderful music collection, and as I grew up, through her—or should I say through sneaking and playing her records when she was out—I discovered the Jacksons, Rick James, and Grace Jones, whose fierceness I still channel to this day. But my sister could always tell when I'd touched her stuff. I swear she must have set booby traps. There must have been single hairs over door openings, ornaments moved two millimeters to the left, black lights, and luminol. Every day was like a scene from *Misery*. I never lost a foot, but I got hit a lot in that room. I still kept touching her stuff, though. I was nothing if not persistent. My sister was an asshole, but she had good taste.

As we grew older, Taiwo's behavior took on a more conniving edge. She would tell me stories of places called children's homes, where there were no adults to boss me around, and I would be able to play all day and do as I pleased. I begged her for information on how to be allowed into one of these amazing establishments, and she told me I would have to make certain sacrifices. I'd have to do some bad things in order to be sent there, and some of these things would incur the wrath of my mum, but it would be worth it when I finally was allowed to enter the children's home to live. Eager to experience this child's utopia, I did everything Taiwo told me to do to facilitate my entry into this heaven, and she was eager to help. She instructed me to do things like drop a plate of my mother's food on the floor as I brought it to her, break plates and cups, and spill red juices on carpets. Her personal favorite was to have me lose my earrings.

As well as the colorful materials and coral beads that Nigerians wear, gold is a treasured addition to that mix. My mother had a huge collection of gold jewelry. Some she had purchased and some were heirlooms passed down to her from family. Gold was not only a precious form of currency but also an outward sign of success and wealth, and she would often adorn herself with it when going to parties, weddings, and other important Nigerian events. The size of some of the pieces she wore would put some of today's rappers to shame. When she took us to these events, she would often drape us in gold too, and I developed a love of jewelry and general body adornment from her. I would cry when we got home from these outings and she would remove all the beautiful shiny metal from my body. The only pieces I got to keep wearing were my earrings. In Nigerian culture, a baby girl's ears are pierced within days of birth, and so I have worn earrings since before I had any discernible memories. Gold is obviously the metal of choice for the ears of Nigerian baby girls, and that was the only gold jewelry I was allowed to wear before my twelfth birthday, when I got my first gold ring, which I had been begging for since the age of five. The girls in our family wore gold studs or hoops all the time, and this is where my sister got me. She would take one of my gold earrings and throw it away, instructing me to tell my mother I had lost it. Mum would be furious and beat me, and Taiwo would stand by and watch. She would later soothe me, ensuring me that I was a step closer to getting the coveted children's home invite. I lost several gold earrings, broke many plates, and incurred a staggering number of beatings due to my sister's deception before I finally decided, at the age of nine, that the kid's home wasn't worth all that pain. I didn't work out my sister's trickery till I was well into my teens, and to this day my mum doesn't know that a significant percentage of the punishment she doled out to me back then was as a result of Taiwo's feelings of abandonment and mistreatment.

3

A Snake Can Only Give
Birth to Long Things

As kids, we were taught to stay away from "bad boys," usually groups of young white teenagers who'd hang around the common areas of the flats, randomly shouting racial epithets as we went about our business. "Wogs," "coons," and "niggers" for us, and "stinking Pakis" for the other families, whether they were Indian, Pakistani, Sri Lankan, or suntanned Greek Cypriots. Funnily enough, racial discrimination was not that . . . discriminating.

Most blocks of flats have a trash-disposal chute accessible from each floor. You squeeze your trash into the chute and it falls down what looks like a grime-filled helter-skelter and lands in huge trash cans on the ground floor. Sometimes those chutes become blocked, or you belong to a large household that produces larger than chute-size refuse, so the rubbish needs to be manually taken to the ground-floor cans. This was one of the chores I'd been promoted to at around the age of seven.

I relished this gig, as it proved I was responsible and trustworthy, and I got to go outside the flat on my own, an extremely rare occurrence due to my mother's overprotectiveness. One day on the way back from one of these trash-emptying occasions, I came across a bunch of white teenagers hanging out and smoking by the stairway that led back to my flat. I did as I was taught and made no eye contact as I nimbly brushed past them and ran up the stairs. One of them shouted, "Run, little wog!" Followed by the sound of hawking as one of them gathered enough saliva in his mouth and spat in my direction.

I was a tomboy at seven but still a girl, therefore still being dressed by my mum, who would scrape my unruly hair into a bun and put me in cute dresses that I loathed. I was wearing one such dress that day and so felt the gob of spit hit me on the back of my thigh as I ran away from those boys. I don't remember being particularly upset by this attack, just mildly disgusted by the spit and that I hadn't been fast enough to escape it. Mum calmly cleaned the spit off my thigh while muttering about bad boys under her breath.

I still emptied the trash the following week but this time wearing jeans. Something I welcomed.

Such was the everyday reality of life in 1970s Bethnal Green.

The mouth of an elder might stink, but it comes from wisdom.

Most children of African parents will tell you their parents were strict. A lot will say they had less freedom than their white or Caribbean peers. Many will even say their parents were overprotective. But what they speak of pales in comparison with my mother's utter obsession with not letting anything happen to us.

My mother did everything humanly possible to keep us at home. Her fear that her children would die if they strayed too far from her was such that she kept a large scrapbook in which she'd paste clippings from the newspaper of bus and train crashes and other fatal incidents, which she used to deter us from going places. Whenever we asked to go anywhere, she'd bring out the scrapbook. "You see these children? They are all dead. You know why they are dead? They left their mothers to go on a school trip and are never coming home. Dead!" No amount of persuasion deterred my mother from these opinions.

My class was once going on a trip to the Tower of London. This historic castle, known as the home of the Crown Jewels, worn by every king and queen of England at their coronation, was also an execution site and prison from 1100 to 1952, holding such prisoners as Elizabeth I, Anne Boleyn, and the infamous East End gangsters the Kray twins. As you can tell from the name, the Tower is in London, in an area called Tower Hamlets. We lived in Bethnal Green. *In Tower Hamlets.* We could almost see the Tower of London from our council flat.

My mum told me I couldn't go on the trip. One of my teachers, feeling pity for my predicament, wrote my mother an imploring, heartfelt letter, begging her to let me join this *local* trip to the Tower of London, stressing how *educational* it would be for me, and personally ensuring that Henry VIII would not come back to life and have me beheaded with an axe. My mother read the letter, crumpled it up, and then, without further thought, gave it to me to throw in the bin. I was devastated. So upset was I that I made the mistake of channeling one of the American kids I saw on TV. "I hate it here! I don't wanna live with you anymore!" As soon as the words came out of my mouth, I knew I'd made a possibly life-threatening error. My mum stared at me hard. "Is that so? Okay, then. Go." *Huh? Okay, well, that was easy.*

At last I was going to head to a local children's home, the one my older sister had been telling me about. I would turn up, and despite my lack of invite, I'd inform them I was an orphan. I was on my way! I went to my room and stuffed a school bag with some clothes and a couple of my favorite toys, then walked back into the front room to say goodbye. I was excited. I was going to a local children's home as an orphan. What could be better than a home with just children?

"Did I not buy you that bag and toys? Leave them here."

Fine. I was sure the children's home would give me new, nicer toys. I put the bag down and turned to walk out of the house. Mum stopped me again. "Where are you going? Did I not buy you those clothes and shoes you are wearing? Take them off." I was still adamant I was leaving, so I stripped down to my underwear, and hoped there was a children's home not too far away; I'd sprint there before anyone saw me. I turned to leave.

"Ah-ah. Did I not buy those knickers?" *Surely not!* I stared at my mum beseechingly as my lips began to quiver. She didn't budge. I slowly removed my underwear. I was in tears now, but I still shuffled to the front door, using one hand to cover my genitalia. I was seven then, so breasts were not an issue yet. I opened the door and stepped out onto the landing. Mum shut the door behind me.

It was the weekend and a sunny day in London. The council estate was bustling. No one was currently on our floor, but there were five other flats on our level, and anyone could have walked by. I didn't know where the nearest children's home was, and I certainly didn't want to be asking for directions from strangers buck naked. And what if I bumped into someone from school? I turned back and hammered on the door to be let back in. Mum took ages to open it.

I didn't attempt to leave home again till I was twenty-three. And I still have never been to the Tower of London.

A goal is but a dream with a deadline.

Latchkey kids—kids who wore the key to their home around their necks, and who came into and out of their home by themselves, seemingly as they pleased—were horribly looked down upon by my mum but greatly envied by us kids. We were not allowed our own key until we were well into our teens. Somebody was almost always home to let us into the house after school, and when they weren't, then tough—we waited until they were. We weren't the kinds of kids who had friends over. As in *never*.

We weren't allowed to go to other kids' houses either. My mother trusted no one. We socialized with each other in the house or with the kids of our aunties—who weren't necessarily our aunties but my mum's small network of friends from Nigeria, also immigrants to the UK—or with the kids of people who owed my mum money.

My and my siblings' social skills were mainly built from school, each other, books, and television. I was a voracious reader. I loved memorizing nursery rhymes. My mum nurtured my love of reading and bought me books as fast as I could read them, and she allowed me to join various libraries so I wouldn't read her bankrupt. I was a massive fan of Enid Blyton's The Famous Five series, about a group of outdoorsy middle-class white kids who had many unlikely adventures. I identified with Georgina—"George"—the tomboyish girl in the group. I then graduated to fairy tales, then ghost stories, then horror. Stephen King and Dean Koontz are still my favorite authors to this day.

I buried myself in American movies and TV shows too. Mum didn't let us go out, but she let us watch pretty much anything we wanted, so my brothers and I shared a love of superheroes like Superman and Spider-Man, and The Hulk played by Lou

33

Ferrigno, and cartoons—Bugs Bunny, Woody Woodpecker. We also loved *Knight Rider* with pre-"The Hoff" David Hasselhoff, *The Six Million Dollar Man* with Lee Majors, and Lindsay Wagner in *The Bionic Woman*, who was my first woman crush. I remember my brothers and me huddling together on the sofa at night, watching old black-and-white horror movies too: Boris Karloff as Frankenstein's monster, Lon Chaney Jr. as the Wolf Man, and Bela Lugosi as Count Dracula.

The dream to one day live in America was cemented by a short-lived kids TV show called *The Red Hand Gang*. It was canceled in the US after just one season, but somehow, a few years later, it ended up on UK television, as America's sloppy seconds, and I loved that show. It was about a group of kid sleuths running around the streets of Los Angeles on cool bikes, solving crimes, and leaving the mark of a red hand on a wall wherever they'd been—it set my imagination on fire! Every kid in the US seemed to have nice clothes, skateboards, dogs, parents who let them go out and have adventures, and there always seemed to be a beach nearby to frolic on. Even the kids' sweets were better than ours. Sure, England imported Bazooka bubble gum from the US, with the Bazooka Joe comic strips wrapped around the gum. But the toys you could order from the back of those comic strips—the catapults, guns, and action figures—were priced in dollars and only available to American kids. Oh, the torture!

I felt victimized, seeing pictures of these amazing toys I could never have. I hated having been born in England, and dreamed of moving to the US, joining the Red Hand Gang, and enjoying the freedoms, sunshine, toys, candies, and general coolness that American kids seemed to have in abundance. I wanted Theo Huxtable as my big brother and Arnold Jackson as my friend. *Diff'rent Strokes* was on constant rotation in our house, and my brothers and I often cracked ourselves up shouting at each other, "What you talkin' 'bout, Willis?"

This dream only grew as I got older and began watching TV shows like *Melrose Place*. Jesus! These same kids had grown up to live in apartment buildings with pools, where they'd hang out with all their cool, good-looking neighbors. Nothing like that existed in London. I was determined to have that life one day.

"Why does your hair smell like chlorine?" Taiwo asked me one day as she was performing her weekly duty of braiding my hair.

"'Cause I'm in a classroom with all of my friends and they went swimming today." I secretly hoped the lie sounded casual and convincing enough to allay her annoying suspicion. I couldn't tell my older sister that I was sneaking to go swimming with my class. At eight years old, I knew her envy and dislike of me was such that she was not to be trusted. She would snitch to Mum. I'd get into trouble and I'd be stopped from swimming. If there was any kind of school activity that did not involve me being on school premises, having a book in my hand, it was *out*. There was no way my mum was letting me near water, unless it was a bath at home. Any other type of water was frivolous and dangerous.

I'm not sure what the situation is now, with all that the UK government has whittled away, but when I was a kid, swimming was part of the school curriculum. All school-age children were entitled to free swimming lessons. If your school didn't have a pool, your class would be bussed to a nearby school that had one, or local private baths, once a week. There was a proficiency system in which you could earn various badges depending on your swimming skills. For instance, if you were able to swim the width of the pool and back, you'd get a green badge. If you could swim the length of the pool and back, you would get a blue badge. Then red, yellow, bronze, silver, and gold.

Of course I wanted to go swimming with all my friends. Mum wouldn't allow me to learn how to swim *in case I drowned*, which made absolutely no sense, but there was no arguing with her. No doubt to back up her assertions, she would have pulled out her scrapbook. "Do you see these children? They are dead, because swimming made them drown! Dead!"

When my class did go to the pool, at first I stayed behind at school with the sick kids or the kids who had verrucae or other contagious ailments. Sometimes I was left in a classroom on my own, with one teacher as my babysitter. They usually felt sorry for me and didn't make me do schoolwork but gave me different colored pens and allowed me to draw pictures, as some sort of consolation prize.

This led to the first of a few deceptions I would undertake in order to escape my mother's oppressive overprotectiveness. I had a friend, Vanessa, a little sandy-haired white girl with bangs, who sat next to me in class. She was sweet natured, and we often spent afternoons playing with ladybirds and caterpillars in the grassy area at the back of our school playground. One day she asked me, "Why don't you ever come swimming with us?" I told her. The next day she opened her backpack and pulled out a half navy-blue, half sky-blue swimsuit with a frilly off-white lace skirt around the waist. "Mummy bought me a new costume. You can wear this, my old one." I was ecstatic. She'd even brought along a spare rubber swimming cap for me. To this day, I don't know whether she swiped it from the trash to give it to me or she'd told her mum she was donating the swimsuit to a poor, starving African kid. I didn't give two shits that I was taking charity, which would have been an affront to my proud Nigerian mother, but I was grateful. At last I was going to swim!

The following week, when the teachers were herding everyone onto the swim bus, I took the costume Vanessa had given me and climbed on with the rest of the kids. I strode with the confidence of a child who had permission from her parents to swim—I mean, why else would I have a swimsuit? I hoped the teachers wouldn't ask. They didn't. I rode that bus to salvation.

I had my secret weekly swimming lessons for several months and was even able to qualify for my green and blue badges. Despite the rubber cap Vanessa had given me to keep my hair dry, that chlorinated water got in around the edges, seeping into my hairline and leaving that telltale smell my sister noticed. But she couldn't prove her suspicions.

My school had those old wooden desks you see in British movies from the '70s, with large lids that could be lifted to reveal storage space inside for books, folders, and general school paraphernalia. This was where I stored my swimsuit. That thing never got washed. I'd wear it to swim, change out of it, and stuff it into my desk to dry every week. There was no way I was going to risk bringing it home to wash. But it didn't take long for the swimsuit to start to smell and become moldy. I didn't care. I'd put it on and get right into that pool with all those unsuspecting kids and swimming instructors. I'm still surprised that my school never became the center of a disease outbreak, and I didn't go down in history as the Typhoid Mary of prepubescent fungal infections. Eventually, though, my suit began to fall apart. The skirt began to fray, the straps broke, then the crotch started to give way. By the time that costume finally gave up the ghost, it was held together by safety pins, Plasticine, and bubble gum—anything I could get my eight-year-old hands on. My benefactor and her family had since moved out of the area, and Vanessa was at another school, so when my little costume fell apart, that was the end of my swimming days.

This is why to this day I have the swimming skills of an eight-year-old.

4

When the Laborer Is Praised, His Cutlass Begins to Cut More Keenly

Hobbies were also a no-no in our family. Immigrants, for the most part, don't understand the concept of a hobby. They move to a country and are consumed with hard work and providing for their families. They rarely have the luxury of non-work-related pursuits. My mum would often say, "Hobby? Who has time for a hobby? So you want to do useless things—for fun?"

So there were no hobbies in our house unless that thing was useful to the family. During my first couple of years of high school, some school subjects were optional—electives. You were able to choose something of interest to you, like woodworking or home economics. As was to be expected in the '80s, all the boys gravitated towards woodworking. Home economics—or cookery, as it was colloquially known—was mainly known as a girl's subject. At first I was drawn to woodworking, but I had little patience as an eleven-year-old. I'd thought that I would be wielding a chainsaw and building tables and cabinets within a week, so when by the second month of class I'd only been allowed to pick up a hammer, I became bored and switched to home ec. It was a pretty easy class. More practical than theoretical, and yes, we did bake a lot of cakes. I discovered an affinity for baking. I had a sweet tooth already, and the opportunity to make my favorite things and have that be part of my education was a dream come true. Every week I brought home scones, apple pies, pineapple upside-down cakes, cream puffs, and sponge cakes, until eventually my mum, on tasting one of my creations, finally recognized my aptitude. "Every Sunday from now on you will bake cakes for the family!" She took the hobby I loved and turned it into a *job*. She bought a bunch of baking tins and ingredients, and every Sunday for the next couple of years I had to get up early and bake for the entire family. I resolved at that young age to stop learning things and to gain no more new skills that my mum could use to enslave me.

Mum had very long, thick, beautiful hair, which Taiwo braided on a weekly basis, as well as braiding mine, as part of her chores. Mum implored me on several occasions to watch and help Taiwo, and learn from her, so I could take over when Taiwo left home. Hell no. I was quite a clumsy child, and I made sure to play up my clumsiness, so Mum dismissed me in frustration. I never learned to braid hair, and I haven't baked a cake since I was fourteen.

A single hair falling off your head does not make you bald.

One of the lines in Lil Wayne's 2008 song "A Milli" is "A millionaire, I'm a young money millionaire, tougher than Nigerian hair." I reveled in that lyric, and whenever that song came on in the clubs, I'd proudly point to my head as I mouthed the words. But that pride was nonexistent when I was a child.

I have had a love-hate relationship with my hair all my life. I have thick, tightly curled hair. On the hair-type chart invented in 1997 by Andre Walker, Oprah Winfrey's hairdresser, which numerically grades hair types from 1A, the straightest of straight, to 4C, the tightest of curls, I am a 4C. My hair is super African. The nappiest of the naps. The word "nappy" has been used as an insult for centuries against the natural state of African hair in the US. In the UK, the insult was "picky"—a word that slipped into the language of Black people in England via the Caribbean. Both words have links to slavery. The thick, spongy texture of Black hair was used as another excuse to consider Africans sub-human, and therefore assuage any guilt about owning and using people like animals. Our skin and hair were deemed ugly, untidy, and dirty when put up against the idealized beauty of white, pale skin and straight hair. In the US, California and New York finally passed laws in 2019 banning discrimination based on one's natural hair. We were discriminated against in work, school, the military, and even wrestling matches because of the way our hair grows from our heads.

After centuries of this attitude being embedded in our psyche, Black women still hot-comb and put straighteners in their hair as early as they can to distance themselves from African "picky heads." Mine is the type of hair that suffers major shrinkage. It can start the day full, luscious, and long, but one rainstorm, one too many sweaty encounters, one errant water hose, and my hair shrinks like a wool sweater in a hot wash.

"Tough" was a word I heard a lot throughout my childhood when it came time to comb my hair. Out of the three girls (ultimately) in my family, my hair was the most tightly curled and most unmanageable, judging by the way my mother tugged, pulled, and huffed when she combed it. My hair broke many combs. The thick plastic combs with glitter inside them, wooden combs that were the thickness of small trees, even a couple of metal ones were bent out of shape by my picky hair.

In the '70s, conditioning hadn't been invented. Well, if it had been, Black people hadn't got the memo, as Vaseline was the hair treatment of choice, used to grease the scalp as the hair was braided. Actually, Vaseline was the Season-All of moisturizers—in my early childhood, it was used on my hair, my body, and my face. My brothers and I often went to school looking like three greasy brown M&M's.

My brothers didn't get the benefit of a barber. That was an unnecessary expense when Mum had two perfectly good hands and a pair of scissors. Yup, a good fade was a thing of the future, but back then, all the Black boys at school had the same haircut. My brothers' haircuts varied in quality, depending on how much of a hurry my mum was in.

My mum tried with my hair until I was around nine. She never braided it. I remember being called a picky head a lot in school. I didn't get to go to school in pretty buns and pigtails with colorful ribbons on the ends—my mum did a thing called African threading. This is a hair styling method used for centuries in Africa. It involves parting the hair into sections and wrapping black thread around each section from root to tip. Problem was, my mum would just cut the ends of the thread with her teeth and leave these threaded bunches sticking out of my scalp at various unflattering angles, so my head looked like a giant spider. Children are extremely honest, and cruel. So a couple of new nicknames were added to the collection I already had: Roots, upside-down tree head, and Anansi, after the West African folktale spider.

Eventually, after much crying and begging, Mum gladly stopped threading my hair and passed on the responsibility to Taiwo, who had taught herself to braid. Cue even harder tugging and more comb breaking, but I gladly took on that pain if it meant I was no longer an uprooted tree. My hair had never looked better. When Taiwo was in a good mood, she experimented with different styles that matched the Caribbean girls at school. She even put beads in my hair on a few occasions. Hair beads were big in the Black community way before the white actress Bo Derek made them famous when she wore them in the 1979 movie *10* (cultural appropriation anyone?), and before Venus and Serena Williams kicked down the doors of tennis with their proudly adorned braids. I loved having beads in my hair. The weight of them, dangling at the ends of my cornrows, meant I could at least feel like I fit in with the other Black girls at school, and I could swing my hair like the white girls. And swing I did. At the end of each school day, there were always a few beads missing.

Having Taiwo in charge of my hair meant I was at her mercy. If she decided I had been disrespectful in any way or just irked her for any reason, she refused to do my hair, knowing that I couldn't manage it by myself, and that once my head got into a bad enough state, Mum would notice it. My mother's solution to my unruly hair was drastic. She would force me to sit down next to my brothers and would shear my hair off with the scissors. She didn't have time for my knotted clumps, and she didn't give a damn about my school cred. I'd be sent to school with a chopped-up, uneven mini Afro, at a time when Afros were no longer in fashion, Black Power or not, and all the girls coveted long braids. My school had a strict dress code, so I couldn't even hide my mum's butchery with a hat. I was a laughingstock.

The trauma of begging my sister to plait my hair, before Mum got out the scissors, stayed with me for a long time. It was my own fault. I'd refused to learn to braid, to escape more housework, but I'd inadvertently screwed myself. I hated my hair for years. I ached for long, smooth tresses that blew in the wind, and through which combs and brushes glided, like in those Head & Shoulders commercials. But I had to wait until I was old enough to make my own hair decisions.

This didn't come till I was thirteen, after Taiwo left home and I was finally allowed to handle a hot comb by myself. I'd watched the many times when Taiwo used the large metal comb to press my mum's hair straight and how my mum's mane was transformed from a large curly halo into something long and shoulder-length. She'd grease up my mum's hair, then pull the comb out of the burner flames on the stove and lay it on old newspapers to cool for a couple of minutes. After blowing on it a few times, she'd run it through Mum's hair, accompanied by the sizzle of grease heating and the smell of hair being burned into submission.

When Taiwo felt generous, she'd do mine too, and I'd also be blessed with flowing tresses, which I maintained longer by not moving too much or going near water, including the bath, as any moisture and my hair would shrivel up like the Wicked Witch in *The Wizard of Oz*, and I'd be returned to ugly duckling status in a hot minute. Those few days I was able to maintain that straightness, I felt on top of the world. My hair was thick, but when it was straight, it outranked most of the dark-skinned girls' hair length at school, and they marveled at it. I felt almost popular. I stomped through school those days tucking my hair behind my ear, untucking it, and tucking it again. I couldn't wait to be allowed free use of the hot comb, and when I finally was, I abused it. The smell of the sizzling 1980s Black hair staple Luster's Pink moisturizer permeated the house as I fried my hair on an almost daily basis. I'd press my hair as straight as I could get it and slick it back. I looked like James Brown and Barry White had had a baby. But to me, I looked good, as long as I didn't get caught in the rain.

On my sixteenth birthday, Taiwo told me to get ready as she was taking me somewhere. After she'd left home, our relationship had improved. She sometimes returned to take my brothers and me out, showing us random acts of generosity and kindness. One year she took us to Wimpy for burgers and milkshakes. This was a big deal to us. Mum never believed in eating outside our house unless it was a school meal, so we hadn't been to any kind of restaurant. That day we'd gorged on cheeseburgers and huge ice-cream sundaes called knickerbocker glories. We thought we'd died and gone to heaven, all previous mistrust towards our older sister dissipating with each bite.

This time she took me to a hair salon. We walked in, and the place was bustling with Black people. People getting blow-dried, getting their hair braided, straightened. It was wondrous. Taiwo wished me a happy birthday and explained that she would pay for me to have my hair relaxed. The first hair-relaxing chemical was invented by accident by Black inventor Garrett A. Morgan, in 1909, while he was trying to figure out how to reduce friction between the needle and wool of a sewing machine. From there, he tested it on a dog and then on humans, after which it became a worldwide phenomenon, and a tool for Black women to fit into white beauty parameters. I was overjoyed.

Taiwo informed the receptionist of our appointment in fifteen minutes' time, and we walked to a waiting area. Three hours later we were called over by the woman who was to be my stylist. "So we ah go relax all ah dis?" she asked in her strong Jamaican accent.

I nodded and looked up at Taiwo, who took charge. "Yes, we're going to relax and style, please."

"All right." She began to comb through my hair, which hadn't been hot-combed for a few days. "Rahtid, your hair tick nah rass!" ("Wow, your hair is thick!" for those who don't speak Ja-maicanese.) She separated my hair into bunches and began apply-ing the relaxer cream from the roots to the tips. My excitement grew. I was going to leave here looking like a million bucks.

As the stylist smeared more and more relaxer on my hair, I began to feel a tingle on my scalp. *No problem*, I thought. *This must be normal.* The tingle increased to a small burning sensa-tion. *You've never had your hair done before. It's fine. Stay calm.*

Within five minutes my scalp felt like it was on fire, being stung by a thousand bees, and being set on fire again. I winced inwardly, clenched my fists, and tried to breathe through the pain. I was afraid to speak for fear of embarrassing my sister and having her put a stop to the outing. I needed to get this hair done, so I was going to suck it up, no matter what.

"How you feeling?" the stylist asked.

"Okay," I squeaked.

"Good. We leave it on another twenty minutes, then me ah go wash it off." *Jesus Christ.*

I sat in agony, sweating, which made the burning even worse.

Taiwo came over from where she sat reading a magazine be-hind me. "How does it feel?"

"It's burning a bit."

Taiwo called the stylist back. The stylist put her hand in my hair to check how well the relaxer had taken. That small manipu-lation of my hair released another set of flames shooting into my scalp under her fingers, and I nearly jumped out of the chair.

"Okay. Time fi take it out."

She led me to the basin, I put my head back, and she began washing my hair out. I asked her to use ice-cold water, but my scalp exploded like the top of a volcano every time her hands rubbed my head to wash out this devil cream. Finally, she poured a neutralizing shampoo on my head for the extremely alkaline cream, and *Oh! Blessed relief!* It was like she'd dipped my head in a pool of Pepto Bismol. The flames died down. The rest of the appointment went without incident. My scalp throbbed, but my hair had taken the relaxer, and I was rewarded with the longest, straightest hair I'd ever had. The stylist curled my hair, and I floated out onto the street with my sister, ready for my future as a Black debutante. I thanked Taiwo profusely and went home.

In the morning I tried to remove the silk scarf that I'd used to tie my hair and maintain my style the night before. It wouldn't come off my head. It was stuck. I was confused. I peeled it off and looked in the mirror, and was faced with the reflection of a burn victim. My head looked like Freddy Krueger's face. It was covered in weeping scabs, and my beautiful hair lay clumped and buried under large discs of dried pus.

Taiwo arrived at the house within the hour. She had to face my mum's fury at what she had let these people do to my hair. I felt bad for her. She had tried to do something nice for her younger sister, and it had ended in disaster. She took me straight back to the salon.

The Jamaican woman was unapologetic. "Why she never tell me she ah bon?" I told her, "How was I supposed to know that burning wasn't normal?" They washed my hair again and did their best to separate the clumps from the scabs, and fortunately there was no damage to my thick hair, just my scalp, which would heal in about six weeks. Just in time for my hair to grow enough that I would have to go back and burn it all over again.

My scalp never stopped getting burned. I'd go, burn my head, let it heal, burn it again, on and off for the next twenty-five years, pausing only when I had dreadlocks for three years, when I followed the London band Soul II Soul, whose style was Funki Dred. Such was the allure of that creamy crack.

You cannot cook yams with your anger, no matter how hot it is.

With a mother like mine, normal teenage experiences were obviously off the table too. I remember, when I was fifteen, a popular girl in my class announced she was having a birthday party, and we were all invited. Normally there were two of us who were left off these invites: myself, as by now everyone knew my mum didn't let me go anywhere, and Annie. Annie was from a family of Indian Muslims. Her parents were also extremely strict, and we bonded on our shared experience of missing out. I took comfort in having someone else who was suffering the same indignities as I was. Misery loves company.

Popular Girl sidled over to me. "You should ask your mum. She'll let you come to my party, 'cause you're only across the road from us." This was true. Popular Girl lived less than a hundred feet from us. We could easily see her family home from ours. I figured I had nothing to lose by asking. The proximity of the party would surely put my mum's mind at ease if all she was worried about was my safety.

I spent three days putting my case and rebuttals together and waiting for the right moment to approach Mum with my party proposal. All the housework was done, she'd eaten, the boys hadn't gotten into any trouble, and she'd just finished a particularly good episode of *Dallas*. This was it. I sat down beside her.

"Mummy, one of the girls in my class is having a party at her house next Saturday."

"Is that so?"

"Her parents will be there, and it's just across the street at 52. Can I—"

"No."

"But it's right across the street."

"And so? Are you arguing with me? I said no."

End of discussion.

The next day at school, everyone excitedly discussed their out-fits for the upcoming party. Annie walked into the classroom look-ing sad. Popular Girl turned to Annie. "You can't come, then?"

Annie frowned. "No."

I began to commiserate with her, though I was internally glad to have a fellow outcast. "Me neither," I began, "'cause my mum—"

"Psych!" Annie interrupted. "My mum and dad said I could go! My brother's gonna drop me off and take me home!"

Everybody cheered and rushed over to hug the excited Annie. I slinked out of the room in despair.

The day of the party arrived, and I still held hope that my mum would have a change of heart. I made sure all my chores were done perfectly, I was as well behaved all day as I could possibly be, and I had secretly selected an outfit of black jeans and a bur-gundy Fred Perry tracksuit top that I had gotten for my birth-day, which was the only vaguely fashionable name-brand thing I owned. I had it laid out on the bed, for a quick sprint and change the moment Mum changed her mind. I sat in the living room, opposite my mum, looking as desperate and sad as I could, as the music for the party began. Mum turned up the volume of the TV. Before long, you could hear the loud and excited chatter of teenagers in the street as they made their way to the party. Mum carried on watching TV as if she couldn't hear it. I sat fidgeting opposite her, becoming increasingly desperate.

The doorbell rang. I went to open the door. Michelle Berry, one of the popular girls at my school, who lived in the council flats nearby with her mum and younger sister, stood in the doorway with Beverley, another girl from school.

Both of them were known to my mum, as we'd been attending the same schools since we were eight.

"Who is that?" my mum asked from the living room.

"It's Michelle and Beverley."

"Oh, hello, girls."

"Hello, Mrs. Iyashere."

The girls came into the front room to greet my mum. "We're going to the party across the road, so we just knocked to see if you're coming." I didn't know whether Michelle was trying to help me or just testing the limits of my mum's overprotectiveness, but I could have hugged her at that moment. I stared at my mother imploringly.

"She is not going."

"Oh, okay. Have a good evening. Bye." And they were gone.

I spent the rest of the night peeking through my bedroom window, watching my school friends having the time of their lives. I was heartbroken. This couldn't possibly be about my well-being. This felt like cruelty. I couldn't get my head around it. My mother could have watched me partying from the comfort of her couch and still ensured my safety. My mum could have shouted for me to come home from the comfort of her couch, and I would have heard her from anywhere in that party. The party was so close that my mum could have slapped any illicit alcohol out of my hand from the comfort of her couch. But I still couldn't go.

I remember truly hating my mother that day.

. . .

Most kids look forward to weekends. They wax lyrical about all the fun things they have planned that school simply gets in the way of. Hanging with friends, playing in the park, riding their bikes. For us, weekends were two days of being stuck at home doing chores and homework, and trying to entertain one another. Friday evenings were stew night. Every Friday after school, while other kids excitedly ran off to begin their weekends of fun, I returned home to spend the evening in the kitchen with my mum, cooking the stew that would feed the entire family for the next seven days.

This was before the days when everything had to be refrigerated as soon as it saw air, for fear of death. In the 1980s African household, one pot of food could be left out on the stovetop, being repeatedly heated, and providing sustenance like a magic porridge pot, until your wooden spoon scraped against the burnt remnants on the bottom. Funnily enough, none of us ever got food poisoning and died. Nowadays, if you leave anything out of the fridge for more than ten minutes or keep anything one hour past its "consume by" date, you have to eat it in a hazmat suit while being injected with antibiotics.

This stew usually contained chicken, oxtail, and various other meats, depending on what was available at the butcher's that week. All the meat was bought fresh, so the chicken feathers had to be singed and plucked, and the meat had to be cleaned and prepared for cooking. This was a laborious process that took hours.

Helping Mum with the stew was one of my chores. Taiwo and my mother had done it when I was younger, but when Taiwo began working, when I was twelve, I was inducted into kitchen duties.

My mum was a hard taskmaster, and cooking was not a bonding experience. I remember getting shouted at a lot. I'm left-handed, and clumsy, so being stuck in the kitchen on Fridays from 4 p.m. till midnight with an impatient Nigerian woman who was trying to prepare me for marriage was not anybody's idea of a fun weekend. I also couldn't understand why the process took so long. I felt Mum dragged it out just to punish me. It was torturous.

After a year of suffering these eight-hour cooking marathons, I persuaded Mum to allow me to cook the stew alone. She was skeptical but agreed. I got that preparation and cooking time down to two hours, and though Mum was suspicious, the stew tasted almost as good as hers, so she couldn't complain.

I had regained some of my Friday evening. Saturdays, though, she'd find us something else to do, like sweeping the stairs. That doesn't sound like much, but our house at that time was five stories of swirly patterned carpet. And vacuum cleaners were an expensive luxury. Why have a vacuum cleaner when you had kids with hands? We would sweep dust from each stair with a small dustpan and brush . . . one . . . by . . . one. My brothers and I were each given a flight. And my mother checked every step. We'd often try to skip some, sweeping every other one, but if my mum found one errant piece of lint, we had to start again from the top. That was half a Saturday in one fell swoop, or should I say sweep. After we finished, we'd all sit upstairs at the windows looking out onto the street, watching our friends riding by on their bikes or just meandering in groups to the local adventure playground. We were like the Flowers in the Attic.

The highlight of the weekend would be getting sent out to buy paraffin. In '80s London, central heating was a thing of the future. That was some *Tomorrow's World, Doctor Who* shit. That was for rich people. Most people's homes either had one open fireplace in the front room that the whole family would huddle around or were heated with dangerous tin boxes with a wick inside that you filled with a highly flammable liquid and then lit with a naked match. These were paraffin heaters. As kids, we'd be sent out to buy gallons of paraffin from the shop (yes, back then corner shops had paraffin pumps), then have to carry those heavy containers home, trying not slosh it on our clothes, as the distinctive smell lingered. And when we went to light the heater, there was the danger of lighting up like Michael Jackson's hair on a Pepsi commercial. But these errands were an opportunity to get out of the house, and we jumped at those small outings.

The heaters sucked the oxygen out of a room while warming it, and released noxious fumes to boot, so we flirted with danger. There were quite a few deaths from carbon monoxide poisoning from these heaters, but we knew no different. London of the 1300s had the plague. London of the 1980s had paraffin heaters.

One time my brothers were fighting in their bedroom, so my mum separated them. Sheyi slept in the front room that night. Come morning, Dele emerged from the boys' room unusually woozy, and covered from head to foot in soot. On running into the bedroom, my mum discovered that the paraffin heater had malfunctioned in the night, and the whole room was coated in black soot. Dele had been breathing it in as he slept. He survived the night on a minimum amount of oxygen, but had the boys not been fighting, and had both slept in the room, one or both of them would have died. We slept in coats without the paraffin heaters for a few weeks after that. But when the winter became too bitter to bear, we went back to flirting with death. We cleaned those heaters and kept it moving.

A child who has no mother will not have the scars to show on his back.

Despite that imminent danger within our household, my mum's fear of the dangers outside knew no bounds, and she had no problem keeping us in line with physical discipline.

When visiting other people's houses, most African kids were

forewarned by their parents that if they were offered anything to eat, the correct answer was "No, thank you," lest their parents look like they couldn't afford to feed their kids. Well, Mum never taught us that lesson, and we had to learn the hard way.

One day my mother took my brothers and me to a friend's house. The woman put a plate in front of us stacked high with all the best biscuits in the world. (Biscuits in England are cookies, Americans.) There were chocolate digestives, custard creams, and bourbons. The kinds of biscuits my mum kept under lock and key, and only brought out on rare occasions. Putting those in front of us was like watching a man crawling through a desert for three weeks, then putting a bottle of Pellegrino in front of him. My brothers and I dove headfirst into those biscuits, and if that wasn't embarrassing enough for my mum, we fought over them like animals, and after all of the biscuits were eaten, Sheyi picked up this woman's fine china plate and licked it. All this while the woman raised her eyebrows and commented wryly, "Your children really like biscuits." Which my mum translated as "Did you not feed your children, you negligent woman? They are positively feral!"

Beating.

In fact, that was the longest rant and worst beating we ever had in our young lives. My mother's fury was unparalleled. She was mortified and furious. We learned our lesson: whenever we were offered food during future visits to people's homes, we broke out in a cold sweat and ran screaming in the opposite direction. To this day my brothers and I still laugh about that beating.

Now, I can already hear some bleeding hearts filling up their lungs to shout, "Abuse!" and wringing their hands about the propensity for violence within the Black community. *Shut up.* The practice wasn't unique to Black people. Every TV show or sitcom produced in England that had a school with a headmaster in it

depicted a dude with a cane who took a little bit too much pleasure in caning kids on the buttocks. White people. Corporal punishment wasn't banned in UK schools till 1986, and kids were still
getting "slippered" in private schools even after that. Teachers
used plimsolls, slippers, and various other footwear on the asses
of other people's kids for the longest time. Again, white people.
The nuns in my school, whizzing around like evil penguins on
flying carpets, slapping kids on their thighs—all white people.
Way prior to that, King Edward VI of England was said to have
had a "whipping boy." These were a popular accessory among
European aristocrats and royalty, apparently. So basically, in the
1400s, if you were a white child who was wealthy or posh enough,
when you transgressed, you could have another child *take your
beatings for you*. At least Black people had the decency to beat the
kid who'd *actually* fucked up—and belonged to them.

Beating your kids is considered a hackneyed topic among
Black comedians on both sides of the Atlantic. Of African and
Caribbean kids who were brought up in the '70s and '80s,
99.9999 percent got their asses kicked. That's it. Kids of our generation got beaten, slapped, whipped with belts, tree branches,
extension cords, a smaller child—anything our parents could get
their hands on. In many Black families, this was the norm, hence
the commonly told jokes and stories among us. Whether it was
right, you guys can discuss among yourselves. Whether it actually
worked is an altogether different discussion.

There is the idea that hitting our children came from slavery
and colonialism. I found evidence online to suggest that many
indigenous African cultures didn't hit kids prior to colonialism.
Regardless of the history, my mum was partial to a bit of physical
violence, as many African parents were at that time. She had a
collection of belts set aside just for the purpose of punishment,

and she was an equal opportunity punisher. Me and my two brothers, all close in age, tended to get into scrapes together and therefore often shared a beating, where we'd all be lined up with our hands outstretched to take our whippings. If I'd been smarter, I might have been able to avoid at least some of the punishments, by telling my mum it was rude to beat her own mother. I mean, wasn't I *Granny*?

The beatings were never as bad as the anticipation of them. My mum's beatings were rarely done in explosions of frustration. They were slow and calculated, like an executioner relishing the sharpening of her blade. She would tell us what we had done wrong and that a beating was going to ensue, but we didn't know when it would happen. It was like living under a death sentence. When it was time for our beating, she would line us up, then go into a rant about what we had done, what had led up to the point of us committing this crime, why she had to beat us, why we deserved it, and the history of our previous infractions. This could go on for hours.

Sometimes the phone would ring, she'd answer it, have a forty-minute conversation with whomever, replete with jokes and laughter, while we stood to attention, awaiting our punishment, hoping that surely she'd get off the phone in a lighter mood, only for her to somehow summon up her previous rage and pick up exactly where she had left off with her rant. Those times we wished she'd stop talking and hit us already so we could move on with our lives.

Aside from eating biscuits offered by hosts or coming home a minute later than was expected, reasons for Mum's corporal punishment varied:

(1) My mum picked me up from school one day, and a teacher mentioned lightheartedly that I'd told her my mum always came

to pick me up from school because my dad had run away to Nigeria. The teacher did not realize she was sentencing me to death, as that revelation fell into the "Never tell people our business" category.

Beating.

(2) My brothers and I made a makeshift catapult, shooting glass marbles at each other. A window broke. We lied that it had been someone out in the street, even though the glass fragments were outside the house. We didn't have the benefit of forensic education from TV shows like *CSI* back then.

Beating.

(3) Mum would tell us to do something, like fetch her some thread for her sewing machine, and sometimes a kind of tutting or involuntary sound of dissent would escape from our mouths.

Beating.

(4) I am cack-handed.

Cack-handed is a term for left-handed. I didn't technically get beatings for this, but definitely I was slapped! I'm the only one in my family who was born left-handed. So I was opposite to everything I was supposed to be, just like my grandmother had predicted. But in African, Middle Eastern, Asian, in fact pretty much in every culture the left hand is seen as unclean. The reasoning behind this was that the right hand was used for eating, handling food, and social interactions, whereas the job of the left hand was to wipe your ass—which technically it is, because I'm left-handed! I'm pretty sure right-handed people wipe their asses with their right.

As a child, my mum tried to force me into right-handedness, which was a common practice among parents of leftie-afflicted kids. She would make me practice writing with my right hand for so many hours that I was ambidextrous for a little while.

Eventually, tired of a sentence taking eight times longer to write with my right hand than with my left, I resorted to trickery, switching back to my left as soon as Mum exited the room. If I gave Mum food with my left hand, that was a slap. If she came into the kitchen and I was stirring the pot with my left hand, slap, and all that food would go straight into the trash. A large part of my childhood clumsiness was due to trying to do things with my less dominant hand and struggling with everything on the planet being made for righties, including scissors, fountain pens, and faucets.

My mum tried to beat it into us that we had to be the best, that we had to work the hardest. That we would not succeed unless we worked at it. To my mum, it wasn't abuse. It was love dosed with some fear. As a Black mother, she may have felt she was preparing us for the world and how we were going to get abused out there as Black people. She probably felt, like so many other Black parents, that she needed to get us straight, and beating was her way of doing it. And it kind of did. There are certain aspects of my childhood that I hated, for sure. Like the fact that my mum never let me go anywhere. It felt stifling and sometimes cruel. But looking back, the discipline worked. A lot of my friends who didn't have that discipline growing up were pregnant by fifteen or sixteen. A lot of them.

There's also a difference between hitting and beating. I don't see anything wrong with slapping a kid on the hand if they've been naughty, but beating is a different story. I don't believe in beating kids. Most of my siblings now have their own children. None of them hit their kids. None of them. It's kind of ironic how we went the opposite way.

5

Going to Church Doesn't Make You a Holy Person Any More Than Going to a Garage Makes You a Mechanic

*When the missionaries arrived, the Africans had the
land and the missionaries had the Bible. They taught
us to pray with our eyes closed. When we opened our
eyes, they had the land and we had the Bible.*

—JOMO KENYATTA, FROM *FACING MT. KENYA*

My mother, like many Nigerians, is notoriously secretive about her past. As she's gotten older, she has kind of started to relax and let some stuff slip, but in general, she has always glossed over the details. When I ask her about her childhood, she answers in platitudes, such as, "Oh yes, it was wonderful." And I'm like "Well, it wasn't really—all your blood brothers ended up dead." Her reply? "Oh yes, they had juju done on them by the other wives, but that was the way things were." Even Christianity couldn't sever my mum's strong belief in the power of juju, despite her being disavowed of traditional Nigerian deity worship at an early age.

From my mum's recollections, she enjoyed her schooling, which set her on the path to become a qualified teacher in Nigeria before she was twenty. Having been born in the heyday of British colonialism, Mum was educated in missionary schools in Nigeria. "They were very nice. Yes, they hit us with sticks, but only when we deserved it."

The missionaries' main purpose was to convert as many people as possible to Christianity while also educating them from a Eurocentric perspective, turning them away from their apparently primitive and barbaric way of life, plus getting them to give up land that was theirs to house churches they never knew they needed. This education included learning the Bible. The same Bible that had been used to subjugate Africans who were stolen and taken abroad. The same Bible with all that worshipping of an impossibly blond and blue-eyed Jesus, with Black people being cursed as descendants of Ham. And with all that obey-your-master, turn-the-other-cheek shit. That stuff that keeps you accepting horrendous abuses in this life with a hope of ascending to heaven in the end.

But despite this, Mum is very proud of her Christian faith. As I grew up and discovered more about our history, I'd throw my two cents in with comments such as "You know Christianity was forced on you, right?" To which she'd respond, "Shut your mouth," then change the subject.

My mother is a Baptist. Despite being a staunch Christian, she was quite unusual among other Nigerian mums in that she didn't make us go to church. I've often heard horror stories from cousins and friends of them being forced to sit still in services that lasted hours. (Although to be fair, when you're eight years old, being forced to sit still for twenty minutes without playing, it feels like a year. If I'd been brought up in the Black churches of the US, like Aretha Franklin, Beyoncé, and the members of Jodeci, maybe I would have been more open to Christianity. Those churches looked way more fun.) To this day, I haven't worked out whether my mum's lack of churchgoing was due to a sense of rebellion or if, after a hard week of doing whatever she could to put food on the table, she just couldn't be bothered to get a herd of kids dressed up in their Sunday best to sing songs in a chilly English church for an hour. Whatever the reason, I'm grateful. I often heard her say the Nigerian adage "Going to church doesn't make you a holy person any more than going to a garage makes you a mechanic." And we as kids were more than happy to agree with her.

My mum's version of Sunday worship was a British TV show called *Songs of Praise*. This long-running religious show was, in my humble opinion, the first reality show. Basically, every Sunday a camera crew would set up in a church and film people "churching." It was a Sunday service, delivered to your living room. That was Mum's church. The flat would be filled with my mum's voice as she sang hymns in front of the TV. *"All things bright and beautiful, all creatures great and small, all things wise and wonderful, the lord God made them all!"*

Although Mum was Baptist, her ambition for her children meant that whichever God we prayed to did not get in the way of our education. Let's just say our religion was fluid, in accordance with whatever was the best school in the area we happened to be living in. If the best local school was a different religion than my mother's, then that's what we became for the duration of our time at that school, whether it be Anglican or Roman Catholic. If the best school in our area had been Jewish, I'm pretty sure my mum would have been giving us bar and bat mitzvahs, and whatever else it took for us to fit in and enjoy the advantages of that better school.

I remember once walking with my mother to be baptized. I was way past baby-christening age, and I was tall enough to bend down so the vicar could wet my head. That's how I ended up at a Roman Catholic primary school from the age of four until I was eight. It was a small school, with a varied mix of kids, from all over Bethnal Green and the surrounding East London boroughs. This school was run by a bunch of hard-faced nuns who had no issue with slapping kids on the backs of their thighs for any infractions, as this was the '70s, a time of smacking kids with impunity and no comebacks. And, again, my mum had no problem with that.

. . .

Mum was overbearing, a hard taskmaster, and unaffectionate, but there was no doubt in my mind that she loved us and would go to the ends of the earth to defend us against outsiders. After all, she did once take a white man to court for me. Let me explain.

My brothers and I were instructed to always come home from school together. This meant if one of us had detention, we all had detention. I often found myself waiting around for the boys, who liked to take their sweet time hanging with their friends, playing Penny up the Wall. This is a game in which a number of players line up a fixed distance away from a wall and each takes a turn throwing a coin of common value towards the wall. The objective is to throw the coins such that they land as close to the wall as possible. Whoever gets their coin closest to the wall collects all of the coins, shakes them in their hands, and throws them all into the air. Before the coins land, the player shouts "Heads" or "Tails" and is entitled to claim all those coins landing the corresponding way. The remaining coins (if any) are then gathered up by the player whose coin landed second closest to the wall, who repeats the shaking, throwing, and calling of "Heads" or "Tails." This process continues until all the coins have been picked up.

Dele was a master at it. I'd once lost two months' worth of pocket money to him in under an hour. Dele and Sheyi often organized after-school Penny up the Wall tournaments, using the game as a way to top up their income. On afternoons like this, I had no choice but to wait around while they gambled.

One such day as I waited, I wandered around outside the empty school. Eventually, tired and bored, I leaned up against a parked car.

"Get the fuck off my car!"

Startled, I looked over to see a white man walking towards me, his face screwed up in anger.

"Get the fuck off my car, you Black bastard!"

My mouth opened before I had a chance to stop it. "Piss off, you *white* bastard!"

"What the fuck did you say?"

He leapt towards me, and I took off running. I was a good sprinter, but I was wearing my school uniform, so my speed was hindered by my school bag bouncing off my hip, by my skirt, and by my sensible school shoes. I was so panicked, I ran in the opposite direction of where my brothers were playing around the corner. I ran into the school grounds, thinking I'd get back into the school building the same way I had come out. As I ran, I peeked behind me, and the man was not far behind, his face pink with fury. I made it to the glass entrance doors of the school and pushed to enter, but they were locked. I caught sight of a teacher inside, walking down the corridor, and I banged desperately on the doors to get her attention. She turned and began to walk towards me, but it was too late. The man caught up to me and began punching, kicking, and pummeling me as the teacher frantically fiddled to get the door open. She finally did, and I stumbled inside as the man then turned and jogged away. Horrified by what had just taken place, she called the police. She recognized him as a father of a child who went to my school, and he was arrested the next day.

I was bruised but otherwise not seriously hurt. Mum accompanied me to the police station the next day to add my statement to the teachers', assuming that criminal proceedings would follow and justice would be served. The man was released a few hours after his arrest and let off with a caution. A police caution administered in England and Wales is a formal alternative to prosecution in minor cases. It is commonly used to resolve cases in which full prosecution is not seen as the most appropriate solution. Accepting a caution requires an admission of guilt. Basically, the police believed that the apt punishment for a grown man who had severely beaten a fourteen-year-old child was a "Don't do that again, naughty boy. Now, off you go!"

That would have been the end of the story, and quite frankly, I was happy for it to be over. I'd gotten away without serious injury, the guy probably wouldn't attack me again, and I just wanted to put my head down and get back to regular life. But Mum wasn't having it.

Although she had been relatively calm and collected throughout the dealings with the police, she was absolutely furious when she was informed about the caution. This man had attacked her child and gotten away with it. He was going to be punished. She bombarded the police with calls to voice her dissatisfaction and to demand they prosecute this man for assault. The police told her the case was closed. I was secretly glad and hoped Mum would give up the fight. She didn't. She decided to pursue a private prosecution against him. This meant that as an individual without the backing of the police or the criminal justice system, she would not have access to a public prosecutor and would have to hire her own. I overheard her discussing the cost on the phone with various lawyers. It was going to cost thousands. This was a woman who bought us sneakers with two stripes on them and told us to draw on the third if we wanted Adidas so badly. A woman who would haggle for thirty minutes over the cost of an apple. Surely she wasn't willing to spend so much money on this. I was wrong.

She eventually hired a lawyer and took my attacker to court. The teacher was called in to testify and told how she'd seen this man beat me as I cowered in the doorway of the school. I also testified and told the court how he had racially abused me before his attack. But this was England in the '80s. I stood in front of an old white judge who simply saw a white man who had been disrespected by a young Black thug. And as if to cement the futility of the case, my mother's lawyer made the mistake of asking this man what he did for a living. He was a firefighter. It was all over then. To the judge, here was an upstanding citizen who saved lives. Sure, he'd made a mistake beating this Black child, but she'd probably deserved it. These Blacks could be so unruly. The judge gave the man an absolute discharge. This is an unconditional discharge whereby the court finds that a crime has technically been committed but any punishment of the defendant would be inappropriate. And the case was closed. Again. This meant there would be no conviction on the man's record despite the fact that he'd admitted to stomping a child. He was free to go. Back to his job, his family, and his racism.

This was my first taste of the difference between justice for Black people and justice for white people in England. My mum showed no outward emotion at the loss, and she never discussed the case again. This experience did hammer home my mum's love for me and how far she would go to protect her children. And even better, I no longer had to wait for my brothers after school. Silver linings and all that.

. . .

When Mum was out working, my brothers and I often made up our own games and built makeshift toys from scraps of stuff we found around the house. Our favorite toys to build were guns. From cop shows to Cowboys and Indians, guns were the most popular toys of the '70s, before it was deemed politically incorrect and dangerous for young kids to point pistols at one another. Remember, this was the time when parents bought their children candy cigarettes complete with red sugar at the end to duplicate the burning embers of the tobacco. That would be the equivalent of making candies for today's kids in the shape of rolled-up dollar bills and coated on one end with powdered sugar. I loved those candy cigarettes, though, and even though Mum never smoked, she bought them for us, as they were just another type of candy. Nobody saw the danger of normalizing smoking for a bunch of four-year-olds! I was disappointed to find out at fifteen, when I bit into one, that real cigarettes tasted nowhere near as good as the sugary ones.

As kids, we often got cowboy outfits, complete with fake Stetsons, sheriff badges, and cap guns. Cap guns were named for the small caps, or capsules, of flammable material that would explode upon contact with the trigger's hammer mechanism. The caps came on a thin roll of paper that was fed through the cast-iron gun. My brothers and I loved running through the house, shooting at each other.

Later, we coveted guns with real missiles, stuff that actually came out of them, and we graduated to water pistols. That was as far as Mum let us go. The more expensive guns that shot pellets, she refused to stump up for, so we began experimenting with making our own. There were toys we couldn't get our hands on because they were beyond Mum's toy budget, and some belonged to another world.

For our first experiments, we tried making catapults and guns that would match the toys we saw depicted on Bazooka gum wrappers. Eventually we had the perfect prototype. It was a catapult shotgun made from two aluminum pipes we salvaged from the legs of the cheap kitchen stools everybody had in their houses in the '70s and '80s. They had vinyl seat pads, and their thin aluminum legs, over time, would splay out and finally collapse under the weight of a particularly fat auntie who came to visit. That happened at least twice in my childhood, and it took every ounce of self-control as kids not to let a laugh escape, or we'd face a harsh beating after that auntie left.

We collected those broken metal legs from the trash and strapped two of them together with rubber bands. At one end, in between the pipes, we made a trigger from a wooden clothes peg, which was held in the cocked position by more rubber bands. A catapult rubber band was attached to the other end of the gun and then pulled back behind the top of the trigger ready for shooting—similar to the action of a crossbow. Glass marbles were our bullets of choice. They were cheap to purchase with the modest pocket money Mum gave us, and through playing marbles with other kids at school, my brothers and I amassed a decent-size collection, as when you won a game of marbles, you got to keep those of the losing child. We pooled our winnings for our ammunition pile. We'd place a marble in front of the elastic band that acted as a catapult. When the trigger was pulled, the rubber bands released and launched the marble out at full speed. The more bands we used, the tighter the catapult and the more powerful the gun. Super dangerous, and much more fun for it. We played with these guns when we were alone in the house, using cans and plastic bottles from the trash as our targets, and we hid them under our beds when Mum was home. None of us lost an eye, but we smashed a lot of stuff. We broke a window once, and we took a vow to accept the beating without ever revealing the guns we'd used to do it.

Mum eventually found out about our shotguns when Sheyi thought it would be a good idea to take his one to school to show off to his friends. One of those dumb friends decided to pull the gun out of Sheyi's backpack in the middle of a lesson. Mum got a call from the teacher to come to the school immediately. When she arrived, she entered the empty classroom where Sheyi sat waiting in terror. "Mrs. Iyashere, your son brought a homemade gun to school, and I'm sure you understand how serious this is." The teacher then pulled the gun out from behind her desk. My mum, who up till that point had assumed she was about to come face-to-face with the equivalent of a peashooter, on seeing the two-foot-long weapon of mass destruction, was so shocked that she burst into fits of uncontrollable laughter. The teacher stared at her aghast. Sheyi thought our mother had lost her mind. Her laughing terrified him even more.

It took Mum a full three minutes to control her giggle fit, then she asked what the teacher wanted to do.

"Well, Sheyi is a good student, so I will take this no further," she answered smugly. "I will allow him back into school tomorrow. But I am confiscating the gun and then—"

"What?" my mum interrupted.

The poor teacher had no idea what she was stepping into. "Well, Sheyi can come back to school tomorrow, but obviously I'm going to confiscate this weapon."

"'Obviously'? Did you not take this gun from my son?"

"Eh, yes."

"And you said no further action will be taken."

"Well, yes."

"Therefore, that gun now belongs to me."

"Well, er, well, I suppose, technically, yes."

"Then technically you will not be keeping it and using it as an example to criminalize my son at a later date. Give me the gun." End of discussion. Nobody messed with her kids.

My mum walked out of the school with the offending weapon in one hand and Sheyi's hand in the other. She didn't punish any of us. But we all disappointingly had to give up our weapons stash.

6

If You Are Eating with the Devil, You Must Use a Long Spoon

W hen I was around five, my mother began a relationship with a man who became our de facto dad—or as I would later dub him, Step-Bastard—for the next twelve years.

Samson Ekhaguere was a Nigerian man who worked as a mail sorter at the Royal Mail and drove a silver Ford Granada. Not many people on the housing estate where we lived owned cars, so the car added to the excitement he brought to the household. We weren't to call him "Daddy," as he wasn't, so we called him "Uncle," a commonly used moniker for any older male. In African culture, anybody who wasn't your mum, dad, or sibling was never referred to by their first name but as either "Auntie" or "Uncle," as a sign of respect. As we were instructed in my mum's Nigerian accent, "Uncle" became "Oncle."

Oncle was a stout, dark-skinned, bespectacled man with a formidable deep voice and big, rough hands with thick fingers. His smile was wide and toothy and reminded me of a crocodile's—I could see the menace behind his grin. He looked like the big bad wolf in *Little Red Riding Hood*, but no one else seemed to notice.

For the first year or so after Oncle had moved in with us at the cramped Bethnal Green flat, he was good to my brothers, coming into the family as a father figure for them. I remember their joy of having a new dad. He seemed enamored with them too. They would hang around his legs, and he would scoop them up onto his shoulders, bellowing, "My boys!" But he didn't have much time or interest for me or Taiwo because, you know, *girls*. Taiwo didn't seem too bothered, as the more he hung out with my brothers, the less babysitting she had to do, so she often was left to her own devices.

Despite my initial wariness of Oncle, I longed to roll around on the floor with him and the boys and roughhouse, and I often tried to join in. I'd go sit in the front room where they played while my mum was on her sewing machine in the corner. I'd laugh loudly, trying to alert them that I was available for play too. I'd clap, I'd giggle, then eventually I'd try to slip closer to the action, only to be shooed away by him. Mum would call me over and try to get me interested in other things. Like sewing. She often spent hours at her machine, making the clothes she would sell and re-creating outfits she had seen on the high street, which she would fashion for us out of whatever material she had. She bought me a mini sewing machine in an attempt to teach me some of her sewing skills, and draw my attention from the boys' rough play. I was not impressed. I fiddled with it for about an hour before becoming bored and disappearing into my brothers' room alone to play battles with their toy soldiers. As I listened to them squealing in delight as Oncle lifted and threw them around, I knew I was being excluded from these activities because I was a girl, and it infuriated me.

The first year of Oncle's presence was filled with my dejection and loneliness. I wasn't part of the boys club, and I was much safer when Taiwo was ignoring me so I stayed out of her way as much as possible. I had no one. Oncle wasn't nice to me, and I didn't like him at all. He had come and taken my brothers, my only playmates, leaving me in the wilderness. Up until that point, I'd not missed being without a father, but around this time I began to pray for my real dad to come rescue me. That he'd show up at our door, swoop me up in his arms, ready to take his family back. He'd drive Oncle away and protect me from Taiwo, and we'd all live happily ever after.

I also had a backup fantasy savior. That was Taiwo's twin brother, Kehinde. I always knew my oldest sister had been born a twin, but he'd never lived with us, and I'd never seen him in pictures or in person. Whenever I asked Mum where he was, she alluded to him being in Nigeria somewhere. I imagined this big brother one day arriving out of the blue from Nigeria, taller and stronger than Oncle, who'd fight his little sister's battles and play with me and me only. It wasn't till years later, when we were teenagers and I was wondering out loud when we'd get to meet this long-lost brother, that my younger brother, Sheyi, who's always been the most intuitive and smart of us kids, retorted, "You do realize Kehinde died at birth, right?" I hadn't. Nigerians don't like to talk about death, and rather than tell us that she had lost a child, Mum had just avoided the subject altogether until one of us worked it out.

In a Nigerian household, kids weren't allowed to just vocalize their feelings. TV made it seem like American kids could tell their parents anything, from dictating what they wanted to eat to how they felt about something. And their parents listened! On American TV, families sat and discussed their feelings, tears were shed, hugs given, and compromises made. That shit didn't happen in my family! Respect for your elders—which meant that children were to be seen and not heard—was a rule heavily enforced in our household, so kids didn't have "feelings." We just did what the hell we were told and shut the fuck up about it. I did not like Oncle, but I never came out and said, "Hey, Mum, I don't like this fella. I think he's a wolf," because even at five, I knew that somehow this man was important to my mum. To her social standing, as she now had a man, and to our finances. I just had to adapt to the new status quo.

It became obvious that the dislike I had for him was mutual when Oncle began to make comments about how boisterous and how much in need of discipline I was. My knees and elbows were always scraped and ashy from playing rough games with the boys at school. I also knew my own mind pretty early on in life and was prone to asking a lot of questions, something that would always get me into trouble. Oncle saw these things as defiance, and so he sought to stifle me. I often found myself being bellowed at and lectured by him, but being told by my mum that I had to behave myself, as we were lucky to have him, and he was now the man of the house. I learned from an early age to stay out of Oncle's way as much as possible.

I hated when my mum was working and he would collect me from school, as this gave him more opportunity to bully and humiliate me. He would turn up at the school gate in a suit, looking every bit the respectable father figure, and make a point of berating me loudly in front of my friends. He would bellow my name. "Dapo! Pull your socks up! Dapo! Why is your hair messy?" or "Why is there mud on your dress? Dapo! You wait till you get home!" From an early age, my family had called me by my middle name, Dapo, prompting kids at my school to rename me Bus

Depot. He made me so ashamed. I continued to pray every night for my real dad or my unbeknownst-to-me-at-the-time deceased older brother to hurry up and come rescue me.

Oncle/Step-Bastard also brought over from Nigeria some of the more imaginative punishments for kids, like Hold the Bottle, in which the child had to stand and hold a glass bottle over their head, straight armed, for as long as was deemed enough for them to have learned their lesson. If those arms moved down an inch, *beating*.

Fun guy.

To be fair, that might be why I'm quite good at yoga.

. . .

When I was six, we welcomed my new, youngest sister, Asiriuwa—Asi for short—to the family. Oncle was overjoyed to have a baby who was his own flesh and blood (though we later found out he had others strewn about the country before he settled with us). He dropped my brothers like hot potatoes and concentrated all his attention on his new daughter.

Poor Dele and Sheyi had no idea what had gone wrong. Overnight they went from being "his boys" and the apples of his eye to being discarded like rice prepared by my left hand. He no longer played with them, and in fact, the disdain he had previously reserved for me was now shared between my brothers and myself.

Not long after my mother and new baby Asi returned home from the hospital, Oncle pulled me aside for a quick conversation, which went along the lines of "You don't like me, and I don't like you. Stay away from my child." As a mere six-year-old, I was slightly disappointed, as I viewed the new baby as a living doll to play with, and I was being denied this pleasure. But

I was unsurprised by Oncle's feelings and was secretly glad to have my brothers back to play with, and to share in my misery. Besides, whenever Oncle was at work, I sneaked into Asi's room to play with her tiny fingers and toes, and Mum sometimes let me carry her.

With this expanding family, the Bethnal Green flat became too cramped, but we stuck it and its perpetual dampness out for a couple more years while Mum and Oncle saved to buy a house. Two weeks before my eighth birthday, we moved into a large five-story house on Lancaster Road, in Finsbury Park. It was a palace! And dry! Downstairs had a cellar and a large front room and kitchen separated by a wall with a window built in so you could still see the TV from the kitchen! At a time when houses typically had just one TV, that window was state of the art. We couldn't believe it. A window *inside* the house.

Looking back, it seems like the previous family must have been on the run from gangsters or the police and left in a hurry, because we discovered a cupboard *full* of toys and, as the months went by, even more toys strewn about the house. It was like the house had been blessed by a fairy godmother.

Our next-door neighbor had a pond in his garden with ducks and swans. I felt like I'd moved into Narnia—but the novelty soon wore off when I realized those ducks were very early risers.

There was also a two-room extension towards the back of the house that became Oncle's man cave, where he had a bed he slept in when he did night shifts plus another TV and his own small kitchenette and bathroom. The next floor had a large family bathroom and three connecting rooms, which became my mum's suite. One room had huge closets, the second was where she kept her sewing machine and materials, and the third had a large brass four-poster bed, complete with heavy curtains.

The ultimate status symbol for my mum was that bed. She'd always wanted one and had insisted on it when they'd bought the house. Though no one but us ever saw the inside of that bedroom, all our extended family and friends knew about that bed, and that Mum was doing well for herself.

Oncle had built that bed. He was extremely handy at DIY projects and took on the laying of carpet, wallpapering, and all the physical work the house needed. He built shelves and cupboards, and put up the curtains Mum sewed. He even installed several doorbells in the house. One for the front door, obviously, but more ingeniously he installed a button in the kitchen and another by my mum's bed, both wired up to doorbells in the upstairs bedrooms, so whenever my mum wanted to call us in the large house, all she had to do was ring that bell, and we all had to come running. On the wall above the staircase, Oncle had hung a massive five-foot poster of Elvis, because both my mum and Oncle loved him. It wasn't unusual for me as a kid to walk past this larger-than-life-size Elvis keeping his eye on our Nigerian British family.

The third level housed the bedroom for the boys, Dele and Sheyi. The fourth had two bedrooms. One was meant to be Asi's room. That's right, the two-year-old baby was assigned the biggest single bedroom in the house, but as she was a *damn toddler*, the room housed all my mum's stuff that she was selling. Mum now had a shop in the house, and Asi slept in a cot next to my mum's four-poster. The last bedroom was the girls' room—as in, I still had to share a room with Taiwo. *Fuck*.

To escape the oppressiveness of sharing with Taiwo, I spent a lot of time in my brothers' room, which became my haven. Being close in age, Dele, Sheyi, and I were like a little gang, the three Musketeers, having the same family experiences. We played, fought, and plotted in that room. It was where I could vent, where

I learned to play table tennis, Space Invaders, Pac-Man, and where I first listened to New Edition and the Jackson 5. That room is where I learned to shit talk, as my brothers and I were always calling each other names and roasting each other before we knew what roasting was. That room gave me a lot of the skills I still use today and was the center of my childhood till I grew breasts.

I was not close to my sisters. Taiwo was like an adult to me. She had not experienced a proper childhood, having spent so many years in Nigeria and then being forced into the role of a surrogate parent to us when my mum had been out trying to make ends meet. As a result, she was not in the least bit fun. During my entire childhood, her feelings for me swung between hatred, disdain for the annoying little turd she was forced to share a room with, and envy, as I had a special place in my mum's heart because of my birthmark and therefore got away with a lot more than she did as the eldest.

And I couldn't have a relationship with Asi—who besides being much younger was Oncle's biological child and so belonged to him. She was the center of his attention, and I, Dele, and Sheyi became the enemies. Oncle kept Asi separate from us, and though we were her brothers and sisters, he instilled an us-versus-them mentality in her. From an early age, she was taught to spy on us and tell on us at every opportunity. We, in turn, began to see her as the enemy and excluded her from our games—hiding from her for hours and telling her that we had been to places like Narnia, and that she wasn't welcome. This was our only weapon against her, as she had everything else.

Oncle spoiled Asi—to the point that she had pretty bad tooth decay at a young age because of the sheer amount of candy, chocolates, and other sweets she was allowed to eat. While Mum rationed the amount of sweets and biscuits the boys and I ate, keeping them under lock and key, Asi had mountains of the stuff, which Oncle kept in his man cave and padlocked at night to keep us out. Every day after school and all day through the weekends, he would unlock the door, leaving it open so we could see the piles of sugary treats. We were warned never to go in that room, and that those sweets were for Asi and Asi alone. She would wander in and out of that room at her leisure, chomping away, while I and my brothers looked on in envy. She never shared any of it with us; in fact, she made a point of eating the sweets with a gleeful slowness, to prolong our agony.

Mum, surprisingly, never really had that much say in Asi's up-bringing, and I always wondered why. Looking back, it seems almost as if Asi was an offering to Oncle to keep him around. He obviously put his foot down about how she was to be raised. He didn't want her to be anything like us. She was special. She was his. And she was going to have everything we didn't.

My mother had been so notoriously overprotective of us, but Asi was not subjected to the same discipline or restrictions, and she was also allowed to go on every school trip. The trips that Mum had made us stay home from. The trips that Mum had told us would kill us.

On Asi's birthdays, Oncle would buy a mountain of toys and arrange them like a damn Hamleys toy-shop display. Then we'd all be dressed up and photographed as a family next to her toy arrangement, and afterwards banished to our rooms while Asi played by herself and gorged on every imaginable confectionary. We were never allowed to play with any of her toys, under threat of severe punishment from Oncle, hence in every one of those pictures from my childhood, me and my brothers look . . . fuck-ing . . . miserable.

Although Oncle worked for the Royal Mail, he had once har-bored dreams of becoming a lawyer. As a frustrated prosecutor, he began practicing his "lawyer skills" on us kids, interrogating us for hours over heinous crimes like "Who ate the last of the cornflakes but left the empty box in the cupboard?," "Who left baked beans in the sink?," "Who put the fork in the knife compartment?," and other equally serious offenses. He became equal parts harasser and bogeyman for me and my brothers, constantly tiptoeing around, trying to catch us doing something bad, or eavesdropping outside our bedrooms, listening to our childish conversations. This is how one day he caught me telling my brothers how much I disliked him. He had been crouched outside the room, ready to pounce, and he kicked open the door as soon as the words came out of my mouth.

I was paraded before my mother and forced to apologize to him. I was then forced to do another dreaded version of Hold the Bottle for a couple of hours. In this version, I had to lie on my stomach with both feet and arms raised off the floor while holding the glass bottle over my head, for as long as was deemed enough for me to have learned my lesson. If those arms or feet moved down an inch closer to the floor, the belt was waiting. It was around this time that, although publicly I called him Oncle, in my head he became the step-bastard. My dislike bloomed into a full-on hatred.

He took great pleasure in punishing me and the boys this way and encouraged Asi to enjoy our humiliation. She would often stand beside him, giggling during our torture and pointing out when our limbs looked like they were about to touch the floor. We three musketeers developed super-acute, ninja-like hearing to where we could pick out the sound of a creak on the staircase from two floors down and know the step-bastard was sneaking, ready to pounce on us, and we'd stop whatever we were doing and pose innocently when he busted open the door.

We weren't total Cinderellas, though. My mum always made

sure we got a decent present ratio at Christmas and on our birthdays, but spreading her income over five kids, she could never match the lavishness of Asi's stuff. Every kid in the '80s had a bike. The most popular ones were the Raleigh Chopper, a low-riding high-handlebar bicycle modeled on the Hell's Angels–type motorcycles, and the Raleigh Grifter, a predecessor in style to the BMX. The boys and I were desperate for bikes.

We all had secretly taught ourselves to ride by begging kids at school to let us ride theirs. We knew we'd never own our own bikes, as they were expensive, and they were on my mum's scrapbook list of things that got kids killed. That didn't stop us from asking, and dropping catalogues open on the bike pages around the house, whenever our birthdays were coming up. My mum completely ignored those hints.

One year the step-bastard bought Asi a bike. She was the first and only child in the family ever allowed to have one. It was a large, gleaming beauty, close in style to the Chopper and way too big for her but perfectly proportioned for my brothers and me. We would have killed to have one like it. We were furious—especially as Asi was quite unimpressed with it and maybe rode it twice. We knew the step-bastard had only bought it because we would never have one, and he took perverse pleasure in our pain. He stood us all in front of the bike and warned us that we were not to touch it, then he placed the bike in pride of place in the kitchen, next to the wall that separated the kitchen from the living room, so we would be forced to walk by this forbidden pleasure multiple times a day. When the step-bastard worked the night shift, my brothers and I used to sneak from our rooms in the middle of the night just to sit on it and imagine what it would be like to ride it around our neighborhood. Dele, by the time he was ten, had become quite the master at taking his toys apart and rebuilding them, and had taught himself how to pick locks. On those bike-sitting nights, we also broke into the step-bastard's man cave and stole some of Asi's sugared treats. Chocolate had never tasted so good.

The bike sat in the kitchen for over a year, then in the backyard, rusting away. Eventually the step-bastard threw it down into the cellar to die. Anything but let us enjoy it.

. . .

The new house meant a new school. Stroud Green Junior School was run by a matriarch with an iron fist. Mrs. Say wore sandals all year round, probably because she had the type of toes that didn't fit in any shoes. As a kid, I was fascinated by them. They seemed to be super long, with an extra knuckle on each one, and they refused to sit in line like normal toes. They piled on top of one another in her stockings like rugby players.

Mrs. Say had no qualms about laying hands on errant children. A week didn't go by without a child caught whispering in assembly being grabbed by the collar and dragged on their ass out of the auditorium. If you got sent to her office, you better believe you were getting a thigh slap.

Most kids were terrified of that. My brothers and I were unbothered, as were a lot of the other Black kids. She didn't have a belt? No shoe? Not even a slipper? *Puh-lease.*

I was most excited about going to this school because the playground, unlike the one at my previous school, was large and spread out, and had an array of swings and other outdoor equipment that the East End lacked. I was particularly looking forward to getting a grip on the large climbing frame that stood center stage, gleaming, in the middle of the playground. I couldn't wait to get on it. The '70s and '80s were much simpler and less safety-obsessed times. Kids didn't wear helmets while riding their bikes. There were adventure playgrounds made from wood and ropes and pipes where you might suffer tetanus from a splinter or break a leg falling off a makeshift zip line. School playgrounds, like this one at Stroud Green, had climbing equipment bolted right into the concrete—no padding, no warning notices, nothing! Back then, if a kid fell off the frame and cracked their skull open, the blood was cleaned up, we poured some apple juice on the scene of the crime for our homies, and we worked harder on having better hand-eye coordination. I knew I was going to love this school.

On my second day, as I happily hung upside down from the bars of said climbing frame, a large dark-skinned girl in the class a year behind me, Esther, strode up to me and said, "I'm not going to be your friend because I'm Jamaican, and you, you're an African bubu." She then spat on me.

That was my first lesson in the animosity between Black people who were the descendants of slaves and those who weren't. It was also my first lesson in climbing-frame defense. If I was ever again hanging upside down and someone was striding towards me with purpose, I would get the fuck down and get my hands up.

I had to learn to be tough because the majority of kids at school were of Caribbean descent, such as Jamaican, Trinidadian, Bajan. Black people from the Caribbean had been fed a steady diet of Tarzan on TV and tended to believe people from Africa were dumb, animalistic barbarians, and so they looked upon us with disdain and, in some cases, hatred. The English had been so thorough in their obfuscation of their part in bringing slaves from Africa to the West Indies that a lot of Caribbean people had absolutely *no idea* they were descendants of Africans. They had never been told. The knowledge of who they were had been wiped out over generations, and it hadn't been in the interest of the English to reeducate them. Many had been led to believe that there were distinct "breeds" of Black people in Africa and the various Caribbean islands, and that we were all different. In America, Black people knew their history because they were all descendants of Africans who had been forced to work on American plantations. That history was woven into the very fabric of the US. They were called African Americans, for crying out loud!

The Europeans had done slavery differently. They had set up plantations in the countries they had colonized, therefore not bringing their dirty work home. The Portuguese had used slave labor in Brazil, Angola, and several other countries, thus the official language to this day in those countries is Portuguese. The French did the same, from Haiti to the Congo. The Belgians, the Dutch—basically, Europeans carved up Africa and the Caribbean like a huge pie.

The Americans, by bringing all their stolen people to the American continent, had done the equivalent of burgling a house, then keeping the stolen goods in their own home. The Brits and the Europeans had also burgled but kept the stolen goods in someone else's house. If you'd gone to England in the 1700s and shouted, "Hey! Thieves! You have stolen Black people," they could have smugly waved their arms across the quiet English countryside and said, "But where?" They had separated themselves from the evidence of their misdeeds.

The British education system helped in hiding what the Brits had been up to. Children studied history for several years in high school, and spent an inordinate amount of time on Henry VIII, memorizing the names of all his wives and becoming intimately acquainted with the lineage of the British monarchy. When it came to the hundreds of years of British slavery, that lesson seemed to last only about half an hour, before moving over to the French

Revolution. The slave trade was also glossed over in a way that made it seem like a benign trade of manpower. I distinctly remember my history teacher using words like "help" and not "people theft," "kidnapping," "rape," or "murder." At the time, looking at that now-ubiquitous drawing of bodies laid out on slave ships, I failed to register the connection between those stick figures and the Black children I sat with in a classroom. All I remember thinking was that the ship looked a little bit uncomfortable.

Not long after that history lesson, the movie *Roots* came out in the UK. Sheyi came home complaining that his best friend at school, whose family were from Barbados, had begun laughing at him and calling him Kunta Kinte. My mum retorted, "Tell your friend he is a fool. *He* is Kunta Kinte, as his people were slaves. Our people were never taken."

The feelings of distrust went both ways. Many Africans believed that people from the Caribbean and African Americans were below them because every image they'd been fed, in movies and TV, was of African Americans as lazy people, thieves, drug dealers, or prostitutes. The images of Caribbean people were very similar, with their predominant stereotype of being criminals. As a result, many Africans saw themselves as separate and "better." Basically, we took the racism directed against us and internalized it. We all believed in these racial hierarchies that had been made up by somebody else, and they still exist to this day.

In the US, "African booty scratcher" is a distinctly Black on Black insult bandied about by children of color against the children of African immigrants. I have no idea when or where the term originated, but if I hazard a guess, I'd say it comes from the belief that Black Africans are primitive and used to live in the jungle, naked and scratching ourselves like monkeys. What is an "African bubu"? I know that a bubu is a traditional garment worn widely in West Africa. I assume it was adopted as a slur in England because of its African origins, and the fact that to kids the word "bubu" would have sounded hilarious. I mean, it is a funny word, "bubu." White people in England had their own derogatory terms for us, like "jungle bunny" and "spear chucker," which were epithets sometimes adopted by the Black kids as well. In fact, it was mainly the other Black kids who used those against me—so much so that when later I discovered an affinity for athletics, I tried everything—hundred meters, two hundred, shot put, long jump—but I tell you what: I never went *near* a javelin.

I remember that day when Esther spat on me like it happened yesterday. I was confused for a second, because I hadn't yet heard the term "African bubu," and I didn't understand how this little girl who looked and sounded just like me deemed me unworthy of friendship before we'd played a single game of hopscotch. But I just shrugged, wiped off the spit, and skipped over to play with some other, friendlier kids. I think the reason I was so unfazed was because back in those days my mum harbored many of the aforementioned ideas about people from the Caribbean, which she invariably had shared with me. I just took Esther's hostility as confirmation of what my mother had always warned me about.

"African bubu" would become a term thrown at me all through school. All this made for a very un-fun school life for me. Most kids of African descent lied about their ancestry, saying they were either half American—I know, what does that even mean?—or from Guyana instead of Ghana. They often Anglicized the sound of their names, so Ola (pronounced like the Spanish *hola* but more aggressively) became "Oh-la," Tunde ("Toon-deh") became "Tun-dee," etc.

I was no different. In high school, I told people I was from the Cameroon, as to me it sounded less African, and people spoke

French there. (Ridiculous.) I got away with that for about a month, till my mum turned up at a parent-teacher conference looking like she'd just come from an African birthing ceremony. She was in full Nigerian costume: a bubu, a loose-fitting blouse, and a wrapper, with colorful material tied around her waist and a matching Gele head wrap. This was the type of outfit normally reserved for large social events and parties among Nigerians, but my mum liked to make an impression when she came to my school, and parent-teacher conferences in her mind were important events.

7

It Is Not What You Are Called, but What You Answer To

When I moved up into high school, at St. David and St. Katherine Church of England Secondary School in North London, I decided I was no longer going to be Dapo or Bus Depot; I was going to use my British first name, Regina, and become a cool, new, unteasable version of myself. I instructed all of my family and any friends who were following me to my new school to address me with my new moniker. I was excited to start this cooler phase of my life.

Nobody warned me that I'd picked the absolutely *wrong* pronunciation of my name.

I discovered this in my first biology lesson. The moment the teacher began discussing female genitalia, the entire class turned to stare at me. The laughter began, and I realized I had made a huge mistake, and ruined the next five years of my life. I went from the seemingly harmless nickname Bus Depot to Regina Vagina. I had jumped out of the frying pan into a damn inferno. Whenever my name was called out, whether in assembly or for attendance, sniggers followed. It was a *Groundhog Day* of humiliation.

Totally my mum's fault. She had given me that name and the pronunciation. She'd ruined any chance of coolness for me at that school, and I was sure she'd done it on purpose. What better way to make sure your daughter didn't get invited to parties or sleepovers and therefore end up dead or, even worse, pregnant?

I didn't enjoy school. I didn't hate it, but I didn't love it either. It was an escape from the monotony of my home life, which revolved around chores, studying, keeping out of the way of Taiwo, avoiding Oncle, and fighting with my brothers, with the odd trip to the park if Mum was feeling generous. I wasn't particularly interested in academics, but I was under pressure to do well enough at school to fulfill Mum's doctor ambitions for me. My mum was happiest when I brought home high test scores, and fortunately I was blessed with the knack of being able to memorize large chunks of information that I could regurgitate at will.

I had school friends in the loosest of senses, in that there was a group of girls I often hung out with. I'd known Beverley and Michelle since I was eight and had attended Stroud Green Junior School with them, but on arrival in secondary/high school, they swiftly disowned me in favor of the more popular friend groups. But I'd gained the respect of Andrea, the proclaimed toughest girl in school and leader of a group, by fighting her on my second day, and thereafter I was allowed to hang in the periphery. There was also Jackie D, one of at least eight Jackies in my school alone— there were a lot of Jackies in 1980s London. In order to stave off constant physical confrontations, I tried to use humor to ingratiate myself with the other kids, or at least slow down the rate of ridicule directed at me. I'd crack jokes, do silly voices, even ridicule my teachers, incurring many detentions in my attempt at popularity. I was the only African girl in my friend group. The rest were all of Caribbean descent, which became a problem when I had a falling out with one, as it tended to spread to the group, and then I was ostracized with the whispers of "Regina Vagina," "African bubu," or "stinking African" as I passed.

The experience of school varied from day to day, depending on whether I had my friend group or not. Most of the time I spent hoping to get picked for team events, and usually I got picked after the popular girls and just before the fat kids and the nerds, even though I was a better athlete than most of the people doing the picking. But such was my social standing as an African girl named after female genitalia. What I looked forward to was my GCE O-level exams, which I would pass, and then get the fuck out of that school.

In England at the time, students from age eleven to sixteen studied for Certificates of Secondary Education, CSEs, or General Certificates of Education, known as GCEs, O levels (ordinary levels) in each subject. The CSE was introduced to provide a set of qualifications available to a broader range of schoolchildren and distinct from the GCE O level, which was aimed at the academically more able pupils, mostly those at independent schools. Basically, your education was based on your class in society.

Private school kids studied for GCE O-level exams, which were more likely to lead to GCE A-level (advanced-level) exams, which in turn would lead to access to university, a degree, and therefore the "better" jobs. Many government-funded high schools operated as either grammar schools, basically free schools for more academically gifted children who couldn't afford private school, or secondary schools, for everyone else.

Every child in the UK who lived in an area where grammar schools operated was tested at age eleven, and those who passed were funneled into the better schools. Unfortunately, those schools tended to be full of middle-class kids. Their parents, even if they were unable to afford private school, were able to manage the extra tuition needed for their kids to pass the eleven-plus exam. This gave their children an advantage over poorer children, and so curtailed the opportunity of the vaunted "upward mobility" grammar schools, which should have been equally as available to more gifted working-class kids, since places at these schools were limited.

Kids who didn't pass the eleven-plus exam, already burdened with the weight of failure at such a young age, went to the much less prestigious secondary schools, which received less government funding and struggled to retain the best teachers. Students there had access only to CSE qualifications, which tended to cover more vocational subjects, like car maintenance and cookery, as the assumption was that these kids would be the bus drivers, gardeners, and manual laborers of the future.

The high school I went to was a comprehensive school—entry was not reliant on academic performance, seemingly leveling the playing field by providing access to study for both GCE O levels and CSEs. The only problem was that kids were still being streamed into different groups according to how their teachers perceived their abilities, and whether or not a kid would be allowed to take O levels or the less academically taxing CSEs was being decided by age fourteen.

My mum had drummed it into my head: it was O levels or nothing. CSEs were for dummies. From age eleven to sixteen, my life was consumed with studying for those hallowed O levels, and making sure Mum had no excuse to call me a dummy.

I also needed to pass O levels in as many subjects as possible because I now had a bet to win. The step-bastard was unconvinced of my potential and found my mother's boasting about my impending medical career unbearable, especially as he had never realized his own dream of a career in law. "None of your children are going to be anything," he'd often announce. One day in a fit of pique, he shouted, "She will get no more than three O levels, and I'll put money on it!" Never one to back down from a challenge, or a chance of free money, I said, "How much?" and a wager was made. He would pay me five pounds for every O level I passed. I was studying ten subjects. A pass in all of them would be quite the windfall, and it would be sweet to take his money and shut his hateful mouth.

After O levels, a kid could leave school and get a job at sixteen, or take an apprenticeship, which was a job but with training and paid vocational study. Another option was to continue their studies to A level, which is another two years of study (similar to junior and senior years in the US high school system). A child's A-level results predicted what universities or colleges they could attend.

Obviously, I had only the one option. I was to get a bunch of O levels, then do A levels, go to university to get a degree, then go to medical school for seven years to become a doctor. Though I had no choice as to whether or not I wanted to do A levels, I believed I had a choice as to where I would study for them. I figured my mum wouldn't mind if I went to another school.

Actually, I was biding my time at D&K until I could restart my life somewhere else. At a new school, I would reinvent myself. A new girl arrived at D&K in my third year there, and I'd found out that her full name was also Regina, but she had had much more foresight than I did and had avoided the years of ridicule I had suffered by changing the pronunciation and shortening her name to Gina. She was now one of the cool girls. My envy of her was so strong that I hated her a little. Why hadn't I done that? Stupid! Oh well. I counted down the two years I had left before I'd be able to start my life anew, and also shorten my name.

When the time finally came to begin taking my exams, I broached the subject with Mum of changing schools after my results, and her response was a resounding no. I was to stay on at St. David and St. Katherine's to study for my A levels, then go to university from there. No discussion. No reason. I was furious but powerless. She was putting all this pressure on me to succeed but giving me no leeway or choices in how I was to do that. I resigned myself to being Regina Vagina for another two years.

If you sell eggs at the market, you should never be the one who starts a fight.

Exam season gave me a little more freedom than I'd experienced up to that point in my life. We were not required to come into school every day, as we were given time off for studying, and so we were only required to come to school for the exams themselves or for consultations with our teachers. On top of that, we were allowed to come to school out of uniform to take our exams. This became a fashion parade, with sixteen-year-olds showing off their latest Sergio Tacchini tracksuits and Adidas shell toes, which were all the rage at the time. I didn't have all that name-brand stuff, but I was a color-coordination master and put together some cheap but cool-looking outfits with my limited budget and wardrobe.

One such day, after I had completed my English O level, confident that I had easily passed the exam, I strolled happily through the playground of the school on my way home. It was not recess time, so all the students were currently in class. I was dressed head to toe in red. I had a red jacket on, similar in style to the very fashionable Members Only jackets but a cheaper non-brand version that my mum had bought at a market. (She sometimes accidentally bought fashionable stuff, and this had been one of those rare but delightful purchases.) I was also wearing matching red cotton trousers and red shoes, and I had fashioned a red belt into a headband tied around my curled tresses. I'd received a curling iron for my sixteenth birthday, and I'd been burning my hair into various bouffant shapes for weeks. It was a lot of red. I looked like a walking British mailbox, but I was happy with my outfit, and I strutted with my head held high.

"Oi! You African bubu!"

I stopped dead in my tracks and looked up to where the insult had come from. Angela, a heavyset, mouthy Caribbean girl from the year below me, leaned out of her classroom window. Angela was one of those girls who had friends only because people would rather be with her than at the receiving end of her cussing. She was a fifteen-year-old harridan who, despite my seniority, had insulted me on many occasions throughout the years.

"Who you think you're talking to?" I shouted.

"I can only see one African bubu, so it must be you, Regina Vagina!" I could see the faces of other students at windows in the room looking down and laughing at me. I had been in such a positive headspace, minding my own business, and this girl, who was in class—oh, and where the fuck was the teacher, by the way—was so affronted by my happiness that she had to make a fool of me in my wonderful outfit. Surely she knew what a ferocious fighter I was. Why was she challenging me like this? Let me give her a chance to back out.

"Call me that again and see what happens!"

"What you gonna do, stinking bubu? You think you look so nice, but you're still an African!"

Okay, then.

I entered the school building and stomped up to her class-room. Angela was in the middle of a mathematics class with Mr. Mohammed, a slight, mild-mannered man from Algeria—a good teacher but one who struggled to control unruly students. He was no match for Angela. Or me. I strode into the classroom and grabbed Angela, pushed her up against the wall, and began pummeling her. She didn't stand a chance as I unleashed five years of pent-up embarrassment and fury on her. I doubt she got so much as a slap on me. Poor Angela must have thought that being in a classroom with a responsible adult would have saved her from a beating, and that the teacher would have intervened before I could get to her, but Mr. Mohammed did nothing. He stood back with the other students and watched. After I'd hit her with a few good flurries, Mr. Mohammed tapped me on the shoulder as if to say, "Okay, you've made your point. You can leave now." And I did. As I left, I swore I saw a small cryptic smile on his face. I mean, he was from Algeria. He was an African too. Maybe he had secretly enjoyed me defending our continent, or maybe he'd just been fed up with Angela's insolence and let me do what he knew he'd lose his career and freedom for doing himself.

He still reported me, though. The next day I was called into the principal's office.

The no-nonsense headmistress cut to the chase. "You dislocated Angela's shoulder, and her parents want to have you arrested."

Oh. Fuck. I imagined my future draining down a massive plughole, and that image then cut to my mother's furious face. I was in deep shit. I was in the middle of taking the O levels that I'd spent the last five years preparing for, and if I wasn't allowed to complete them, I would be screwed. Leaving school with no qualifications and labeled a criminal was not an option. I might as well have walked out of that school and in front of a train.

"Luckily for you," she continued, "I talked them out of ruining your future, but you will not be allowed to return to this school to continue your A-level studies in the sixth form."

"But I'll still be allowed to do my O levels, right?"

"Yes, but after that you will not be allowed to step foot on school property."

Phew. I didn't give a flying monkey poop about not going to D&K for my A levels. I'd been wanting out of there since that first biology lesson at eleven years old. Compared to what could have happened, I thought I'd gotten off pretty easy. All I'd have to contend with was my mother's anger, but if I could get to her before and maybe soften the blow—

"I've called your mother and informed her of my decision." *Shit.*

My mum screamed at me for hours. I was sixteen now and too old to beat, but my mum could beat me just as hard with her tongue. She screamed at me for acting like a homeless ruffian, for embarrassing her, for nearly ruining *our* future doctor opportunities, for making her now face finding me a new school at such short notice, all the while refusing to listen to my side of the story or acknowledge the years of abuse I'd suffered that had led up to that point and the immense pressure I was under.

I returned to my bedroom furious and at the end of my tether. *Fuck Angela and her big mouth! Fuck the school, fuck these O levels, and fuck you, Mum! If you hadn't given me this stupid name, and actually let me go places and have friends, maybe none of this would have happened. All you care about is how good you look to your Nigerian friends, as you boast about how well I'm doing, but you don't actually care about me. I hate my life! I don't want to live anymore! You believe in reincarnation. Maybe I'll come back to a better family!*

I rushed to the medicine cabinet in the bathroom and pulled

out a tub of aspirins. I returned to my room and proceeded to swallow all the pills left inside. There were approximately thirty left. *That should do it*, I thought. *I hope Mum finds my body and lives the rest of her life in regret.* I decided to write a quick note before I fell into unconsciousness, detailing my anger, pain, and unwillingness to continue carrying this burden of expectation, then I left it pinned under the empty aspirin tub on my side table while I lay down on my bed and waited to die.

Fifteen minutes later I was still conscious. *When does this shit kick in? I could go down and get more pills, but somebody's bound to come looking for me shortly, as I never get more than twenty minutes alone in this house without being summoned to do something. I better just close my eyes and be unconscious until I am unconscious.* I lay still, with my eyes closed, for another fifteen minutes, then I heard the bell on the landing outside my room ring. I ignored it and repositioned myself to look suitably unconscious. The bell rang a few more times, and then I heard footsteps on the stairs. I played dead.

Taiwo walked into the room. "Mum wants you now." I played dead. "I know you heard me. Mum is calling you. Didn't you hear the bell?" I played dead. I heard her walk over to the bed and stop. Then I heard the rustle as she picked up the note and read it. She then began shaking me. I played dead. Never one to miss an opportunity to bestow a little violence, she pinched me. Then she slapped my face. Hard. And then again. And again. My cheeks stung. I played dead. She ran out of the room.

I later learned she called an ambulance, then went to Sheyi to help her break the news to Mum. My youngest brother, who was thirteen at the time, for some reason was the calmest and wisest in the family, often finding himself counselor and confidant to the older family members. (He still holds that role to this day.) He rushed with Taiwo to tell Mum what was happening. As they approached my mum, Taiwo's exact words to her were "Your precious daughter has taken an overdose." So much for telling her gently. Faced with the potential death of her sister, Taiwo's festering resentment still couldn't help but seep out. My mum screamed and collapsed, writhing and wailing on the floor. The ambulance arrived, and after that, there was no time to get Mum calm enough to deal with the situation. There was a flurry of activity.

The whole time I was conscious, and annoyed that overdoses didn't work like they did on TV. I had hoped that I would fall into a deep sleep, die peacefully, maybe float around for a bit to gloat over my mum's misery at my passing and watch her berate herself for not being nicer to me, then dissipate to be reincarnated into a loving white American family like the Brady Bunch. Instead, I'd taken a bunch of bullshit pills and had to pretend to be dead.

The paramedics were not fooled. I heard one of them ask what I'd taken, and on hearing that it was aspirin, he noted, "Then she ain't unconscious." He then leaned close to my face and said, "Come on, love, stop playing. Let's walk downstairs and get you to the hospital."

But I was committed. I kept channeling a possum. Those poor guys had to carry me down four flights of stairs into the ambulance while my mum was still collapsed in her room, screaming in the background. *Serves you right*, I thought. I was still angry enough to want to die out of spite.

Taiwo rode with me to the hospital while Sheyi stayed behind to get Mum coherent enough to follow later.

I had not done proper research into suicide methods, otherwise I would have seriously considered jumping off a high-rise, walking in front of a bus, or battering my own skull in with a rolling pin had I known what was coming next. I was wheeled into an operating room. I'd feigned waking up at this point, just in time to hear the doctor say the words "gastric lavage." Posh words for "stomach pump."

I was held down while they forced my mouth open with some kind of metal torture instrument, then they fed a large, long tube into my mouth, down my throat, and into my stomach, and proceeded to siphon out my stomach contents. No anesthetic. The whole time I was awake, crying, gagging, and choking. Holy shit, I'd just tried to kill myself, and it felt like they were trying to finish the job! It was like they had chosen the most barbaric deterrent for suicidal teenagers. *That's right, we'll vacuum your insides like a wet carpet. Now go tell your friends what happened here!*

After the procedure, they kept me in overnight to observe and make sure no further damage had been done to my system by the drugs. They moved me to a private room and asked me if I wanted to see my mother. I said no. Two minutes later she walked into the room, because when had what I wanted ever mattered?

Now, if you are a partaker of soppy American movies, you'd be forgiven for thinking that after a suicide attempt, a near death of your child, there might be hugs, tears, maybe a mutual apology. Nope. This was my Nigerian mum. She stood by my bed as cool as a cucumber, nothing even resembling the screaming mess she'd been earlier. She'd obviously been told that I was alive, and probably fine, and so had gathered herself and rebooted, returning to her normal stoic exterior.

She stared down at me and asked, "Are you okay?"

"Yes."

"Good."

Then she followed up with the question she really wanted to ask: "When is your biology exam?"

Fortunately, I'd tried to kill myself on a Thursday. My biology exam was the following Tuesday. Plenty of time to recover and still be on track to become a doctor.

. . .

The suicide attempt did not foster a new era in Nigerian mum-daughter relations. After I came home from the hospital, my mum refused to talk about what happened, except to tell me how stupid I'd been and how I had nearly ruined my future, which was pretty obvious, as dead people tend to not have those. There was no processing of what had led me to take an overdose, no family meeting to discuss our feelings and how we all might have been affected, and absolutely no talk of me, God forbid, seeing a therapist. *"So you want me to waste money for you to be telling our family business to a stranger? You have really gone mad!"* My mum was too busy working hard to make sure all her children succeeded. She had no time for a child for whom she'd sacrificed so much giving up because of stress. This word just didn't exist in my mum's vocabulary. It was in the fairy-tale realm with "art" and "yoga." *"So you want to give up on all this opportunity because you are stressed? Keep talking this nonsense and I will give you real stress. Idiot."*

So my mother did what she does best: suppressed her feelings, put her head down, and set about finding me another school, while my job was to shut the fuck up, finish my O levels, and get the grades that would allow me access to another good school. And that's what I did.

I took my exams for each subject in June. To be accepted to study for A levels, I had to pass at least six subjects at O level with A, B, or C grades. Any grade below that was pretty much a fail. I would then sweat till my results were mailed to me in mid-August, and my results would tell me what I'd be doing come September.

My mum found me a school: Camden School for Girls in North London. I had been in mixed schools my entire school life, but Mum had obviously decided that crunching a girl's shoulder was a stepping stone to prison, pregnancy, and crack addiction, in no particular order, so a girls school it would be, and as usual, I had no say in the matter. Camden Girls is a highly rated school. Started in 1871 by Frances Mary Buss, a known campaigner for women's voting rights and the first woman in history to use the title "headmistress," the school was set up to provide affordable education for girls. To this day, it is one of the highest performing schools in the country and produces the best exam results in the area outside the private-school sector. Although Camden is a government-funded school, it has high standards for the students allowed to attend, and so my place there in September was dependent on my exam results. A point my mother had no qualms about repeating on a daily basis. *You do know it was precisely this kind of pressure that had me gobbling aspirins like a Nigerian Pac-Man just a few weeks ago, right?*

I didn't care what school I ended up in, as long as it was far enough away from D&K for me to complete my reinvention and not come across anybody from my previous life. Camden fit the bill, and I hoped I'd get in for both my and my mum's peace of mind.

One morning about six weeks after I had completed my exams, my mum excitedly called me into her bedroom. As I entered, she grabbed me by the shoulders and kissed me on the cheek. I recoiled in shock. My mother had never hugged or kissed me in my life. Physical affection was not practiced in our family.

Once, after a steady diet of American kids shows, with their abundance of hugs and kisses, I made the mistake of asking: "Mummy, do you love us?" To which she responded, "I *like* all of my children!" She couldn't even bring herself to say the word. I'd never seen any kind of physical affection between her and the step-bastard, though there must have been *something* she'd initially liked about him besides the car. And they did have a daughter. Even when we were watching TV and a couple began kissing, she would make noises of disgust: "Pleh, pleh, why so much kissing and cuddling! Ugggh!" And turn the TV off. So kissing was not a thing in our family, which is why I nearly fainted when she face-planted me.

"What happened?" I asked.

My mum waved an envelope in my face. My exam results. They'd come. And although they were addressed to me, she'd opened them. I wasn't surprised or upset. Just relieved. I'd passed nine O levels. The only subject I hadn't passed was chemistry, for which I'd gotten an E. I had been terrible at chemistry from the beginning, so I had skipped studying for it and concentrated on the other nine. That had paid off big time. Mum was ecstatic and proud, and I was rich. I'd be starting my new, better life in another school, after enjoying the rest of my summer with forty-five pounds of the step-bastard's money in my pocket. He had bet that he would be paying me no more than fifteen pounds. He was about to eat some humble pie laced with shit. Mum marched me straight to him, brandishing that letter like a flag, and watched him reluctantly count the money out and put it in my hand, while she chuckled.

A few days after that, my mum received a phone call from the principal of St. David and St. Katharine's. Apparently the school wanted to congratulate me on my excellent exam results, and let me know that they had had second thoughts about my expulsion and would be more than happy to welcome me back to the sixth form to continue my A level studies. Second thoughts my ass. They simply hadn't expected me to do so well, and now they needed to add me back into their system to bolster performance statistics. Mum took great pleasure in turning them down.

8

If You Sleep with an Itching Anus, You Will Definitely Wake Up with Your Hand Smelling

Before I learned to use my humor to defuse stressful situations, I decided that at school people would leave me alone if I was the craziest and scrappiest, and so if someone tried to humiliate me, I would launch myself at them, no matter their size, age, sex. I soon got a reputation, and most of the teasing became whispers behind my back, as no one actually wanted their ass kicked.

I had to develop a reputation as a tough girl to protect myself from the teasing, but the first and only time in my life I actually threatened the life of another person was when I was sixteen years old, after coming home from what was supposed to have been my first day at my dream weekend job at Topshop.

Part-time work was a coming-of-age thing in the '80s. Every fifteen- and sixteen-year-old yearned for a Saturday job to supplement their pocket money, or allowance. In my case, a job meant independence and an escape from my mum's overprotectiveness. A job meant money, which meant better clothes, which meant acceptance, which meant a better teenage life. Money was also a step closer to buying a car, which—most important of all—meant freedom. Mum wouldn't be able to open up her scrapbook of death and threaten me with the dangers of all the rapists and murderers lurking on the night bus when I could drive myself home to safety.

I had taken my O levels in June, and school was finished for me until September, when I would start studying for my A levels at Camden Girls, instead of finding an orphanage for teenagers, as if I had failed my O levels, I suspect my mum would have gladly surrendered me to one. This meant I had over two months off. I was sixteen now, so too old to be stuck in the house, begging my mum to let me go to the park every once in a while. I was old enough to work.

The dream place to get a part-time job as a teenager in London is the West End, a district where the majority of London's main tourist attractions, theaters, entertainment venues, nightclubs, and shops are located. Our version of Midtown Manhattan, Causeway Bay in Hong Kong, or the 8th arrondissement in Paris. It's the UK's shopping Mecca.

When I was younger, and not allowed to move more than seven feet from the house on weekends, I'd often hear kids at school on Monday talking about spending their Saturdays in "the West End." It sounded amazing, and I was desperate to go. I had romanticized notions of this magical, forbidden area of London, where kids roamed free, then came back with cool clothes and stories, and I couldn't wait until I was old enough to sneak there. I finally made it when I was in my last months at D&K. I had two free periods between lessons, which gave me a two-hour window to visit the mysterious land and return to school with no one any the wiser. I jumped on the London Underground to Oxford Circus, which brings you out snap bang in the middle of the West End. I was excited.

I ran up the steps of the station, expecting to exit into a shopping version of Narnia. I was sorely disappointed to find myself on a regular London street. A slightly busier London street, but still a London street. With shops. *This is it?* I thought. *This is the West End? Just bigger shops?* After years of hearing about this place, and having it be forbidden to me for so long, I had been expecting . . . something! Brighter lights, different signs, better-looking people. Different-colored buses. Anything not so ordinary.

I walked around for about twenty-five minutes, peeking into shops, with exactly three pounds in my pocket, then returned to school. I came to appreciate the West End later, as the best area to get a Saturday job, because prestige pays, but I never forgot that initial anticlimax.

There was a hierarchy of part-time jobs. Bakeries, supermarkets, and grocery stores were at the bottom. The money varied, depending on the company and its size, but bakeries and fast-food joints paid the least. Perks came in the form of how many free burgers you could stuff down your gullet during your lunch break, and at bakeries you could take home some of the more perishable pastries at the end of the day.

The first and only bakery I worked at was called Coombs, and I was paid £1.25 per hour. I gained about ten pounds in the two months I worked there. Luckily for my arteries, I was fired from that job. The shop typically opened at 7 a.m., when the cakes were fresh out of the oven, which meant I had to be at work at 6:30 a.m. Which meant I had to be out of bed by 5 a.m., which meant, as a non-morning person, I was never going to last in that job. I was late. A lot. In fact, if I remember correctly, the only time I was on time was for the job interview. Bakeries and early mornings had to come off my job list.

Supermarkets were the next step up. The hours were more to my liking—a 12 to 8 p.m. shift I could do. The pay at the big ones like Sainsbury's and Tesco was average, around that time £2.50 per hour, for either stacking shelves or working on the register. The register jobs were the most coveted, as you got to sit down, and you had a good view of the whole store, so you could watch the boys you liked. Plus all the store gossip came through the cash registers. Who kissed who in the back of the storeroom last week, who got caught stealing and was sacked, who was seen in the pharmacy section picking up discounted herpes ointments. Handling money also always felt more responsible. A perk with food retailers was that you got to take home the nearly out-of-date stuff at a huge staff discount. And that included baked goods. *Fuck you, Coombs!*

I worked at Sainsbury's later, when I was seventeen, and I even went out with a little Irish boy there for a few months, because that was what girls were supposed to be doing, and though I'd had crushes on girls and female teachers at school, I hadn't actually realized what that meant. I hadn't yet consciously thought about my sexuality. Besides, I still liked boys too. Just not as much.

My little Irish boy, John, lived nearby, so he would take me home and we'd eat lunch with his parents there, and I remember them being very sweet and welcoming. His dad worked at Sainsbury's as well. John was nineteen years old, but we never had sex. We used to just make out, which I remember enjoying immensely. Later, for my eighteenth birthday, John took me to the first nightclub I had ever been to. Up until that point, as you well know, I wasn't allowed to go anywhere. That day I packed my nightclub outfit in a bag and changed into it after work so I could sneak off with my boyfriend. But when I got to the club and realized that no amount of supermarket overtime was going to explain my getting home at 5 a.m., I was terrified. I went to a phone box and called my mum, just blurting into the phone, "I'm eighteen now! I'm calling from a nightclub!"

"Okay. Good night." And she hung up.

I was flabbergasted. It was like she had known this moment would come and had been prepared for it. I couldn't believe it—I was free!

That was the beginning of the end, as every weekend from then on I went out clubbing. Every. Weekend. From eighteen till I left home at twenty-four.

But I digress . . . back to my threatening the life of another person . . .

At the very top of the part-time-work hierarchy were the department stores and fashion retailers. The top department store chain was Marks & Spencer, an international retailer established in the 1880s. They were known for carrying the best quality British-sourced groceries as well as British-made clothing. Their clothing wasn't that fashionable, but they were world-renowned, and their customer service was unmatched. As long as you had proof of purchase, you could return any item, no matter how long you'd had it. *No matter how long you'd had it.* You could wear a sweater for ten years and return it, faded, sweat marked, food stained, run over by a car, in six different pieces, for a full refund, no questions asked. People would travel from as far away as Saudi Arabia to shop there. Most important for me, they paid £3.20 per hour. The big bucks. They were great employers, and they knew it, so it was notoriously competitive to get into, and those who did never left, so you had to have your ear to the ground or have friends who worked there so you would get the heads-up when the company was recruiting.

Such was the prestige of working there that kids who got in had to let everyone know they were one of the chosen few by wearing their M&S uniforms *all the time*. I knew a dude who wore his uniform out on the weekends, just so girls knew he was balling. And that shit worked. Older guys swiveled their BMW keys around their index fingers. Teenagers wore their department-store uniforms.

Working at Marks was the holy grail, and I eventually ended up getting a job there when I was eighteen, but a good fashion store was almost as prestigious, and that is where I wanted to work at sixteen. Those stores didn't pay as well, but the clothes were more fashionable, you received discounts, and there was no uniform. You got to wear the product, plus you were in the middle of cool-kid central on the weekends, as everyone flocked to these shops to buy their weekend clubbing garb.

Topshop was at the top of the fashion-store list. A huge, multilevel place, the main store housed all the newest designer clothing, accessories, and sneakers. It was and still is located on the corner of Oxford and Regent streets, the first store you see after exiting Oxford Circus station. This store was the first port of call for *every* teenager and twenty-something who passed through the West End looking for something cool to wear. It was a combination of T.J. Maxx, Manhattan's Century 21, and a day party all rolled into one. There were cool, good-looking sales staff of different classes and ethnicities (take note Abercrombie & Fitch), loud up-to-date music playing throughout the store, and a general vibe of too-cool-for-school-ness.

Every open position advertised for this store promptly received applications from every young person within a two-hundred-mile radius. So when I applied for a Saturday job there a couple of months after my sixteenth birthday, I was not hopeful, but I still filled out the application like I was applying to be an astronaut. I listed all the subjects at school for which I expected to get good exam grades, I listed hobbies I didn't have, I feigned a love of fashion, and I even made up a few extracurricular activities, like skiing and volunteering in orphanages. I was overjoyed when I was called in for an interview, and though my wardrobe was limited, as my mum had no interest in buying me the latest fashions ("You can buy all the clothes you want when you become a doctor!"), I had enough pieces to cobble together a decent outfit.

I removed the breast-pocket school insignia from my old navy-blue school blazer and rolled up the sleeves, Duran Duran style. Underneath, I wore a cream satin shirt with a chained brooch—those were all the rage then, and luckily cheap to buy in costume-jewelry stores. I matched that with acid-washed jeans and a pair of leather boots I'd gotten for my fifteenth birthday—the only fashionable boots my mum had bought me, after two years of begging. I was lucky they were still fashionable. I'd worn them so much that the soles had holes in them, and I put plastic bags inside the boots so my feet wouldn't get wet when it rained. My unruly hair was curled into a high bouffant and finished with a matching headband fashioned out of the belt that had come with the shirt. The hair alone took me an hour. I looked the shit. I was half Janet Jackson, half Spandau Ballet. I was the epitome of cool and fashionable; I deserved to be working in the trendiest shop on London's Oxford Street.

I arrived forty minutes early for my interview, so I watched as other immaculately dressed teenagers traipsed in and out. When it was my turn, I was led into a small office where I sat opposite a balding white man in his forties. He introduced himself as

Robert and proceeded to ask me questions about myself, what I was doing at school, and why I wanted to work at Topshop. I went on the charm offensive. I told him that I wanted to work in the fashion industry when I left school, and Topshop was the perfect training ground with their support of the new wave of fashion designers, from Mary Quaint in the 1960s to brands like French Connection. I'd gone to the library and researched all this, as these were pre-Google times. Robert was extremely impressed, and after a friendly twenty-minute chat, he offered me a job on the spot. I was to start work in two weeks. I'd be working Friday evenings and all day on Saturdays, with an option to work full-time during the summer holidays.

I thanked Robert profusely and floated out of the store. After years of being Regina Vagina at school, I had finally entered the cool phase of my life. I would be starting work at the coolest shop in the West End as Gina. I was going to get a staff discount on all these cool designer clothes. I was going to get an equally cool boyfriend, and we'd go to all the cool nightclubs. Life was about to get infinitely better. I went home and phoned everyone I knew to tell them the good news, then spent the next two weeks methodically arranging outfits for my first week at work.

That two weeks dragged on interminably, but the day finally arrived for my first day of training at Topshop. I was up and dressed early. My mum was up also, as were Dele and Sheyi, as she was dragging them to the market to do the weekly shopping. I arrived at work thirty minutes early and wandered for a few minutes around different departments, wondering which one I would be working in, before making myself known to the floor supervisor. I was Gina, the new girl, here to begin my training. She looked confused. She brought out a roster and, skimming it, informed me that my name wasn't on it. No problem, I thought. Maybe Robert had me down for another department, maybe women's shoes or lingerie. I had no interest in selling knickers, but hey, it was still Topshop.

The supervisor lady led me to a chair outside Robert's office, where I was left sitting for the next forty-five minutes. I was slightly perturbed, worrying that I'd wasted one of my few outfits on today, when I was probably about to be told they'd mixed up the dates and I'd be starting tomorrow instead. Annoying but still workable. I was looking forward to a chatty reunion with Robert, a laugh about their mess-up, then returning the next day to begin my fashion work.

Robert finally arrived looking flustered and seeming hesitant when he approached me.

"Hi, Robert! There seems to be a bit of a mess-up with the roster. I definitely have the date correct, as I wrote it in my Filofax."

"Please come into the office, Gina."

Uh-oh, I thought.

When we got into his office, Robert sat down slowly and heavily behind his desk. A feeling of dread started to settle in my chest, but I was still hopeful. Okay, maybe I'd be starting work in three weeks. Shit, but still doable. Maybe they hadn't been that impressed with my cobbled-together outfit and I'd need a makeover before I started work. Still doable. Maybe Robert had had a family emergency and had forgotten to add me to the roster. His screw-up, so I still had a job, right? All these thoughts whizzed through my head, but none of them came close to what actually came out of his mouth.

"We called your house last week, to see if you could start early. Your father told us that you had stolen his money and run away, and that he didn't know where you were."

My body temperature seemed to drop 20 degrees in a split

second, and suddenly I could feel my heart pumping in my ears. Whatever Robert said next, I didn't hear, as I felt like I was underwater, and all I could hear was my blood coursing through my veins. Over the rushing noise of my increasing blood pressure, I stammered: "But, but, I don't have a father. I mean, I do, but he's . . . That guy who answered, he's not my dad, he's my stepdad, and he's lying! It's not true. I'm here. I can start now!"

Robert looked at me with a mixture of pity and mild disgust. "I'm sorry, Gina. We gave your position to somebody else."

I couldn't believe what I was hearing and began hyperventilating. All my hopes and fantasies of the last few weeks began shredding before my eyes. "But it's not true!" I shouted.

Robert flinched, and I saw the fear in his eyes. That made me clench my nails into my palms to calm myself down. He'd actually been, for a split second, frightened that I was going to attack him. And if he thought this young Black girl was violent enough to hit him, a mere stranger, then how much of a stretch would it be to steal from her own dad?

I struggled to steady my voice. "My stepdad is a malicious liar. He made that up. None of that is true. I just came from home. Is there another position available? I'll work in any department. Please. I'm a fast learner."

Robert retorted, "Afraid not. You could maybe reapply in six months."

With the terseness of his response, I knew at that moment I was never going to work in Topshop. I was marked as a potential thief. No matter what I said, I was tainted. I wanted to cry, scream, and throw things around, but I didn't want to be dragged screaming from the store, past a line of cool girls shaking their heads and tutting, *"She'll always be Regina Vagina. Why does she keep trying to be one of us?"*

I thanked Robert for his time and walked slowly out of Top-shop with my head held high, past the supervisor lady, who looked like she was trying not to smirk at the silly criminal who thought she could gain entry into this hallowed space, and past all the other young workers, who seemed to be deliberately busying themselves and avoiding my eye as I passed them. I tried to appear nonchalant, though my stiff gait probably revealed I was anything but. My back was ramrod straight, and I had to concentrate to bend my knees and put one foot in front of the other.

When I was a safe distance away, I found a nearby McDonald's, sat in a bathroom stall, and prepared to cry my eyes out. But I couldn't. The urge to cry had dissipated on the short walk to that bathroom stall. It had been replaced by a white-hot fury. I was consumed with anger and hatred towards that man, the step-bastard. He had truly lived up to the name. Fairy tales were full of stories of evil stepmothers, as if only women were capable of such nasty, vindictive things, but this man had taken conniving and cowardice to a new level. Not only had he ruined this opportunity for me but he also had gleefully watched over the last two weeks as I had prepared for this job and discussed with my brothers the cool stuff they'd be able to afford with my staff discount. I had no doubt he had listened in on my phone conversations with my friends, who were all excited and jealous at my good fortune. I had not realized how low this man was willing to stoop. That morning he had watched me dress. He'd watched my mother wish me good luck in my new job. He'd watched me skip out of the house to a job he already knew I no longer had. That fucking snake. Ever since I'd passed my exams, therefore winning the bet, he'd been waiting for an opportunity to punish me. I was going to kill him. As I'd grown older, taller, and more confident, the step-bastard had become more fearful of me. I was more outspoken and had begun to question his authority. He still tried to assert it by trying to goad me into anger, so he could report my disrespect to my mum, knowing that she would not tolerate any disrespect towards him no matter how unreasonable he was. I knew what he had been trying to do, and I had spent a lot of time trying to contain my fury.

One Friday evening while I was cooking the weekly stew for the family, he entered the kitchen on some pretense and began to try to pick a fight with me. Although he had never cooked the stew, he stood at my shoulder, shouting that I was doing it wrong, that I was not seasoning the meat correctly, and that I was useless. As much as I wanted to batter him around the head with the wooden spoon I was holding, or at least tell him to fuck off, my Nigerian upbringing to respect my elders repressed my natural inclinations. I refused to engage, which infuriated him even more. He screamed at me to get out of the kitchen, and I gladly left. Both he and I knew my mum would be furious if she came home and the food wasn't cooked, and the step-bastard also knew that if it wasn't done tonight, I would have to spend my Saturday cooking. He could no longer physically beat me, because he could see in my eyes that I would be the child to grab something and kill him with it, but he could inconvenience me at every opportunity. I wouldn't stand for it. I returned to my room, wrote out a meticulous list of ingredients and instructions, and persuaded Dele to sneak down to the kitchen and finish the cooking. My brothers and I, in times of crisis, had one another's backs. When Mum came home two hours later, she was surprised and somewhat amused to find her son in the kitchen, putting the finishing touches on the simmering pots of chicken, oxtails, and jollof rice.

The step-bastard's behavior had become increasingly unreasonable over the years. As Mum's business had become more successful, she was less reliant on him financially. She had gone from selling stuff out of the spare bedroom in our house to having a network of people in England and Nigeria selling stuff for her. She was making her own money, and the step-bastard could feel his power eroding. They were fighting more, and I'm unsure at what point he became physically abusive towards her—or if he had been all along—since my mother hid it well. She never appeared cowed by him, and she refused to let him shout her down, even though she would have known what was coming. We kids were usually sent to our rooms at the top of the house, but we would hear the bumps and crashes as they fought.

I remember when I was around age ten walking into the front room and seeing my mother bent over with her arm held behind her back by Oncle. They both stopped dead, like statues, when I entered the room. "Dapo, go upstairs. We are just playing," my mum said, and I did as I was told, convincing myself they must have been playing a game of Twister, although we had never had that game in the house.

Rather than go to couples counseling, the Nigerian custom for a married couple having issues was for them to sit down with an elder couple from the Nigerian community who would act as intermediaries. Mum and the step-bastard tried this once. Dele, Sheyi, and I were sent upstairs while, for some reason, Asi was allowed to stay with her father during this intervention. We hid by the staircase on the next floor, trying to listen to what was happening. The couple were invited in, and they all entered the front room to talk. Within ten minutes, the step-bastard's voice rose as he shouted over my mum. Suddenly there was a series of the familiar bumping and crashing sounds, accompanied by four-year-old Asi screaming, "No, Daddy, no!" and the couple shouting, "No! You cannot do that!" The step-bastard, incensed by something Mum had uttered, had lost control and beaten her up in front of the mediators.

After that, they began to lead increasingly separate lives in the same house, only coming together for trips to the market to buy food for the house, and only *if* he felt in the mood to drive her. If not, Dele, Sheyi, and I had to get several busses with her to the market to help her carry all the shopping home. The more separate their lives became, the more erratic his behavior. And the angrier, more conniving, and vindictive he became. On a few occasions we'd come home to find the house locked and bolted from the inside, so we couldn't get in. He and Asi were in the house, while Mum and the rest of her kids had to walk around the neighborhood for several hours until he decided to let us back in. Mum refused to leave the house, as she had put up most of the money for it. His name was on the mortgage, as he had had a job with a paycheck, which had been required for the loan, but Mum insisted she was not letting him take this house from her and her children, so we stayed.

Things grew stranger and stranger. One evening, when I was around fourteen, Step-Bastard insisted that everyone leave the house with him on some errand. When we returned, he opened the door gingerly and announced that we had been burgled. Mum pushed past him, saw the house had been ransacked, and immediately collapsed, screaming. On further inspection, all of Mum's expensive gold had been stolen, some of which she had been trading and selling. A lot of her shop inventory had also gone. Although Mum had had her jewelry in a secure hiding spot that only family members knew about, the burglars had found it and had had time to sift through it, taking only the real gold and leaving the costume jewelry. Almost as if they'd known exactly where the good stuff was and how long the house's occupants would be gone. Strangely enough, Step-Bastard had had only a few minor things taken, and all of Asi's expensive toys were untouched, including her gleaming, never-ridden bike, still standing in the hallway.

Luckily the house contents were covered by insurance, and a claim was made. Several months later, frustrated at still not having received recompense, Mum called the insurance company, only to be informed that they'd already sent a check for £3,000, which was a lot of money in the '80s, and that it had been cashed. Mum was furious but decided not to confront Step-Bastard directly. Instead, she sent Sheyi downstairs to ask him for her share of the insurance payout.

Step-Bastard still exploded. "You are sending the boy to ask for the money? Why don't you ask me yourself?" he bellowed up at my mum, who stood on the landing above him.

"Okay, then. Where is my money? They sent the check, and you cashed it months ago!"

"Who told you this, and what are you trying to say? *Say it!*"

The shouting brought Dele and me out of our rooms. We stood next to Mum on one side while Sheyi stood next to her on the other as they continued to argue. "Where is my money, *oyie*?"

At that Edo word, Step-Bastard roared and began bounding up the stairs towards my mum. *"Who are you calling 'thief'?"*

Dele and I both jumped in front of Mum and ran down the stairs to meet him halfway and block his advance. Sheyi put himself in front of Mum, as the last line of defense, in case he got through Dele and me. Step-Bastard screamed and frothed at the mouth as he tried to bulldoze past Dele and me as we clung to the wall and the banister. Some of the spindles of the banister snapped as Step-Bastard tried to push through the human-child barrier to get to Mum, but we held strong.

After several minutes, he was spent and gave up. He stood, calmly rearranged himself, and spoke directly to Dele, Sheyi, and me. "She's lucky you are here. I would have killed her. Tell her I will give her a thousand pounds of the money when I see fit. The rest is mine." He then disappeared back into his man cave. Mum never saw a penny of that money.

From then on, he slowly grew crazier and crazier, and it became more impossible to remain in the house with him. On one trip to the market, as Mum was stepping out of the car, he drove off at speed, with one of her legs still partially in the vehicle. She managed to get her foot out just in time to avoid being dragged to her death. Later, he made a sly observation about men getting away with killing their wives. Mum never got in his car again and began making plans to leave.

Besides my mum, I seemed to be the main focus of his wrath, so I had resolved to be out of the house as much as possible. A part-time job after school and on Saturdays was the perfect solution, which is another reason why I had ended up interviewing for that position in Topshop.

If you fail to take away a strong man's sword when he is on the ground, will you do it when he gets up?

The entire Tube ride from Topshop Oxford Circus back to Finsbury Park was a blur. I barely remember the twenty-minute walk from the station, just the repetitive clenching and unclenching of my fists. I was going to hurt the step-bastard so bad, damn the consequences. All I could imagine was the satisfaction I would feel as I pummeled the years of pent-up fury into his face. My hands shook as I struggled to get my front-door key into the lock. As soon as the lock turned, I threw open the front door so hard it smashed into the wall behind it. I stepped in just in time to see the step-bastard scurry behind the door of his man cave, slam it shut, and engage the door's bolt. I rushed to the door, screaming at the top of my lungs. "I'm going to fucking kill you!" I kicked, pummeled, and threw myself against that door. I screamed some more, I called him every name that I'd ever called him in my head. "Where's your Hold the Bottle now, you fucking coward! I'm going to wrap it around your fucking skull! *Come out!* Come out and see if you can still beat me, you fucking weasel!" He didn't. He stayed in that room while I paced up and down outside for several hours until my mum and brothers returned home.

"Dapo, what is going on here? What are you doing?" my mother asked when she got home.

"I'm going to kill your husband!" I declared, with all the years of my pent-up fury finally unleashed. I somehow managed to explain what he'd done, and my mother began speaking to him through the door in her mother tongue, Edo. I didn't understand what she was saying, but I could tell—from the fact that her voice had lowered a couple of octaves and each sentence sounded like it ended in daggers—that she was cursing him out, and somehow that calmed me. She was on my side. She was not going to force me to apologize to him and show him respect he did not deserve. Mum stood with her daughter against this tyrant, and the fury drained out of me in that instant.

The police turned up five minutes later. Of course he'd called them. Piece of shit. He'd told them that a young woman had broken into his house and was trying to kill him. No mention of the fact that this was his stepdaughter whom he had terrorized for over ten years. When they entered the house, he then shuffled out of his hiding place, looking sheepish and weak.

My mum explained the situation to them, that this was nothing more than a domestic dispute. They left, but not before lecturing the step-bastard about wasting police time. My mum, myself, and the boys then walked upstairs to our rooms, followed by Asi, who unbeknownst to me had sat at the top of the first landing and witnessed the entire confrontation with her father from start to finish.

The next few weeks in the house passed without incident. Mainly because untethered from our binding contract to show the step-bastard respect, my brothers and I were free to ignore him completely while going about our business. No longer were we forced to say "Good morning, Oncle," "Good afternoon, Oncle," "Good night, Oncle." My mum knew better than to insist on this anymore. And best of all, he knew. The whole house had witnessed how he'd cowered when confronted by me, and so the fear he had used to run the household was gone. Kaput. Finito. Over. We saw him for the child-bullying, woman-beating coward that he was. He spent all his time scurrying between work and his cave, with fewer and fewer visits from Asi as she gravitated closer to us.

A month after the Topshop incident, Mum called us all into her suite of rooms and told us that we needed to pack up all our things, as we would be leaving in two days. She had organized temporary accommodations for us, and she would fight for her share of the house from afar. She asked ten-year-old Asi what she wanted to do. Asi had a choice to stay behind with her father or leave with us. Although spoiled by her father at home, she had not made any friendships at school with other children, and so despite her disdain for us, and my and my brothers' ambivalence towards her, she chose to come with us, and was sworn to secrecy.

Forty-eight hours later, a huge moving truck turned up outside the house on Lancaster Road. My mother and her four remaining children loaded up that truck in silence with all the clothes, toys, and whatever possessions we could carry while the step-bastard looked on in dumbfounded shock. When the truck was fully loaded, we all climbed in, and the driver pulled away with all of us looking straight ahead into our new future. Not even Asi turned back to look at her father.

Years later, I asked Mum why she, such a strong, self-sufficient woman, had stayed with him so long.

"You young ones can just have babies all over the place, no husband, nothing. In my day, it was shameful. How many men would have taken on a woman with four children already? Heh? Abandoned by not one but *two* useless men? I took what I could get. He was a good provider."

"But he hit you!" I blurted.

"So what?" she responded. "I have a sharp tongue, and I pushed him too far sometimes!"

While Nigeria is a multicultural society comprised of hundreds of ethnic groups, each with its own traditional value system, the prevalent belief is that men are the authority figures and women are expected to show due respect for that subordinate position at all times. This is the tradition Mum had been raised under, and although she was headstrong and independent, she still held those beliefs.

I remember once a friend of the family discussing with my mum how her daughter, a doctor, had complained that her husband had been physically abusive towards her. Mum had responded, "Well, maybe she was rubbing it in his face that she is a doctor.

She needs to be more humble and make him feel like a man." The doctor's mother had agreed wholeheartedly, and undoubtedly had rushed home to tell her daughter to try harder in her marriage. Mum's mindset was that the physical violence she suffered was just another facet of marriage and a by-product of her being unable or unwilling to bite her tongue. The straw that finally broke the camel's back was a combination of the step-bastard's theft of her money, his threats to her life, and her fear that I would in fact ruin my future by slitting his throat.

9

Where You Fall,
You Should Know that It Is
God Who Pushed You

After we left Step-Bastard, we moved into temporary accommodations for a couple of weeks. We were basically squeezed into a hotel room, paid for by the council, until a suitable flat or house became available. Mum had everything planned, so we were soon able to move to Crouch End, a wealthy enclave in North London inhabited mainly by actors, filmmakers, and other entertainment industry types. It had originally been an area beloved by students and artists because of its cheap rents, but as is often what happens to neighborhoods made desirable by artist communities, gentrification brought in wealthier buyers.

Fortunately at that time there was still a good amount of social housing in the area, and Mum was able to successfully apply for a council flat in a small building, Williams Close, tucked behind all the massive, more expensive houses. It was a nice little flat that was part of a block of six apartments, and we were on the ground floor. It had three bedrooms, one of which my mother shared with Asi. The second bedroom was for the boys, and the third was for me! I had my own room! Okay, it could hardly be called a room, as it was a tiny little box that could only fit a single bed. No room for a side table. In fact the bed was so close to the wall that had my feet been any bigger than a size 6 I'd have had to get out of bed sideways. And definitely no wardrobe. My clothes hung in the coat closet in the hallway or were folded in bags under my bed, but I didn't care. It was my room, a space that I had full ownership of for the first time in my life. And best of all, we were all free of the step-bastard's oppressive presence.

Mum, by this time, had secured a little stall to sell her clothes and bags at the famed Ridley Road market. Well, sort of. Technically it wasn't a stall, and technically Mum wasn't in the market, but it was as close as Mum could get.

Ridley Road market was the go-to weekly shopping spot for every Black person I knew. Immigrant mums would go there with their kids in tow, pulling large wheeled trolleys that by the end of the day would be filled with all the meat and vegetables needed to feed their families for the week. It also sold clothes, bags, shoes, and household goods. I had spent many miserable Saturdays dragging Mum's trolley around that crowded market, trying not to run over people's feet as I struggled to keep up with her. She would whip through the market, squeezing plantains and taking bites out of random apples to test their ripeness, but God forbid if she turned around with an onion and I wasn't there to take it from her to put into the trolley. Every market trip took hours, as Mum bargained at every stall. "I will give you two pounds for that chicken! No? Okay, then, I am walking away . . . Last chance!" Sometimes I felt my mum haggled more for sport than necessity. The market was also where Mum caught up with her friends. If she bumped into one of her Nigerian companions, that often had added a good forty minutes to my torture.

Ridley Road market was where Mum wanted to sell her wares, but getting a stall there was nigh on impossible, unless a stall-holder died or you wanted to pay a humongous premium while also giving out sexual favors. My mum, always resourceful, instead found the leaseholders of a dilapidated old warehouse across the street from the market and rented a corner of it, where she could store her stuff and set up a little stall outside. That became her shop, and she was there seven days a week, rain or shine, setting up, selling, chaining everything back together, and doing it all again the next day.

At that time, my brothers and I complained about being expected to help out at the shop some evenings and weekends, but looking back, I appreciate how hard Mum worked to provide for us on her own while also following her dream of owning her own business. I wanted to take myself off that list of burdens Mum was carrying, and I was still on summer holidays, a month away from starting my new school, so I began working full-time in bakeries, stores, and supermarkets to at least provide for myself. Mum had always said, "You want all these fashionable clothes? Then you pay for them yourself!" Now I actually could. Or so I thought.

Mum demanded half of my earnings. She expected it. Taiwo, before she had moved out and bought her own house, had handed over half her salary to my mum every month. When she began work at her first full-time job as a trainee auditor, she made the huge error of letting my mother see what she earned, complete with a projection of yearly wage increases as she progressed up the corporate ladder. My mother had demanded half my sister's income for her "keep," and she had made a copy of that projection, bringing it out every year to ensure she got a raise that matched my sister's.

I was thirteen when Taiwo had started working. I had watched, learned, and vowed to *never* let that happen to me! When my time came, I told my mum that I was earning half of what I actually was earning, then gave her half of *that*. If I earned ten pounds on Saturday, I told her I'd made five, and she'd take two pounds fifty. She never saw a pay stub. I tore them all up and threw them in the neighbor's trash. I always told her I was paid cash in hand.

Later, when I began working full-time as an engineer, I refused to tell her what my salary was, which infuriated her, but instead I negotiated a mutually agreeable monthly amount for the rent for my bedroom and to help with household expenses. I was happy to contribute, but I was no fool.

The two years we lived in Williams Close were some of my happiest. We children were a little older—me, sixteen; Dele, fifteen; Sheyi, thirteen; and Asi, ten. Mum felt confident enough to concentrate on building her business and letting us fend for ourselves at home, but she would still cook one pot of stew for the week, from which we kids would feed ourselves when we got home from school.

In the early to mid '80s, VCRs were pretty new technology and very expensive to purchase, as were good-quality televisions. Most people rented them from British companies like DER or Rumbelows, which had branches all over UK high streets. Some of these companies also rented VHS movies to go with the VCRs and became one-stop shops for all your at-home entertainment. These companies were eventually put out of business by the availability of cheaper, more reliable equipment, meaning more people could afford to buy instead of rent units, and also by the advent of Blockbuster Video, which had made its way over from the US in 1989, completely obliterating all competition and taking over the UK movie-rental market share. But pre-Blockbuster, Mum's

TV and VCR rental setup included a free VHS movie every day for the first year.

We kids were in heaven. Every day after school we would congregate in the video shop and take turns picking a film to watch. Horror was a favorite genre. Through that little shop, we watched 365 movies, never missing a day. *A Nightmare on Elm Street 1, 2, and 3*; *Robocop*; all the *Alien* movies; *The Entity*; *The Exorcist*. We spent many an evening with the curtains drawn, huddled on the couch, scaring ourselves to death, and we loved it!

On the weekends, Asi would travel back to Lancaster Road to visit her father, the step-bastard, and on the days my mum didn't take the boys to the stall with her, we'd sneak out to the local funfair. Whatever money I'd earned that weekend from my supermarket job I would blow on a day of fun for my brothers. One day in particular I spent thirty pounds just on the bumper cars alone. We rode those for several hours at fifty pence a ride until my money ran out. This was the most freedom we'd ever had, and my favorite summer holiday as a student.

If you think education is expensive, try ignorance.

When summer ended, I began my new life at Camden School for Girls. Although not a private school, this was an upper-middle-class establishment, as was reflected in the subjects some of the girls took, all of which Mum would have classified as "useless": Latin, History of Art, and Classical Civilizations. Mum picked most of my A-level subjects based on "our" daughter-doctor dream, so she erred towards all the sciences. But I've always loved languages, and I wanted to take French. Thankfully, she wasn't too bothered, as long as the other two subjects (biology and physics) were enough to get me into medical school. It also helped my case when I explained that being a doctor who could speak other languages would be much more lucrative. I had no idea if that was true or not, but it sounded legit, and my mum bought it, which was all that counted.

With my new name, half a wardrobe of supermarket-wage-purchased clothing, and my finely tuned personality and humor skills, I strutted into this new school and made friends easily. In fact, I became cool. Coming from a distinctly working-class background in comparison to the other sixteen-year-olds, who'd had mainly sheltered and coddled upbringings, my embellished stories of council estates and skinheads had them enthralled. There was only one other girl, Columbine, who came from a similar background to mine, and we secretly giggled at how gullible these girls were to my stories. I became everyone's cool Black friend.

Our sixth form of approximately a hundred was made up primarily of white girls along with four first-generation Indian girls, Sian (a biracial girl), and me. Sian's mother was white and her father Nigerian. We bonded over our shared Nigerian heritage and the fact that both our fathers had been absent from our lives. At one point we became excited by the possibility that we might even have the same father and be long-lost sisters, like in an American sitcom in which she had been raised by her middle-class mother in relative comfort and I had been banished to the council slums of London's East End.

I reveled in my new status at Camden Girls and became a social butterfly, flitting easily between different friend groups. I could hang with Columbine and laugh at the posh girls. I could hang with the Indian girls, enjoy our shared brownness, and laugh at the posh girls. But I could also hang with the posh girls while maintaining who I was and not trying to be them. I was aware that to some of them I was a fun token, validating their own coolness by my proximity to them, but I didn't care. I preferred the "Your hair is so pretty. Can I touch it?" well-meaning racism to people who had the same hair as me abusing me at the drop of a hat. Because I was the cool Black friend. You wouldn't have believed that we were only in Camden, North London, a mere four and a half miles from Bethnal Green and just three miles from my previous school. But it felt like another world, and I couldn't have been happier.

Camden was one of those pretty progressive schools. We sixth formers were considered young adults, and therefore treated as such. We had a smoking room—yup, a room dedicated as a safe space for those sixteen- to eighteen-year-olds who wanted to smoke their cigarettes in peace. That had not been included in the school brochure, as my mum would never have sent me here in a hundred years had she known. She was puritanical in her belief that cigarettes led to weed, which led to crack, heroin, robbing your own parents, prostitution, death, and shame on your family. In that order.

Mum had often accused me of being an "alcoholic, just like your father," based on the fact that I loved *Coca-Cola*. Not a sugar addict, which is what I really was, an addiction actually mirroring her own, but an alcoholic, based on my love of a sugary nonalcoholic drink. For the record, I don't believe my father was an alcoholic, just a regular guy who liked a beer or five at parties, sometimes got drunk, and found himself facing the wrath of his wife, the lifelong teetotaler. At worst, my father was a lapsed Muslim.

The smoking room was where all the cool girls hung out, so naturally I began to smoke cigarettes and found myself in there a lot, in between classes. After a month of being a smoker, though, I turned to some of the girls. "This is shit. I'd rather be eating a Snickers bar right now. I'm done!" And I gave up smoking. Just like that. Several girls bet me money that I would be back, but a nicotine addiction never got ahold of me. I wasn't willing to keep forcing myself till it did, and so I never smoked again. For all my mum's fears of her offspring falling under the spell of peer pressure and their lives careening off the rails, she should have trusted that she'd raised some pretty strong, self-sufficient kids, who would obviously make mistakes but ultimately lead fruitful lives.

My two years at Camden were my best school years and set me up to move forward in life with a renewed confidence.

When the elderly ones in a house travel, the younger ones grow in experience.

When I began studying French in high school, I became fixated on getting to Paris and conversing with real French people in their actual country. How I would do it with Mum's overprotectiveness, I didn't know, but I was going to get there and work things out when I arrived. And you know what? I did it. In retrospect, I'm impressed with how determined I was to take my dreams and destiny into my own hands. As I stood at the Gare du Nord, a huge hub train station serving northern Paris, I thought, *I made it!* I stood amidst the Parisian hustle and bustle and under the high, ornate ceiling, excited. I was going to walk the Champs-Élysées, see the Arc de Triomphe and the Eiffel Tower. I had enough money to afford one or two McDonald's meals a day for the week, which was plenty for an excited, skinny teenager, but not much money for anything else.

I was then seventeen and had figured out a way around my mum's restrictions to go off to France on my own. How, I hear you ask, when your mum never let you go on any school trips? Let me tell you.

A-level French promised to be intensive. There would be both written and oral parts of the exam that had to be passed in order to gain the overall qualification. I would have to demonstrate my fluency by being able to hold a proper, high-level conversation in French with a native French-speaking person, and my proficiency would be graded on that.

At around this time I found out that the council was giving grants to language students to do exchanges at colleges and universities in different countries to take short language courses. These local government grants covered course fees, travel costs, and accommodations for up to a month. I knew someone who was studying German and going off to Berlin to further her language studies, and I was sure that if I went to France, it would put me in a much better position to pass my French exam.

I went ahead and applied for the grant without telling my mum. I'd figure out later how I was going to get her to agree to let me travel alone to another country when she was the type of Mum who, if she could, would use one of those stargazing telescopes to watch me in school all day. A few weeks later, I got a message that I was approved for a grant to study at a school in Southern France! My excitement was tempered, though, as I had to come up with a plan.

I decided to tell my mum I *had* to go on this course in France because it was a compulsory module of the A-level exam, and the entire class had to go, and I'd be failed if I didn't. Failing would mean I'd have only two A levels when the minimum requirement to get into university was three. The word "fail" is like Kryptonite to Nigerian parents, and I swear I could see my mother physically shrink at the word. I added that all the expenses for this trip would be covered by the council so she wouldn't have to pay any money, which was helpful at the time, because although we weren't dirt poor, Mum was still struggling. I also told her that I'd be living at this university (which was true) and I'd be going there with my teacher and all the other students (not true) so I'd be safe. And would you Adam and Eve it (Cockney slang for "believe it"), she agreed to let me go! On the condition that I called collect every other day and sent postcards (remember those?).

Woo-hoo! But also . . . *Shit!* As this now led to the next hurdle in my escape-to-France plan. I knew for a fact that, as her first child to travel not only alone but also to another country, she would definitely come to see me off at the station. How was I going to pull this off? I concocted a plan as close to perfect as I could get. I persuaded a bunch of my Camden School friends, about twelve of them, to meet me at the train station, carrying suitcases, as if we were all heading off on this school trip to France together.

Luckily for me, some of them were actually going off on their own trips to other countries anyway, and the rest were just down for the fun of taking part in this ruse. I prepped them all with the same script, for when my mum asked any questions. We were all going to take the same course in France, and the teachers were there already, meeting us when we arrived. We would be chaperoned for the entire month, and we'd live in an all-girls dormitory. All my friends, God love them, turned up and acted convincingly. I waved my mum goodbye and got on the train with my friends, who then all exited at the next stop to either continue their own respective journeys or go back home with their empty suitcases, leaving me to adventure onwards.

The French course I took was at a school in Touraine. It was a three-week course, but I had told my mother it was for a month so I'd have some time to go off and explore France alone afterwards. This was the first time I'd had *any* freedom, and I wanted to enjoy it.

I fell in love with the freedom, and this was the trip that truly sparked my love for travel and adventure. I was completely free to do what I wanted, to go to bed when I wanted, eat what I wanted, socialize with whomever I wanted, and even kiss someone if I wanted! The irony was that although I had this complete freedom, I didn't go crazy. I enjoyed myself, but even to this day, I've never done drugs, I've never done any binge drinking, I've never engaged in casual sex. It turns out that all I wanted to do was be able to socialize with people and have clean, innocent fun. Which is what I did.

I even managed to have a little romance while I was in Southern France. An older guy from Cameroon was taking an English course at the same school, and we'd just kiss and hold hands, and I was able to practice my French with him. It was innocent and sweet. I mean, he was twenty-seven, so he did try to persuade me to have sex with him, but I made it clear that wasn't going to happen, and he was very cool about it. Our time spent together meant my French improved, as did my French kissing. This was my first experience with the opposite sex, and it was a good one.

The course was attended by a mix of people from all over the world. Folks from the US, Canada, Spain, Germany, all came to this place in Touraine to do these French courses, and I was excited to meet the world through them.

There were several different classes, and each class had about twenty-five to thirty people. Although I thought I was quite fluent in French, I was placed in the intermediate class, which I was a bit peeved about. I thought my spoken French was good, but apparently it was not good enough.

I enjoyed the course, and there was plenty of free time to explore the local town with my fellow students, but after the three-week course ended, I had my sights on Paris. Never mind that I had no accommodations set up, I barely had any money, and I also had no idea how I was going to get there.

Luckily, I had made some great friends during this course, and there was a girl, Helga, who had an Interrail Pass, whereby as a sixteen-year-old she could travel around Europe for next to nothing. She lent me her card, to use with the instructions that I was to send it back to her when I was done with it. The card had her picture on it, but this being the pre-card-swiping late '80s, nobody truly checked these things, so I was able to get to Paris by pretending to be a blond Scandinavian.

This is how I ended up at the majestic Gare du Nord alone. I had no idea where I was going to sleep, and as I stood in the middle of the station staring and looking around in awe, like the vulnerable young girl I was, a white guy strode up to me and began to converse with me in French. When I told him I had just arrived and that I didn't know where I was going to stay, his face lit up like he'd just won the lottery. He turned and started frantically signaling for another white guy to come over, like *"We've got one! We've got one!"* I saw the second guy sprint over, and I was suddenly sandwiched between these two dudes telling me they could help me, that they knew all the good youth hostels, and to come with them immediately. I may have been a seventeen-year-old sheltered kid on my first trip abroad, but I still had some street smarts. My Spidey sense began tingling immediately at their obvious excitement. I told them thanks but no thanks, and they left disappointed. I never gave it another thought till years later, reading stories of young runaways being kidnapped and trafficked, and I was hit by the sudden realization of how close I had come to being one of those girls.

There were a lot of other young people, backpackers, runaways, and adventurers like me at the station, and I quickly made friends with some of them. This is how I got the scoop on how to survive in Paris with no digs. The key was to spend your days sightseeing and exploring the city, then go back to the station to sleep at night. I was advised to sleep at a certain end of the station, because the guards would come out early in the morning and hose people down in their sleep—you'd be woken up by their screams, a morning wake-up call to pack your shit up and bounce. I had a little duffel bag with my clothes that I used as a pillow, and I slept at the station for a couple of nights, washing in the train station bathrooms, while adventuring around Paris in the day. I had one of those cheap little Polaroid cameras with seven rolls of film, and I had reserved my final roll just for Paris. I skipped a meal to save my last few French francs (as this was pre-euro) to pay to get to the top of the Eiffel Tower. Being on top of that tower was a symbolic triumph for me. I had always wanted to visit ever since I began studying French when I was eleven. Seeing the great expanse of Paris from so high above—the River Seine, the connection of bridges, the Arc de Triomphe—was like sticking a flag on the moon and claiming the territory of my own life. It was exhilarating. While up there, I asked a stranger to take a picture of me, since I was alone and had no companion to document this moment. That picture I still have to this day as a reminder of that carefree month and my coming of age.

During the last couple of days in France, I met an old Black guy while on one of my daytime jaunts. We chatted for a while, and he discovered I was sleeping at the Gare du Nord. He said, "Why are you sleeping in this station? Come with me. I'm not gonna touch you, nothing like that, but you need a proper bed to sleep in." Maybe he seemed fatherly, maybe the novelty of station camping had worn off, maybe I was just tired of sleeping with an ear open for water hoses, but for some reason I cannot fathom to this day, I trusted him and followed him into the unknown. I hung out with him for a day. He was quite coy about the details of his life, but I learned he was from Guadeloupe, an archipelago in the Caribbean and one of France's many colonies, via the slave trade. He'd left the island as a young man to live and work in France. He'd worked at the airport as a luggage handler till he'd left (fired, left, or retired, I wasn't sure). That night, when it was time to sleep, he took me to an apartment. Before he knocked on the door, he turned to me and said, "This is my friend's daughter's apartment. I'm gonna tell them you're my niece and you're visiting so that we can sleep here." That's when it dawned on me that he was homeless. All day I had assumed that I'd be staying with him and his family. To this day I have no idea if he even had anybody. A young woman with a toddler in tow opened the door to the apartment. She wasn't exactly ecstatic to see this man standing at her door, but she didn't tell us to piss off either. He spoke quickly, obviously relaying his concocted story. She raised an eyebrow at me and allowed us into the apartment. She told us we could stay one night, and we shuffled in. At this point I felt a twinge of embarrassment. This wasn't how I had been raised. My proud mother would have had a stroke had she known I was begging to sleep in a stranger's house with a man I didn't know. I silently vowed to extricate myself from this situation and get my ass back to England the following day. We slept on the floor in a spare bedroom of the apartment. All that for not even a bed! In the middle of the night his hand crept over my thigh. I slapped it away so hard that he withdrew like he'd been burned, and he didn't try that shit again for the rest of the night. Nevertheless, I did not sleep well, and I silently berated myself all night for being so stupid. Time to go home. This adventure had run its course. The next day I thanked him for everything and left to get my prepaid ferry back over the English Channel. And aside from being mistaken for a prostitute in the southeastern city of Grenoble, to which I had been able to respond in French, *"Va te faire enculer!"* ("Go fuck yourself!"), it was, all in all, a delightful adventure.

I passed my A-level French a year later, and Mum was none the wiser of my adventures in France. As I see it, my grandmother had already predicted, before she died, that when she came back, she would travel the world, so I was merely fulfilling that prophecy.

10

Procrastination Is the
Thief of Time

When I was a kid, there was a TV show called *Jim'll Fix It*. It was hosted by Jimmy Savile, who, years after he died, was exposed as a colossal pedophile, but at the time he had the biggest kids show on TV. The premise of the show was that you wrote him a letter with some desire or wish you wanted to come true, and if you were one of the lucky ones, he'd read your letter out on TV and invite you on the show to grant your wish. Kids got to ride roller coasters while attempting to eat pies, perform with their favorite TV actors, and one kid even got to ride on a luggage carousel at the airport, like a suitcase. Every fun wish was granted.

At eight, I casually mentioned to my mum that I'd love to write to Jimmy to get a tour around a real-life chocolate factory, because, well . . . I was eight, chocolate is delicious, and that's the kind of shit eight-year-olds wish for. My mother became incensed. "Idiot! Why don't you ask for something useful? Tell him to take you to a hospital and show you how to be a doctor!" My mum was able to take the fun out of a fantasy.

I have a joke in one of my stand-up routines: My mum, while

pregnant with me, is approached by someone who asks her, "Are you having a boy or a girl?" To which my mother replies, "I'm having a doctor." My mum mapped out the future professional lives of her children based on characteristics we may or may not have had when we were toddlers. My mum told me I was clever, and therefore I had to do well at school. I believed her and internalized that narrative. I *assumed* I was smart, but looking back, I think I was pretty average academically. I strove to achieve the grades that would match my mum's idea of my intelligence, and win Oncle's money, so I did better at school than I might have done otherwise. My mum had used the best kind of reverse psychology on me.

When I was thirteen, kids were meant to pick the optional school subjects they were interested in. English, math, PE, and religious education were some of the compulsory subjects. My mum picked my optional subjects: physics and biology, due to "our" doctor aspirations. I never particularly enjoyed the sciences but scraped by with manageable grades. I picked German, as I'd discovered my love of languages, and since my school didn't teach Spanish, I added German to the French I was already learning. I again sold this option to my mum by telling her that a multilingual doctor probably earned a lot more money.

Drama was also a compulsory subject up to age thirteen, but in later years it became optional. It was dropped from my curriculum, as Mum was not having me waste time with acting. Due to my boisterous character and my penchant for telling hilarious stories in class, with full act-outs, my drama teacher had once made the mistake of trying to convince my mum to let me continue with drama classes, as I had real acting talent. "She can act like a doctor until she becomes a doctor!" That was the end of the conversation.

Halfway through studying for A levels, kids are supposed to pick the universities they want to attend and apply to degree programs pending their exam results. There were schools to visit, forms to fill out, and advance arrangements to be made. I had done none of that. The reasons were twofold: One, I'm a huge procrastinator. I leave *everything* to the last possible minute, including studying for exams, which I tended to cram for two weeks before. Luckily, I've been blessed with a knack for memorizing stuff. Any subject that included coursework to be completed throughout the year, I avoided, as I would have failed. Anything that entailed me memorizing facts and formulas, I was good at. Two, university applications were long, laborious affairs that required an organized approach. Lots of filling out forms. I *hate* paperwork. You hear stories about accountants stealing millions from their celebrity clients, and on the one hand you think, *How could they be so stupid? I would know if someone took thirty dollars!* But on the other hand, I would sign any form you put in front of me if you told me you'd already read the other fifty pages of that form and it was all good. To this day, if you want to hide anything from me, put it in an application form. I'll never see it. My attention span is too short for that amount of detail. I could see myself getting robbed blind because of my paper phobia. Suffice to say, I didn't do any of those applications, and since Mum didn't know the system, I managed to get away with it for a while. She just assumed I'd pass my exams, then pick any university I wanted afterwards, based on my results. Taiwo had left school and studied accounting while working, so I would have been the first child to go to university. But Mum didn't find out that I'd not started the process until it was too late.

I didn't want to go to university. I did pretty well at school but didn't enjoy it. I hated studying, I was bored by most subjects, except French, but I would have put up with all of that and gone to university if I'd been able to go to school outside of London, where I would've been boarding on campus. I.e., away from home. I.e., *freedom!* My mum wasn't having that. She wouldn't let me go to a university that wasn't in London, where she could keep an eye on me. That meant staying at home, which meant three more years of being financially reliant on my mum. Which meant three more years of no freedom. Nope, nopey, nope.

I've always been squeamish about blood. When people cut themselves and then lick or suck the wound, I am beyond disgusted, and as a teenager when I began menstruating, I could barely look down when I was changing my sanitary products, so grossed out was I by the sight of blood, even if it was my own. And yet, such was the brainwashing of my mum that I *still* thought I was going to make a career of dealing with people's biological functions at probably the ooziest times of their lives. I was seventeen and studying advanced-level physics and biology when I realized this phobia was going to seriously hinder my doctoring abilities. When we had to dissect a rat—as in, cut through the flesh and watch stuff ooze out like a furry lava cake—I was too busy vomiting and fainting to complete that particular class.

A week previously, however, as fate would have it, we'd had a visit at the school from the Engineering Industry Training Board, a government-funded entity that had done a talk to encourage more girls to go into engineering. At the time, I found the idea of building things, working in different places, and not being tied to one location interesting. I briefly flirted with switching vocations but then thought of my mum's reaction to having two engineers in the family and no doctor.

Dele was supposed to be the engineer. He'd actually had an aptitude for taking his toys apart and rebuilding them, so that kind of made sense. He was meticulous and patient at re-creating anything he saw. In fact, before the London buses and the Underground switched to digital travel cards, Dele had managed to slice individual numbers and letters off several old cards, using a razor blade, and forge his own card, therefore riding buses and trains free for years and pocketing the travel allowance Mum gave him. Talented, I tell you! (He was also a phenomenal artist. He could draw absolutely anything, but "artist" was not on the list of African careers, so my mum had no interest in that ability.)

Sheyi was to be the lawyer because he talked a lot—that was my mum's main criteria.

At first, I thought I didn't need the hassle of destroying Mum's carefully thought out career formula. But after the rat incident, I knew I had no choice but to bite the bullet and inform her that I was switching from biology to math A level, and that I was now interested in engineering. Luckily for me, she was not too perturbed. It was still on the list of her preferred careers, and besides, she had a solution. Turning to Dele, she declared, "Dele, now *you* will be the doctor!"

If your only tool is a hammer, you will see every problem as a nail.

I figured that to be a good engineer, work experience was more important than being just book smart, so it would be better if I got a full-time job as a trainee engineer after finishing school, and study for my engineering degree part-time in the evenings and on weekends. I'd still be fulfilling Mum's dream of having kids with degrees but while having money.

It was important to me to earn my own money. Money meant

freedom! I would still live at home, which was a win-win for my mum since I'd be contributing to the household expenses while training as an engineer, but my first few paychecks would go towards a car. That way she wouldn't be able to use the idea of a young woman roaming the streets at night as an excuse to stop me going out. As soon as I hit eighteen, those floodgates would be open, and I'd be out partying every weekend for the next six years till I left home for good.

Getting an engineering job after school was pretty easy. My exam results were good enough for me to get into university, and there was a dearth of female engineers, so employers were falling over themselves to recruit me. There was an abundance of employment out there for trainee technicians and engineers throughout the industry.

I applied for a trainee position in aeronautical engineering with British Airways. Repairing and maintaining planes sounded fun. I passed the initial interview and exam, and I got myself a second interview, but on discovering that the pay as a trainee was a good £3,000 per year lower than other engineering trainee positions out there *and* that I would have to commute an hour and a half each way to Heathrow Airport, I didn't bother to turn up for my second interview. I had options.

I worked briefly for the Inner London Education Authority as a trainee engineer, which was basically a government job. The money and benefits for a teenager straight out of school were good. I was able to have one paid day off a week to study for my electrical/electronic qualifications at a local college, and government jobs were coveted, as they were practically jobs for life. I lasted less than three months. Their idea of a trainee engineer was someone who sat in an office filling out charts and forms all day, with the odd visit to a school or college to check that their VCRs were safe to use. My boredom level was so high that at one point I started imagining things like what it would be like to tattoo my own eyeballs with a BIC pen.

My next trainee position was with British Telecom. BT at the time provided all home communication services in the UK. Mobile phones were still in a fledgling stage, and the monthly cost of one was around the price of a small mortgage, just so you could look like a douche on the bus. Everyone still had landlines then. My job was as a telephone exchange technician, or what they called in the business a "jumper runner." I worked in a building near Caledonian Road, an area of North London famous only for being the home of Pentonville Prison, built in 1842, which had housed people like Oscar Wilde and George Michael.

When I say "telephone exchange," I don't mean the type you see in movies from the '20s and '30s. I was not one of those women, fully made up, wearing a blouse and a pencil skirt, sticking cables into holes and saying, "How may I direct your call?" Every telephone line in the area came through this building. The installation engineers would connect the phone lines in people's homes and offices to the cable boxes outside in the streets. From those boxes the lines came into the exchange, where the wires ran through a series of relay switches and circuits that organized and connected every call. These switches and circuits were arranged on huge frames that ran the length and breadth of the telephone exchange building and extended from floor to ceiling. Attached to the frames were rolling ladders that we, the engineers and technicians, climbed and rode along on whenever we had to run more wires to connect new telephone lines or change lines from one circuit to another if someone changed their phone number. This was also before everything was computerized.

We each carried screwdrivers and soldering irons to connect

and disconnect wires to the mainframe. We ran maintenance and repairs on these lines all day and every day. For fun, we'd sometimes connect our listening equipment—which was used to check for dial tones on specific lines—to eavesdrop on people's conversations, and sometimes we pranked the people on the line by interjecting with dumb advice, giggling, or just using our favorite horror-movie ghost voices to call them by name and freak them out.

BT was a pretty solid equal-opportunity employer. Originally all telecommunications in the UK were under the remit of the Royal Mail—the same post office that had recruited large numbers of West Indians to sort mail in the '50s. A number of those postal workers also worked in the telecom industry, so at my exchange there was a mixed bag of nationalities. My supervisor, Roy, who was kind of the father figure and ruled us with an iron fist, was from Trinidad. Among my coworkers was Benjamin, an older man from Barbados whose accent was so strong that only Roy could understand him and would translate for the rest of us. I think this annoyed Benjamin, because he never spoke much, but when he did, it was like a scene from *Snatch*, with Brad Pitt as the Irish gypsy who sounded like he was talking gibberish. We'd all just stand there and stare at his mouth and wait for Roy to tell us what he'd said. There was Lisa, a white woman who practically bathed herself in the perfume Poison, which was very popular at the time. As soon as you walked in the front door of the building downstairs, you knew whether Lisa was working that day. She was very popular with the installation guys who came in to give us our cabling instructions; they would take turns trying to chat her up. She ended up marrying one of those guys, and they are still together to this day. Nobby was a young guy from Birmingham whose parents were Indian. He sported a mullet and a moustache and was the same age as me. We became firm friends and formed a little gang with Alwin, a young British guy of Jamaican parentage. He was tall, lanky, and had a firecracker of a personality. Every Monday morning he would regale us with stories of what he'd gotten up to on the weekend, from nightclub brawls to bank robberies. We were enthralled. The stories were so engrossing, and convincing, that Benjamin looked at us incredulously one afternoon and told us, "You know all those stories are bullshit, right?" Well, Benjamin said it. Roy translated.

That was our little exchange family. More like a foster family. I was there for about eleven months. Once I'd learned how to "jumper run" at BT, I was keen to move on to the next thing. Whenever I learned how to do something, another new thing to learn had to be lined up or I felt I wasn't progressing.

The engineers who worked outside the exchange seemed to have a more fun existence. They went to different buildings every day, installing systems, putting phones in people's houses—they had variety. They even drove company vehicles that they could take home. And they had pagers! Before cell phones became affordable for all, pagers were the cool thing to have. If you weren't even an idea to your parents in the late '80s to early '90s, I'll explain: These were little electronic boxes that you clipped to your belt. They were the first forms of mobile communication. If someone needed to get ahold of you, they called a number and relayed either their phone number or a message to an operator, who then relayed the info to your pager, which would beep or vibrate on your belt. You would then find a phone and call the number of the person who had paged you or the operator to retrieve the message. Yup, that was the height of technology in the early '90s. Our parents' generation walked fifty miles to school. Our generation had to get to a phone to have someone read us a message. Pagers seemed to be ubiquitous in the US, according to TV and movies, with everyone having them, but the UK was well behind on that technology. Here, they were not readily available for purchase. They were the sole domain of companies that could buy them in large quantities and distribute them among their mobile staff. Basically, to have one, you had to have a pretty important job in which you had to be easily contactable. Having a pager was equivalent to twirling your car keys in a nightclub to get girls. A pager hanging off your belt meant you had not just any job but a *good* job, an important job, and you drove the minimum of a Ford Escort. (Ford Escorts were cool back then.) And if you had the souped-up, sporty XR3, with a . . . wait for it . . . 1600cc engine, you were king or queen racer out in these streets!

I wanted a *good* job. I wanted variety, excitement, responsibility, and a damn pager. I began making requests for a transfer to the installation team six months into my time at the exchange. A position wasn't forthcoming. These were popular jobs within the company, and everyone wanted them. There was a long waiting list. I was nineteen, well qualified, and a Black girl in an industry desperate for people like me. I was a hot commodity, and I wasn't waiting for shit. I decided to leave British Telecom.

People thought I was crazy. BT was one of those companies in which, once you got in, you had a job for life. Nobody ever left a government job or BT.

I managed to leave both in just over a year.

11

The Same Sun
That Melts Wax Also
Hardens Clay

When my letter of employment from Otis arrived just a week after my interview, I was overjoyed. I was to be the first female lift engineer in Otis UK's hundred-year history. For Americans, lifts are what you guys call elevators. Usually Americans are the ones who tend to go for the more literal, obvious words to describe things, like "fall" instead of "autumn" (presumably because the leaves are falling), "sidewalk" instead of "pavement" (because, of course, you are walking on the side of a road), but on this occasion, the Brits must have decided to give it a try and go with the box that "lifts" things.

When I was younger, I was actually afraid of lifts. I avoided them as often as I could, and when I couldn't, I never got inside one alone. I would wait for at least two other people, so if anything went wrong, we'd all go screaming to our deaths together. Misery loves company. I didn't understand how they worked, and I'd seen too many horror movies in which lifts plunged down the shaft, pulverizing everybody in them (*The Towering Inferno*), or they were taken over by the child of Satan and cut unsuspecting scientists in half like a sandwich (*Damien: Omen II*). So when I left school and gravitated towards a career in engineering, lifts were the absolute furthest thing from my mind.

The following Monday I was supposed to report to the Isle of Dogs office to begin engineer training, which would involve following an engineer around who maintained all the lifts in that area. The Isle of Dogs is an area of East London that doesn't have any more dogs than anywhere else in London, so the name is a mystery. It's a part of East London that at the beginning of the century was full of bustling ports and trading, but it fell into disuse and poverty and was earmarked for regeneration. Glistening new apartment buildings had since sprung up among the existing drab council estates, and a whole new financial district was in the works.

I turned up on Monday morning, excited and ready to get started. I was assigned a uniform of a blue Otis sweater, matching blue trousers, and steel-toed work shoes, which I changed into, and I stood in the general area outside my new manager's office, waiting to be assigned a work partner. A steady stream of white, male Otis engineers passed by to pick up their assignments for the week, and they all stared at the young Black woman dressed identically to them.

I had seen the advert for the job in the *Evening Standard*, a daily London newspaper with a great job advertisement page. Thursday was engineering day, so every Thursday, I scoured the paper's job listings, looking for my next adventure, and this was where I found the advert that changed my life: a trainee engineer position with Otis, the largest lift company in the world. I had thought this would be a perfect way to overcome my fear as well as have a job with plenty of excitement, physicality, and travel.

That job advert had pictures of young, smiling guys wearing hard hats, holding complex-looking electrical meters, inside tall buildings with happy, smiling clients in the background. The advert promised great pay, opportunities for promotion, and, best of all, a company van after training completion. I was hooked for three reasons. One, the previously mentioned benefits. Two, I would learn exactly how lifts work, providing an opportunity for me to overcome my fear, or at the very least let me know if all that horror-movie shit was accurate. Three, and the most important reason, Otis was an *American* company. My childhood dream to live in the US hadn't abated, and my plan was to gain all the experience and qualifications needed to work my way up in the company, then transfer to the States, to work on gleaming American skyscrapers during the week and dance on *Yo! MTV Raps* at the weekend.

I sent in an application and secured myself an interview. The Otis UK headquarters was in a large gleaming building that stood out like a sore thumb among a long stretch of council flats and fried chicken shops on Clapham Road, South London, just half a mile from The Oval cricket grounds. When I walked into the area where several other interviewees were waiting, I found that not only was I the sole female applicant—this part didn't surprise me too much; after all, this job entailed climbing up lift shafts and presumably dressing in a boiler suit and steel-toed Doc Martens every day—but also I was the only Black applicant. I saw a sea of white, expectant, male faces that all turned in unison to stare at me as I took my seat. I didn't feel self-conscious at all. In fact, I was extremely confident. I had great exam results from school, I had already begun studying part-time for my electrical engineering higher qualifications, *and* I already had a year of practical engineering experience under my belt. Most of these boys looked like they'd been forced to be there by their dads. *"Get a trade, son!"* I was like a raisin in a bowl of white rice.

My interview was with three white men in suits who bombarded me with questions that I answered easily. I'd done research on the company beforehand, to show my enthusiasm, and to demonstrate my ambition I discussed the career arc I envisioned for myself within the company. Within a few minutes of the interview, I knew I had the job. I thought I'd take a risk: I informed them of my current studies and that in my previous job I'd had a paid day off each week to go to college, plus I attended two evening classes a week, and I was expecting the same benefits at Otis, if I was to reach my full potential. They agreed that if they offered me the position, they would allow me to continue with these commitments. This was the opportunity I'd been waiting for.

But as I waited excitedly on my first day, I heard what seemed like a low rumbling argument coming from my new manager's office, then I clearly heard the words "Why do I have to have her?" Followed by mumbling as the voices lowered. That was my first clue that my pretty uneventful journey as a pioneering female engineer was about to change. The office door flew open, and a small, scruffy, balding man stomped out, followed by one of the men who had interviewed me for the job, David.

"Hi, Gina. Meet Pete. You'll be working with him for a bit, and he'll show you the ropes."

Pete walked past me towards the exit and mumbled, "All right, come on, then."

I turned to follow him. Obviously Pete wasn't happy to have me, and I wasn't happy to not be wanted, but we were stuck together for the foreseeable future. I got into the passenger side of the blue-and-white Ford Otis van. "I ain't got a problem wiv you," he started, "it's just I was promised a mate, and instead I get some sort of fucking diversity experiment."

Most lift engineers in service and maintenance travel in pairs, one a qualified engineer and the other either a young apprentice, aged sixteen to eighteen, learning the trade, or a mate, which in the industry is basically an assistant and a general dogsbody to the qualified engineer. The mate carries the tools, gets the tea, and basically does all the shit jobs the engineer doesn't want to do, while they learn the trade and, in some cases, move up the ladder to qualify, in turn, to have their own mate. I wasn't a mate. I wasn't experienced as a lift engineer, but on paper, I was more qualified than Pete and was the same grade as him. I was not going to be his skivvy, and he was understandably pissed off.

I let him know that I wasn't just an experiment, that I was quite qualified for my job and that I was there to learn as quickly as possible and move on, so it was in both our best interests to get on with it. He agreed and started the engine, and we soon drove off to our first assignment together.

I spent a few months with Pete, on call in East London. We did monthly maintenance checks on lifts in the area and were called out on breakdowns. If you were stuck in a lift, it was most likely us who got you out. They called the fire brigade and they called us. Pete's pager would go off, and we'd have to rush to a location as quickly as possible to get there before the firefighters, as their priority was to get people out, and they didn't care how much damage they caused to the lift while doing it. A few times we didn't beat the firefighters, and we'd arrive to find the lift doors peeled open as if with a giant can opener. That would cost Otis thousands in repairs and got Pete a good old bollocking from the boss.

In order to repair lifts, we worked in the room where the motor and all the electronics were housed. Sometimes we had to work in the bottom of the lift shaft, called the pit, where we would repair the wiring at the bottom of the lift car, as the car dangled above us. I often also rode on top of the lifts to observe their behavior, and I had ample opportunities for serious injury or death. There was the risk of crushing, whether by falling off the car as it traveled, falling down a shaft, or miscalculating the ceiling space left as the lift reached the top floor.

The job was pretty exciting. There was always the possibility of electrocution. We were dealing with high-powered machinery. I was once blown across a motor room, when my bracelet created a short circuit as I worked on a control unit. I was luckily only slightly injured, but that lift was out for three weeks, as I fried all the circuit boards. Which is why engineers are not supposed to wear jewelry on the job. I was also nearly decapitated when I was working on top of one lift that I had stopped in the middle of the shaft. It was one of a bank of lifts that had no separating walls. The others were still in regular service, carrying unsuspecting passengers up and down. As I leaned over the side of the car I was working on, one of those lifts hurtled up towards me. I got my head out of the way just in time. The job was dangerous, and I *loved* it. My mum had never let me have a bike, in case I died on it, and here I was cheating death every day in one of the vocations *she* found acceptable for her kids! We worked on everything from state-of-the-art glass-enclosed lifts that traveled along the outside of buildings (wall climbers) to old metal council-estate ones that were rusty from years of people pissing in them. We found all manner of things thrown down the lift shafts, from old toys to packets of cocaine discarded in police raids. My mum had *no idea*!

Pete taught me as best as he could the practical side of engineering, while I studied engineering theory two nights and one day a week at college. We parted ways with a grudging respect for each other. I don't know if he ever got that mate.

Ashes fly back in the face of him who throws them.

Canary Wharf, on the Isle of Dogs, was undergoing a massive regeneration. The developers, Olympia & York, were building an entirely new financial district in London, spanning a hundred acres. A slew of gleaming skyscrapers and office blocks were being constructed, and Otis had the huge contract to install all the lifts and escalators on the site.

David called me into his office one day to inform me that my training period in maintenance was up, and I was now to transfer into construction. This was to be the next part of my training: I had to learn how to build these lifts. Although I was happy to be moving on, I felt David's relief at being shot of me, like I was being handed off to the next unlucky department as a booby prize. I thanked him for the opportunity, and prepared to face the suspicion and disdain of a new set of colleagues. I was sent to work in the building that would become the Canary Wharf Tower, the tallest building in the UK when it was completed. It was to be an exact replica of the two smaller towers of New York's World Trade Center, which Olympia & York also had built.

When I got to Canary Wharf, construction had already begun on the tower as well as several other buildings. The foundations were finished, and the first ten of the fifty floors were up. Otis would construct the lift shaft as the building went up, and I would be one of the team.

Otis not only had engineers from all over the UK on the project but also had brought them in from Central Europe and the

US. Over four thousand engineers, electricians, plumbers, and various building contractors were on the site, but there were few Black people, and the only women I saw were in the canteen serving food and our onsite nurse. Because of this, the toilet facilities were dire. I had to hike fifteen minutes across the large site to find the only ladies' room. Most of the time, I just pulled my hard hat down over my face and used the men's. I wasn't welcomed by my fellow engineers. The introduction I'd had with Pete paled in comparison with what I went through at Canary Wharf. You could say it was a baptism by fire. I couldn't understand the level of resentment directed at me. I worked hard and could lift anything they could, proven when they publicly challenged me on several occasions.

The men made a point of telling the most misogynist and racist jokes while looking at me sideways for a reaction. Porn was openly consumed in front of me, and men loudly commented on women's physical attributes. There was a large hut where each engineer had their own station to hang their work gear to change in and out of. I didn't have separate changing quarters, nor did I ask for one, for fear of differentiating myself further, and in the morning I'd often find pictures of monkeys stuck above my station, and banana skins. I'd pull them down while the men sniggered behind me. I refused to let them see how much it bothered me. I learned to develop different coping mechanisms. Every weekend I would hit my favorite nightclub, The Fridge, in Brixton or another nightclub, called Dance Wicked, under the railway arches in Vauxhall and dance my aggression out. The Running Man became my anti-racism outlet.

At Otis, there were three men in particular whom I hated the most. One was Bill, a skinny, pale English bloke whose entire face was covered in red welts and pockmarks. He was loud and often very funny, roasting his fellow engineers relentlessly, but his humor was much more mean-spirited when it came to me. One of his favorite lines was to tell me that my name backwards was "a nig." I didn't tell him my full name was Regina. He would have had a field day with that.

Bill made a point of constantly trying to humiliate me in front of the other guys but disguised it as just friendly workplace banter. All of his jokes about me were based on my race. When I would challenge him, he'd say he wasn't racist, as his wife was brown and from Mauritius. I'd often fantasize about pushing him down a lift shaft or smashing his head in with a hammer.

Timothy was a young guy, just a few years older than me, who lived in an area of southeast London called Eltham. This area was to become infamous a few years later with the deadly stabbing of a young Black man named Stephen Lawrence by a gang of racist thugs. Timothy would openly proclaim that he would not tolerate niggers moving into his neighborhood, among other, equally unsavory comments. He'd make statements about Black people's criminality, that we smelled, and that we were animals.

I argued with Timothy constantly, but he never raised his voice. When you imagine racists, its often violent men, with their faces screwed up in hatred and fury—skinheads, hooded KKK members burning crosses, carrying out beatings and lynching. English racism could at times be a lot more genteel. Timothy was very calm and matter-of-fact when he made his statements, as if the things he was saying were just obvious facts. If you only watched his body language as he spoke, you would have thought he was discussing something as innocuous as the weather. This infuriated me more than Bill and his racist jokes, because some of my colleagues agreed with Timothy and were emboldened by his seemingly logical delivery.

Eventually, after months of listening to him spew his shit, the next time we were alone, I informed him that I knew where he lived and I had two brothers I would be glad to send to his house if I ever again heard the word "nigger" come out of his mouth. I think he got the message, as he never uttered another word to me, and I was glad for it.

I hated Timothy, but the person I spent every working hour wishing death upon was Clinton. He was a dark-skinned Black man, three years older than me. He was good-looking and he dressed well, and he had his hair straightened and slicked back. When he arrived on the site a few months after me, I was over-joyed, as I thought I now had an ally, someone whose very presence would help me keep the racist banter under control, if not end it completely. Within a few days, he began making deroga-tory comments about my appearance. "Man, you Africans are so ugly!" Timothy and Bill sniggered. Emboldened by the laughter of his white coworkers, Clinton continued his onslaught. "Careful you don't eat your fingers while you're biting that chocolate bar. You might like it! You damn cannibal!" Oh, how the white guys laughed. They patted him on the back, and he reveled in their acceptance. I returned fire, calling him a fool if he didn't know that his origins were in Africa just like mine. He scoffed. "White people rescued us from Africa, and they mixed with us, so we don't have your big noses and fat lips!" I was speechless. I spent the next few miserable weeks getting into screaming arguments with Clinton. He triggered my fury more than any of those white men ever could, because I felt so hurt, betrayed, and stupid for believing that our Blackness would be our bond.

One day while Clinton and I verbally abused each other, I looked at Timothy, Bill, and the others and took stock of them standing back and laughing at us both. My mouth snapped shut, and I resolved to just keep my head down, work, and no longer be goaded. I stopped speaking with Clinton that day, but that didn't stop me fervently praying that Clinton's sperm were all duds and he would never have children. Now, when I look back, I feel sad and embarrassed for him. I still despise him, though.

This was my work environment for two years. Despite the abuse, I learned a lot on that job, and I enjoyed the actual engineering. I was somehow able to compartmentalize so as not to let my coworkers affect my performance. Funnily enough, I got on quite well with the American engineers, who took me under their wings, and I spent the last few months of the job working with them and avoiding the Brits. I grilled them about opportunities for work as an engineer in the US, as my childhood plan was never far from my mind. Two engineers in particular provided the most solace. James Williams, better known as Rocky, was a stocky African American from Brooklyn, New York. A happily married Christian, with a son the same age as me, he adopted me as his on-site daughter and often took me to work areas of the site with him, shielding me from my tormentors. He is still my adopted dad to this day. I've been a guest of him and his wife, Berniece, in Brooklyn on several occasions, and they have also been guests of mine in both Los Angeles and London.

There was also Big Dave, a huge white guy with a head of thick dark hair and a moustache to match. He looked like a bear and a lumberjack had a baby. Despite his gargantuan proportions, he was a kind, sweet-natured guy who took pity on the weird little Black girl with blond dreadlocks, and we remained in touch for several years after he'd gone back to the US. A couple of years after we worked together I visited New York on vacation with a group of friends, and I called him to see if he remembered me. He was not only happy to hear from me but also invited me to meet him at his new job, as chief elevator maintenance engineer at the World Trade Center. Perfect! The world-famous Twin Towers were at the top of our tourist-destination list. When we met, he asked my friends if he could borrow me for an hour, and then he took me on a lift-engineer tour of the buildings.

Otis had provided all the lifts for the World Trade Center, and Big Dave was in charge of a team who kept them running, repaired any breakdowns, and regularly serviced them. We went up to the control room, and I observed the sheer size of the motors these lifts were attached to. Remember, our tallest building in the UK at the time was Canary Wharf Tower, which was the same height as the two baby towers that flanked the Twin Towers. These motors carried thousands of visitors a day over 110 floors at speeds up to nearly 40 miles per hour. They were *huge*. Each one was the size of a midsize office. I'd never seen anything like them.

Although I had left the company by that point, Big Dave decided to risk his career and put me in an Otis uniform. He wanted to take me for a ride *on top* of one of the lifts. We did not put it in service mode but rode it, while it carried passengers, so it traveled at its full speed. *Holy shit!* No roller-coaster ride will ever top that. As the lift careened towards the top floor, Dave stood at his full height. Having worked on lifts where I'd often had to duck to make sure I wasn't crushed between the lift and the ceiling of the lift shaft, I began to do just that.

Big Dave teased me, "Stand strong!"

"Fuck no." I ducked. There ended up being plenty of clearance, but I didn't give a shit.

I would later watch in horror and fear when those towers came down on 9/11, hoping that my friend Dave was not at work that day. I spent the day desperately trying to get ahold of him and Rocky, but as was to be expected, the phone lines were jammed with desperate callers from all over the world. Finally, after two desperate days, I got through to Rocky to ask him if Dave had been at the Twin Towers that day. A flood of relief washed over me when he said, "Probably not. We lost the maintenance contract last year."

. . .

After my stint at Canary Wharf, my training as a lift engineer was complete, and I was promoted. This meant that if I stayed in construction, I would now be able to manage a small site of my own, and if I went back to service and maintenance, I would have my own service route, complete with a company van, a pager, and a mate. I'd already been told by supervisors and managers that my chances of managing my own construction site were slim to none, as "the lads ain't gonna take orders from a bird." And after the two years I'd had at Canary Wharf, I had no intention of continuing to work with large groups of men.

I opted to go back to callouts and maintenance, and I ended up paired with a young engineer of Indian heritage, Salim. Salim had completed an apprenticeship with Otis and had been newly promoted like myself. We were not meant to work together—each of us should have had our own service route—but he found himself in the same position Pete had been in two years earlier, stuck with an engineer the company had no idea what to do with. (Otis had enjoyed the cachet of having their first female engineer. They'd even put my face on their diversity brochures and had me do newspaper interviews for them, but they were unwilling to afford me the responsibility my position entailed, choosing instead to palm me off to various babysitters.) Salim and I came to a compromise: some days we worked together, and some days I'd drive my own car to one of his buildings, where I'd service the lifts there by myself, while he'd go and do the lifts somewhere else. This arrangement came to an end when one day, while working on the lifts in a home for senior citizens, I came out to find a van load of police officers waiting for me. The residents of the building had assumed that this Black woman was impersonating an engineer with a view to robbing them of their peppermints and Uno cards. I became extremely frustrated with the situation, and so I met with my manager several times to try to gauge when I would finally get my own route. "I'm sorry, Gina," he told me one day. "The company would rather you work with another engineer, just in case you have an accident. You know, you could fall down a shaft and hurt your womb or something and then sue Otis if you can't get pregnant later. It's for your own good."

"Oh, really," I responded. "Do you say the same to male engineers, that they could fall and squash a testicle?"

"Don't be crass, Gina."

It was at that point I decided to bypass my manager and go to the top echelons of the company to set up a grievance hearing due to discrimination. No other Otis engineer of my grade had ever been denied the right to do the job for which they were qualified. I wrote a statement and went through the internal channels. A date was set. I contacted my union rep, whose job it would be to represent my interests as a four-year paying union member. He refused. "I don't know anything about this women's lib stuff," he told me. When the date of my grievance hearing came, I went alone and unrepresented. Unsurprisingly, I was overruled, by yet another room of white men, and I was sent back to engineering purgatory with Salim. We limped on for a few months, but I no longer wanted to be in this job. I was fed up and could see no future with this company.

In the mid-1990s, the building industry in the UK went through a slump, and Otis was affected. They began to lay people off in the construction department. On hearing this, I marched into my manager's office and demanded they make me redundant, even though I was no longer in construction. I made it clear that I no longer wanted to be their token Black female face on their diversity brochures, and that it would be in their best interest to let me go away quietly. Obviously with a redundancy package.

They agreed. A week later, I walked away from engineering with a lump sum of approximately three months' salary, and what turned out to be for good. Salim was sorry, but not sorry to see me go, and without a Black-woman-shaped albatross around his neck, Salim rose through the ranks at Otis; he is now a high-ranking manager.

I became a bore at the movies whenever there were elevator crash scenes, as I would loudly proclaim where they had made technical mistakes or had used artistic license for Hollywood effect. To date, the movie *Speed* is the only film to handle technical details correctly.

Oh yeah, and I'm no longer afraid of lifts.

12

Success Is 10 Percent Ability and 90 Percent Sweat

After I left Otis, I decided to take the summer off, because for a long while I'd been either studying or working or both. I'd never had much time or the freedom to explore my own interests. I figured this finally was my chance. I had always been bad with money, and with a lump sum in the form of a decent severance pay, I thought, *I'm going to enjoy this summer, probably blow the money, and then come winter, I'll get another job.* Being a qualified engineer meant I'd have no problem finding employment. There was always the good old *Evening Standard* with their engineer listings on Thursdays. I would still look through them every week, keeping an eye out. But I was going to spend the summer just enjoying myself.

I had a little black Honda CRX sports car that I loved and had bought with cash, so my only large monthly expenditure was my monthly rent. I had finally moved out of my mum's, out from under her watchful eye, when I was in my early twenties. She had grown tired of my constant weekend clubbing routine. As far as I had been concerned, I worked hard during the week and contributed towards the household expenses with my monthly rent payment to her, therefore, as a working adult, I should have been allowed to spend my weekends however I pleased. This had meant recording every episode of the hip-hop TV show *Yo! MTV Raps* and spending hours practicing the dance moves in the videos to unleash Friday and Saturday nights at various nightclubs around South London till the early hours of the morning, then sleeping all day Sunday before returning to work Monday morning. I did not drink, smoke, do drugs, or disappear with random dudes. As I had been the only one in the household with a car, Mum had often dragged me out of bed to drop her places, which I had done with only some complaint. As far as daughters go, I thought I was in the top percentile. All I had wanted to do was meet up with my friends on the weekends and dance my ass off. She had had major issues with this, and after one too many shouty "You treat this place like a hotel" lectures, I had decided to leave home.

Through my good friend Bev, I had managed to secure an interview with a housing association. In the UK, housing associations are private nonprofit organizations that provide low-cost social housing for people in need of a home. They are regulated by the state and often receive public funding. In the mid-1990s, before government cuts adversely affected the young, the poor, and the middle class, housing help was readily available. Bev, who already had her own heavily subsidized one-bedroom flat, talked me through the process of being considered for one of these coveted properties. A hard-luck story was a must. "My mum doesn't like my clubbing" wasn't gonna cut it. I had to have a better story. After coaching from Bev, at the housing association interview, I told a story of evil stepfathers, abusive partners, and unwanted pregnancies, followed by abortions. It worked! I was given a room in a hostel, a shared private house with four other girls, with super-cheap rent, where I lived for eighteen months. Afterwards, I qualified for my own cute one-bedroom garden flat in Tottenham, North London, where I lived for three years (after which I was making enough money as a comedian to buy my first property).

With my redundancy payoff and cheap rent, I was able to spend a summer experimenting with different activities and interests, and I decided to try my hand at drama again. I took a free acting workshop, which ended in a performance. I was never one of the main actors, more of a glorified extra, but the experience reminded me how much I liked to perform. The other young adults in the class were actual students of drama, and I was in the background with no lines. I'd always thought plays were boring and didn't relate to me, but the one we performed used music from the album *Diary of a Mad Band*, from the hottest R&B group at the time, Jodeci. The music was great, I was in a show, and even though I never uttered a word throughout the performance, I couldn't have enjoyed the experience more. I hadn't been on a stage since I was thirteen, when my mother had put a stop to it. I'd forgotten how good it felt.

After the workshop ended, I figured that I'd have a few weeks of frivolity, then get another job and return to real life.

It is not fishing if you do not have a net; it is simply bathing.

The racism I had been exposed to while at Otis made me want to know more about Black culture and to connect with more Black people. I found some meetings in my community where Black people got together and had interesting conversations about politics and culture. I discovered later that I was actually attending meetings of the Nation of Islam, also known as the Nation.

For those of you who don't know, the Nation was founded in 1930 in Detroit, specifically for Black Americans, and it soon spread throughout the world. Some of the most famous Nation of Islam followers include Malcolm X (before he left to follow a more orthodox style of Islam), Muhammad Ali, and Louis Farrakhan. The Nation promotes social reform within Black communities and economic self-reliance, and it seemed to have been instrumental in turning around disenfranchised young Black men in the US, giving them pride and purpose. I witnessed this effect starting to take hold in London. Suddenly street guys I knew in Tottenham were eschewing the hood life, educating themselves, wearing sharp suits, and exhibiting newfound confidence and pride in their communities. I was impressed. Anything that offered some sort of dignity to Black men was great to see.

But the other side of the Nation, the one that gets a lot of attention in the media, is that it harbors extreme views—like the belief that white people were made in a lab by an evil Black scientist, Yakub, and that all white people are the devil. In fact, it is designated a hate group by the Southern Poverty Law Center. But at the time I began attending the Nation meetings, I was unaware of this, and so demoralized by the racism at Otis and desperately looking for Black comradery that I was willing to overlook these beliefs.

During my short time there, I learned about Kemet—"land of the Blacks"—one of the original names of ancient Egypt. I wanted to learn about Africa in ways other than the messages I'd been fed all my life. Africans were more than caricatures with bones in their noses, chasing white men to boil them in pots, and being outwitted by Tarzan on a weekly basis. Africans were more than sad-eyed children with flies buzzing around their eyelashes, begging for donations. When my friend Bev and I realized the meetings we were attending were those of the Nation of Islam, we were already hooked on the knowledge and the bean pies, and we didn't care.

If you didn't already know, the bean pie seems to be an essential aspect of the Nation of Islam's financial structure. As well as the *Final Call*, the Nation's self-published newspaper, the Fruit of Islam (the bow-tied male disciples) would sell these pies, more often than not baked by the women of the Nation. These pies were not dissimilar to a sweet potato pie or a pumpkin pie, and they were de-fuckin'-licious. I ate tons of them, warm with cream poured all over the top. I was addicted to them, and was convinced they were healthy—after all, it's beans! I gained so much weight. During that time, I gave up pork and all non-halal foods, began covering my hair, and prayed four times a day. Muslims are supposed to pray five times a day, but I could never quite make that crack-of-dawn prayer. Devout I was not. But I enjoyed feeling part of something, and I quickly began announcing to everyone who would listen that I was now a Muslim.

My mum was bemused by this, but she never tried to talk me out of it, as after all, my father had been a Muslim. She also knew how I gained intense interest in things, only to become bored months later, so no doubt she assumed it would be one of my "fads."

Some of the Nation beliefs I could not quite get my head around. After my treatment at Otis, my general experiences with white people throughout my life, and the history of slavery, colonialism, and genocide, I didn't find it too difficult to believe that the white man was the devil. Not the mystical two-horned deity but by way of their action against indigenous peoples all over the globe. What I couldn't understand was the belief that the white man had been invented by an evil scientist named Yakub. So white people had been made in a test tube like alien spawn? Naw. I began asking questions. I did not find the answers satisfactory. I continued asking questions. Still no satisfaction. I asked some more. And this is where my disillusion with the Nation began to set in. You see, for a woman, I was too outspoken. I talked too much. I was too aggressive. I began to notice the dynamics between the men and women of the Nation.

Although the men were always super respectful of the women, referred to them as queens, and the word "sister" always precluded our names, it was the men who did all the speaking, who ran all the meetings, who dictated how things were done. Women were visible, but our roles were meant to be more along the lines of the traditional family dynamic, as in we were supposed to first and foremost support our men, look after the kids, and bake the bean pies. Just by virtue of who I was, my natural tendency was towards rebellion.

Members of the Nation traveled around the country for events with their counterparts in other cities, and Bev and I often went to these. These were exciting day trips and a chance to see the size and might of the Nation of Islam in the UK. It was on one of these trips that I realized my time with the Nation was up. We were heading to an event in Birmingham, a city approximately a hundred miles from London. We all met at a designated spot to travel in a large convoy. At that time, I had a souped-up Ford Orion. (I can tell what was happening in my life by what car I was driving at the time.) It was the bigger, four-door brother to the Ford Escort, but because it wasn't considered a boy-racer car, the insurance was cheaper. I had added a full body kit to it and expensive rims. I had room for passengers, besides Bev and I, so a couple of the brothers without vehicles opted to jump in with us. Now, I am a fast driver. Fast, but not reckless. I don't believe in showing off and driving above my ability to impress people, but if it's a dry, sunny day and there's an open road, I'm putting my foot down on that gas pedal. Hard. Although my hair was covered by a hijab, my driving apparently was not becoming of a good Muslim woman. All of a sudden, I heard a male voice. "Uh, sister, you're driving too fast." I answered, "All right," a little peeved but respectful. I slowed down a little to what I considered a decent speed. After all, we were on a motorway. But then he continued. "Sister, uh, pull over the car . . . I'm going to drive." Excuse me? Who the fuck did he think he was? I asked him, "Whose car is this? I don't remember you making any payments on this car, or paying my insurance, so if you don't like the way I drive *this car that I own*, I suggest you flag down the rest of the convoy and get in one of theirs. You ain't commandeering my vehicle." Bev was my only passenger to Birmingham that day, and I left the Nation soon after.

It was probably for the best. I couldn't make a decent bean pie for shit anyway.

Being with the Nation led me to another organization, Pan-African Community Enterprise, or PACE. Although also run by members of the Nation, brothers Derek Muhammed and Barry Muhammed, PACE wasn't so strict and accepted all types of people, whether Muslim, Christian, agnostic, or atheist. It was more of a community group, doing such things as getting food to people in need and raising money for after-school programs. I still got to meet up with other Black people and continue to learn more about the culture, and I didn't have to wear the hijab to do so.

One day PACE was putting together a community fundraiser. They needed poets, singers, dancers, and performers of any kind. At the time, jungle music—a fusion of dub reggae bass lines and techno, which was the predecessor to what we now know as drum and bass—was huge in the UK. I hated the name of the music, especially as it was a predominantly Black genre. I decided to write a short play about the stupidity of the name, even though I loved the sound.

Two other friends with whom I had attended the Nation, and subsequently PACE meetings, were Lola and Edire, who like me were of Nigerian descent. We were always messing around, imitating the accents of our parents. I wrote the short play, in which Lola and I played a Nigerian mum and auntie, and Edire played the young daughter/niece who was playing this loud music in her room. Our characters admonished her about this noise, the inappropriateness of the name, and the fact that she should be connecting to her African roots. We then finished with a choreographed African dance to Fela Kuti.

It was meant to be a humorous one-act play with a message—something people of different generations and backgrounds in the community could relate to. I don't know whether people got the message, but they laughed their asses off. I realized that I had written not a one-act play but a comedy sketch. It was exhilarating, and highly addictive, that laughter. And I wanted more.

After that PACE performance, we named ourselves Fusion and began performing the sketch at other talent shows. And we kept winning them. After a couple of months performing the same piece over and over again at various events, Edire left the group, to be replaced by another friend, Lynette. It also became obvious at that point that it was time to write another sketch, but I'd already hit writer's block and struggled to come up with another idea for the three of us.

At about this same time Bev's older sister, Veronica, who had seen us perform, approached me one day. "Have you heard about this stand-up comedy thing?" She told me that she had signed up for a stand-up comedy workshop that would meet every Sunday afternoon for four weeks, run by two reasonably known comedians on what was known as the Black comedy circuit. At the end of the workshop, you got to perform in a little theater, in front of an audience, endorsed by the comedians. She invited me to go to the workshop with her, and I thought, *Why not?* The two men were pretty established and could give us access to more performance opportunities, which could help get my creative juices flowing again, and I had both the money *and* the time, as I had not yet begun to seriously look for another engineering job after Otis. I was going to continue enjoying the summer off, maybe even longer, and return to regular work in the winter. The workshop brought in a mixed bag of people. From an older, shy lesbian, who wanted to increase her confidence enough to stand and speak in front of a room full of people, to a performing poet, who wanted to add humor to her pieces, to a young guy with confidence and swagger, who fancied himself as the next Eddie Murphy.

I turned up for the workshop with a large notebook already brimming with ideas and what I didn't know at the time was a five-minute set already written. I had plenty of ideas for stories and jokes but nothing sketch-wise yet for the girls and me. I'd also become bored of performing that one sketch, and for a reason I couldn't quite fathom, I felt restless. Fusion had one more competition to take part in and then either I'd have to come up with another piece or we were in trouble.

On the night of the competition, I arrived early, as I liked to do, to get a feel of the room and watch the other performers we were going up against. I let the promoter of the show know that Fusion was in attendance, and he informed me that we would be up sixth in the show. I settled in at the back of the room and waited, but Lola and Lynette failed to turn up. The show began with a mixed bag of wannabe R&B singers, some dance troupes, magicians, but as far as I could tell, we would be the only "comedy" act. As the show went on, I began to become apprehensive that the girls had still not arrived. As the time drew closer for our performance, I approached the promoter and asked him to push us further back in the show. He did. We were now to be the last performance of the competition. I paced up and down, intermittently worried and furious. No Lola, no Lynette.

The promoter finally approached. "We're about to bring you up. Your girls here yet?"

"Nope."

"So whaddya wanna do? Pull out?"

Hmmm. Forfeit this performance and lose our chance to get through to the final, after having driven over an hour across London to get here and sat through three different renditions of Brandy's "I Wanna Be Down," or go onstage with whatever jokes I could remember from my little notebook and at least try to salvage this disaster. Fuck it. "No, I'm gonna perform some stand-up comedy. Just tell 'em one of the members of Fusion is gonna tell some jokes." The MC did just that, and I walked towards the stage with all the confidence I could muster.

"Hey, everybody. My name is Obedapo Ebuwa Bolatito Iyashere. But you can call me Gina." That intro received a nice chuckle, and my confidence bloomed. "I'm from a Nigerian family. So repeat this phrase after me: 'Am-eh-nawo, Odukwe, Mamakusa.' That means . . . No idea, I just made that up, but it sounds pretty African, eh?" Big laugh. *Holy shit, I'm killing it!*

I did a very respectable five-minute set and walked offstage to enthusiastic applause and cheers. The audience and judges' votes came in soon after, and with my solo performance, I had managed to get us through to the final!

After the show, the MC approached me. "You're a stand-up." He told me, "You don't need the other two girls."

I wasn't ready to dump my friends—well, at least not till I found out why they'd left me hanging—so I smiled sweetly, thanked him, and went about my business. I later found out that Lynette's house had been burgled, and Lola had been helping her make a police report. It had been a stressful evening for all, but those burglars had actually done me a favor.

At the end of the four-week workshop, the two comedians running it hosted the planned stand-up performances with the workshop's alumni in a small, fifty-seat theater in South London, and the show sold out three nights. All the Black promoters and comedians working in the industry came by to see the next generation of talent coming through. The comedians considered the strongest were me, Bev's sister, Veronica—who was already writing strong, observational material that could easily cross over into the mainstream (meaning the white circuit)—and Glas Campbell, a guy from Leeds, about two hundred miles north of London. His shtick consisted of mainly old one-liners, previously told by the white, working-class comedians of the '70s, but his performance, his swag, and the way he strung those lines together into a killer set made him unbeatable, compared to us green comics with our jokes about African parents and stolen front doormats. He headlined all three nights of the alumni showcase and blew the roof off every night.

I was no slouch. I had come up with a killer ten-minute routine, and at the end of every show, Black promoters approached me, offering me money to perform at their events. Money! People wanted to pay for my little jokes! It wasn't a lot—we're talking anywhere between five and fifty per show—but at this point, with my cheap rent and my bought-for-cash car, I didn't need a lot of money to live on, and I was having fun.

I began to play with the idea of taking a little bit more time away from engineering and seeing how this played out. I became enamored with stand-up and threw all my energy into my new passion, neglecting my sketch group, Fusion. But Fusion limped on. I've never been good at ending relationships, always slowly pulling away till the other person gets completely fed up and does the dirty deed for me. Fusion was my first foray into this technique. Our brainstorming meetings became more and more sporadic while I explored my exciting new stand-up comedy world. I was struggling to come up with another sketch for Fusion, compounded by the fact that I'd lost interest and already emotionally moved on. I attended our meetings as much as I could, although my heart was no longer in it, and the girls could feel it.

One evening I turned up at Lola's house, where we were set to meet and finally come up with a new sketch together. There was another girl there. "Who are you?" I asked somewhat abruptly. No one had told me we were taking on a new member. She looked down in embarrassment and waited to be rescued.

"You haven't had much time for us lately," Lola began, "so we decided to bring someone else in to take your place."

I was relieved but still furious. The gall of throwing me out of the group I had put together. "Fine, do your thing, but you can't perform my sketch, 'cause I wrote it. You're gonna have to write your own." I wished the new girl good luck and left Fusion to continue on my stand-up adventure.

Baby me.

Me at eighteen months old.

(Left to right)
Dele, Mum,
and me.

The three musketeers.

Me around
six years old.

(Left to right) Me, Dele,
Sheyi, Taiwo, and Asi.

Asi's third birthday; me looking ecstatic in stripes.

Mum in the seventies.

Mum and Dad *(on the right)*.

In France,
at seventeen
years old,
with Helga.

(Left to right)
Me, Rocky, and
Maggie in Brooklyn.

"Funki Dred."

The Fridge nightclub days.

At twenty-two years old, with my beloved Honda CRX.

Me, the elevator engineer.

(Left to right) Me, Nasima, Maggie, and Tucker at Marks & Spencer Christmas Party, circa 1989.

One of my first headshots, taken on the set of *Blouse and Skirt*.

One of my first show flyers, Upfront Comedy Club, circa 1996.

The first time I met Thea Vidale, Edinborough, circa 1996.

Tanya, the character created for *The Lenny Henry Show*, circa 2005.

(Left to right) My stepsister, me, and my dad in Nigeria.

(Left to right) Taiwo, me, and Dele in Bethnal Green.

Me at Canary Wharf, aged twenty-one.

Me at seventeen, at the Eiffel Tower, Paris, France.

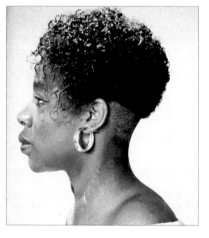

Me at nineteen: Leisure curl. Not Jheri curl!

13

However Hard a Lizard Does a Push-up, It Will Never Have an Alligator's Chest

When I was around ten, I was looking through one of my mum's magazines and something caught my eye. It was an article entitled "Women Who Don't Like Men." I was intrigued and began reading hungrily. The article was about women who loved women—in other words, lesbians. As I previously mentioned, I was a tomboy when I was a kid, climbing whatever I could get away with. I detested the dresses my mother made for me, and besides my brothers, I didn't particularly like boys—I found them stinky and rude. But I coveted their freedom. I wanted to be free to be whoever I wanted to be without being told I was "unladylike." That word was bandied about in relation to me for most of my childhood and deep into adulthood by everyone from teachers to friends to family members to even wannabe boyfriends. One guy once told me, "You're pretty, but you walk like a barbarian."

For as long as I could remember, Mum had ranted consistently about the perils of men. We girls were to keep away from boys at all costs. They were dirty and only wanted one thing, to use us, then dump us, and she would not stand for our education being ruined by pregnancy and shame. Penises were generally the work of the devil, until you were married and needed one for babies. As I read this piece in the magazine, everything seemed to make sense. I ran to Taiwo, triumphant in my epiphany. "Look!" I brandished the magazine, open at the page. "Mummy wants us to be lesbians!" By my childish deductions, it was completely logical. Lesbians didn't like boys. Lesbians didn't touch boys. Therefore, as per Mummy's wishes, we were supposed to be lesbians. Taiwo was somewhat taken aback and tried to explain to me that she didn't think that was exactly what Mum wanted, which only confused me more. Then made me suspicious. Maybe Taiwo was just upset that I'd worked it out before her, because what else could Mum possibly want? I wondered . . . but I soon forgot about it and continued on with life.

My mum's plan had been for her daughters to avoid the opposite sex completely until we were qualified doctors, lawyers, engineers, or accountants, then meet Nigerian men, from the same tribe as us, who were also doctors, lawyers, engineers, or accountants, marry them, have kids, and produce more doctors, lawyers, engineers, or accountants. And preferably more than her friends, as immigrant parents always seemed to be in competition with one another over who had the most kids, the most successful kids, the most grandkids, and the most successful grandkids.

I continued being a reasonably happy tomboy and didn't think again about sexuality for several years. But I always found myself drawn to particular types of characters. In my favorite book of Enid Blyton's The Famous Five series, the horsey, short-haired, active female character George was the one I identified with most. In *Little House on the Prairie*, it was the rough-and-tumble Laura Ingalls I liked the best, and in the movies, I liked the girls who were scrappy and as powerful and strong as their male counterparts. I had no time for the damsels. I loved the old musicals as a kid, and Calamity Jane was my hero.

Calamity Jane, the ultimate tomboy, played by Doris Day in the 1953 movie of the same name, was everything I wanted to be. She could fight, she rode horses, she shot guns, and she was uncomfortable in dresses, but she was still pretty enough to get the man. Even as a tomboy, I knew I was still expected to get married at the end. At school, I wasn't popular, and boys didn't look at me. I concentrated on being the loud, funny one and helping my friends get boyfriends while not really having interest myself. At that time, I believed my lack of interest was because I was concentrating on my education. I was a late bloomer, and anyway, everyone knew I wasn't allowed to hang out with boys, so even if a boy had been interested, there would have been no place to hide for illicit love-ins, unless we skipped classes. And I never skipped classes.

My first inkling of my lesbianity occurred when I was around fourteen years old. Looking back, it was obviously my first girl crush, but at the time, I had no idea. She was my biology teacher, Mrs. McInnis, a petite, soft-spoken Scottish woman who often joked about how her husband was over six feet tall, a full foot taller than her. I found myself vying for her attention all the time, but in the most disruptive ways possible. I constantly talked back to her, made loud jokes in class, and generally made a nuisance of myself. I thought I was just showing off how rebellious I was in front of my sometimes friends, who often egged me on in my terrible behavior. In hindsight, I didn't know how to articulate what I was feeling and was willing to do anything just to get her attention.

She'd often become extremely exasperated and throw me out of her class, but I still looked forward to biology, though she must have dreaded every time she saw my name on the roster. My grades in biology were too high for her to have me permanently excluded from the class, so the poor woman suffered at my hands for several months.

One day it all came to a head. She pulled me out of the classroom. "Okay," she began, "I don't know why you hate me so much."

Huh? I was genuinely confused. I'd really just thought it was a little banter that sometimes I took a little too far. "I don't hate you!"

"Well, can we call a truce, please?" she asked me.

"Okay."

We shook hands, and I became one of her best students.

The next few years passed by uneventfully on the sexual-awareness front. At around age seventeen, boys began to show an interest in me, and though I enjoyed the attention at long last, being reassured that I wasn't ugly or abnormal, I didn't start reciprocating any interest until after I had returned from France. I had traveled alone to another country and had had a relationship of sorts with an older man, so I felt I was ready for the big leagues. I had a few flirtations with boys that I mostly enjoyed, but I felt no real attachment to any of them.

There was Ewart, a young British Caribbean guy who chatted me up outside a library near my home in Williams Close. He rented a room from an old white man in Watford, a town some fifteen miles northwest of Central London. I took a train to see him, and he was my first kiss and dry hump, in a stale '70s-style bedroom while the old man slept downstairs. I saw him twice, then decided he wasn't worth the train journey. And there was John, the Irish boy who asked me out with a Valentine's Day card, which he hadn't signed but had left sticking out of my locker at our weekend job at Sainsbury's supermarket. He was my longest relationship with a guy. We dated for about six months, but we never had sex. We were both virgins, and he seemed quite relaxed with where we were sexually. He was the boy I defied my mother for, sneaking to a nightclub with him after work on the night of my eighteenth birthday. I never felt totally comfortable seeing him, as I was afraid of my mum's reaction to me having not only a boyfriend but a white one at that! I hadn't even told my friends who worked with me at Sainsbury's.

At that time, though there were plenty of instances of Black guys dating women of other races, it was extremely rare for Black women to do the same. I had never seen it with my own eyes, and being the first frightened me. I swore John to secrecy, and we pretended not to know each other at work, while I spent many evenings eating pizza with his parents and younger brother and sister. I eventually grew tired of trying to find time to sneak and see him, and I wanted to get back to an easier life, of work and study, and not spending our entire time together fearing we'd be seen. Our dalliance fizzled out.

After John, I concentrated on work and hanging out with my new crew of friends. I'd met Maggie, Antoinette, Nasima, and Tucker while working evenings and Saturdays at Marks & Spencer, and I stayed friends with them afterwards. We all enjoyed the same types of music and fashion, and we dreamed of traveling abroad together—particularly to the States—and set about saving to do just that. In the early '90s, Soul II Soul hit the charts in the UK and the US with such hits as "Keep On Movin'" and "Back to Life." They were also an extremely successful sound system and ran popular club nights in London, the biggest being a Friday night residence at The Fridge in Brixton.

As I mentioned before, this club was my favorite. It was iconic, having been at the forefront of several music genres, from punk to trance to dance to techno. It was a huge venue that had previously been a movie theater and was easily recognizable by the full-size fridge that hung as a banner from the ceiling. After I had gone to that first nightclub with John, I spent the next few years on a nightclubbing rampage. And The Fridge on Soul II Soul's Friday night was the place to be. The line to get in used to stretch around the block every week.

Soul II Soul played an eclectic mix of soul, funk, reggae, and the latest hip-hop, to which we spent hours doing the Running Man, the Wop, and every dance move we'd spent the previous weeks copying from *Yo! MTV Raps* and practicing in front of our mirrors. Seeing as I was the first of my group of friends to purchase a car, I would drive all the way from North London to South, pick them all up, spend forty minutes trying to find a space near the biggest club in South London on a Friday night, then we'd wait in line, often in the freezing cold, for up to an hour and a half to get in, but boy was it worth it. As well as spinning, Soul II Soul—steered by their founder, Jazzie B—often invited artists they met on their tours to do sets at the club. I saw Public Enemy, KRS-One, De La Soul, Jazzie B, and N.W.A perform there.

Every week was also a fashion parade. At the time, I sported Leisure Curl on my head, which was similar to the now much ma-ligned Jheri curl, but dryer. It didn't leave the huge greasy patches on your pillow but achieved the same moist-looking curls. I would shave the back and sides of my head to make it look more edgy. Denim dungarees, Doc Martens, and bomber jackets were the accompanying style. This look had originally been the uniform of punks and skinheads, but it was then co-opted by the gay community and left-wing skinheads, who wore the uniforms in defiance of its racist connotations. Somehow it made it across to regular street wear, as an alternative to the baggy jeans and white tee hip-hop style. That became my style. Doc Martens were cool *and* comfortable, and those soles were so thick and the leather such good quality, they lasted for years, which was great when you were fashionable on a part-time supermarket-worker budget. Bomber jackets were quite reasonable to buy, and the fashion was to cover them in badges. The more badges you had, the cooler you looked. The Superman insignia was a popular one, as well as a sheriff's badge, which was odd, as we didn't have the same sorts of sheriffs in England, but the badges seemed to be relatively easy to come by. Every kid's cowboy outfit had one. Being as competitive as I was and always wanting to stand out, I searched far and wide for my badges. From market stalls to antique shops, from army-navy stores to car boot sales. My jacket was a bejeweled marvel. It wasn't till years later that I realized some of those badges were actually lesser known Nazi symbols. I had been so focused on filling the space on my bomber jacket, I hadn't researched what I was pinning to it. Blind fashion.

When I became immersed in the Soul II Soul scene, I began to move towards hip-hop in my music tastes and style. Soul II Soul was a mixture of a kind of beatnik style and hip-hop. Their motto was "A happy face, a thumpin' bass, for a lovin' race!" And their style was categorized as Funki Dred, which was a head of dreadlocks but with the sides of the head shaved. I loved the style and emulated it. I grew locs, and then I also shaved my head at the sides. My mother was furious. "So you are wearing your hair like those Jamaicans?" Dreadlocks were synonymous with

Rastafarianism, a religion with origins in Jamaica. Proponents of the religion grew locks, ate vegan, and smoked weed—everything that was anathema to my mother. But at this time I was working, driving, and paying Mum rent, so my life was very much my own. I reveled in this freedom.

Again, being the personality that I was, I needed to differentiate myself from all the other Funki Dreds, so I bleached my dreads white blond. Then I bleached my eyebrows to match. I looked like a damn Q-tip, but I didn't care! My style of clothing became a mixture of the funky, beatnik style and the Kangols, sneakers, gold chains, and leather puffer jackets of the hip-hop scene of the late '80s and early '90s. I liked the large door-knocker earrings made fashionable by Salt-N-Pepa, the hugely successful female rap duo. I would often spend a Saturday afternoon shopping for the latest gear in the West End and turn up at The Fridge the following week proudly sporting Adidas sneaks.

But I wanted to go to the States, the land of *Yo! MTV Raps* and my hero, Downtown Julie Brown. I had been a fan of hers ever since I'd heard her distinctly British accent coming at me from one of my favorite American TV shows, *Club MTV*, which she hosted for several years in the late '80s. She had made it out of the UK and was living the life I dreamed of in the US. I wanted to be her so badly! These were the days before the internet and Wikipedia, so I had no idea how she'd done it, but I was determined to at least *get* to the States, and I would work out a plan of action from there.

All this was while I was still working at Otis. In the UK, most jobs come with a minimum of four weeks paid vacation per year, but my engineering job at Otis had come with five weeks, so I saved four of them for my trip to the country I had dreamed about visiting since I was a child. That's right, with my new crew of friends I began to plan a month-long visit to America. I couldn't wait. We all saved hard for over nine months to pay for those flights, and to make sure we had enough cash to buy up all the gold and sneakers we could fit in my three suitcases. Yup. Back in the '90s airlines let you carry three suitcases at no extra cost. I had one case with the clothes I would wear on the trip and two empty ones for all my US booty I'd be bringing home to show off at The Fridge.

In early 1990, our ragtag gang of young female hip-hop fans flew to the States for our first girls' trip. First stop was Fort Lauderdale, Florida. Tucker (her first name was Jennifer, but Tucker sounded cooler) had an auntie who lived there, and we were going anywhere we could get free accommodations. Tucker's auntie also had a house with a pool! For a bunch of working-class girls from London, this was the ultimate in luxury and Americanness. It was the dream. When we arrived at the house, we marveled at the size of the place. Looking back, it was a regular ranch-style three-bedroom, single-level house, but to us at the time it was a palace. And did I mention it had a pool? Tucker's auntie even had a water-bed. We'd never seen those either. She looked on, bemused, as we jumped and rolled around on it like a bunch of toddlers. I thought she must be a millionaire. In fact, she was a nurse who had emigrated from the Caribbean in the '70s. Nurses seemed to have a much better lifestyle in the US than in England, that was for sure. No British nurse had a pool in her backyard and a bed you could swim in. We immediately dumped our suitcases in our respective rooms and dived into the pool, where we spent the next four days.

When it came time to explore Fort Lauderdale, we discovered that the main pastimes were going to the beach, the mall, and the movies. That was it. Fort Lauderdale was mainly occupied by old white people, so we were in completely the wrong place for the hip-hop parties we'd envisaged. There was no way we were accidentally bumping into Big Daddy Kane in any of these sleepy cul-de-sacs. We went to the beach, the mall, and the movies on rotation for two weeks. We saw *Ghost* three times, *Problem Child*, *Chucky*, and every 1990 movie that was out. Fort Lauderdale was *boring*. Even the pool and waterbed no longer entertained us. We had a glass vase engraved with our names during our final trip to the mall, and we presented it to Tucker's auntie to remember us by. We thanked her profusely for putting us up, and we left early to go to New York, to stay with another of Tucker's aunties, who lived in the projects in Brooklyn. She definitely did not have a pool.

The building she lived in was reminiscent of my Bethnal Green home. So this was "the projects"—just an American way of saying "council flats." They had the same piss-smelling elevators, dark, foreboding corridors, and guys hanging in the stairwells, except this time no white skinheads, just young Black dudes catcalling as we walked by. I didn't care. I was in New York! Every day my friends and I got up early and spent the day buying stuff to fill our suitcases and eating McDonald's apple pies. Yes, we had McDonald's in England, but for some reason in 1990 the British outlets were still frying their apple pies. We had discovered McDonald's baked apple pies on our second day in New York, and our belief that the US was far superior to the UK was confirmed. What bullshit had England been passing off as Micky D's? This was the real deal. We ate McDonald's pretty much every day after that. I estimate that I consumed fifty baked apple pies in those two weeks.

We hit every shopping spot we could. All the department stores we'd seen in American movies, like Bloomingdale's and Macy's, but the real scoop was finding where to get the best hip-hop gear.

I'd heard Canal Street and Delancey Street mentioned in a few rappers' songs and interviews, so I already knew where we needed to go to pick up gold dookie chains, Gucci link bracelets, door-knocker earrings, and name rings. Everyone in the US back then had gold rings and matching necklaces with their names in cursive. The jewelers in England hadn't worked out how to do those yet and were still struggling with the two-letter initial rings; further-more, gold was much cheaper in the US. We bought *everything*! Canal Street was for the gold, and Delancey Street was where to get good leather jackets. There, I picked up a leather puffer jacket with a fur collar and goose-down feathers that I'd seen worn by some of my favorite rappers in their videos. By that time, they were less fashionable in the US but still über cool in England. Because of that, I was able to get this coat for just $160—£80! I couldn't believe it! The US was a nonstop half-price sale! We got sneakers on Broadway—Adidas shell toes with fat laces, and the new kid on the block back then, Reebok Pumps, a shoe with a pump in the tongue that you pushed to inflate and provide extra hold around the ankle. It was the most expensive shoe out at the time, going for $170, and I bought two pairs. These shoes had definitely not made it across the pond yet, so we would be going back to England with clothing and knowledge from the future, like fashion time travelers.

Before broadband internet, mobile phones, and streaming media, there was always a large time delay between the US and the UK when it came to fashion and movies. When a movie came out in the US, the film reels were sent over to the UK via carrier pigeon six months after its US general release. *Six. Months.* Okay, I may be embellishing with the pigeon, but it really was that long before we got to see US films in Europe. So going to the States, watching all the movies, and buying up the swag gave us the best bragging rights and upgraded our social standing ten-fold. We shopped, went to every tourist destination, and soaked up every New York experience we could think of. We saw the 1960s *All for Freedom* singing group Sweet Honey in the Rock in the parkland area that surrounded the World Trade Center. We marveled at the Empire State Building. We got motion sickness on the Staten Island Ferry. We got lost in Central Park. And one day in Washington Square Park, while wandering around to work off the McDonald's baked apple pies, we stumbled on an impromptu show.

Two guys stood in the middle of a crowd that had gathered around them. They had no instruments, did no tricks. They just talked. They told funny stories, and had the crowd enthralled. I had no idea what this was, but it excited me. Little did I know, I had attended my first stand-up performance. Looking closely at one of the men, my excitement tripled. I'd just seen this guy on the big screen the week before! It was Rick Aviles, the guy who murders Patrick Swayze in *Ghost*! I pulled out my trusty Kodak 110 camera and prayed I had enough film left on the roll to get a couple of snaps. I then threw up another prayer, that when I sent them off to get developed a few weeks later and waited with bated breath for them to come back, I wouldn't end up with thirty-six pictures of my finger. This was the best trip ever. We were bumping into movie stars!

After the days spent sightseeing and shopping, the nights were spent hitting as many parties and clubs as possible. We loved the twenty-four-hour subway, and we rode the graffiti-stained cars at night, completely unafraid. We wanted to see how our dance skills stacked up against the Americans'. We went back repeatedly to a multilevel club we found in the Meatpacking District, a place called Mars. Each of its four floors had different genres of music: hip-hop, house, reggae, and rock. We had learned about this club from a bunch of cool kids we'd become friendly with at the McDonald's on Broadway. They had told us that Mars was the place to be any night of the week. Those apple pies led us to many adventures.

The first night we arrived at Mars, we lined up dutifully to get in. It was a hot summer's evening, and there was a varied mix of people hanging outside. This was no sleek, built-up area. The club looked like an abandoned warehouse, and this image was very much confirmed by random piles of rubble dotting the surrounding area from which rats dodged in and out. I was wearing one of my brand-new pairs of Reebok Pumps, so I kept a wary eye on the rat activity. When we finally got into the club, we excitedly explored all floors but finally settled on the hip-hop floor, where we danced till 7 a.m., and slept happily on the subway back to Brooklyn. We went to Mars three nights in a row, but on the last night, a Sunday, as we approached the club, we noticed a distinct change in the clientele. The surrounding area was packed with people I'd heard of but never seen in real life: cross-dressers, men dressed just like the characters from the pop group Village People, drag queens, and a lot of girls who were dressed similarly to us but were holding hands and kissing! Oh! We'd obviously turned up on gay night. We still wanted to go to the club, so we all hatched what we thought was a novel plan. We'd pair up and hold hands, *pretending* we were lesbians so no one would bother us.

I grabbed Maggie, Antoinette and Nasima paired up, and Tucker and Lara, another friend who'd joined us on the trip last minute, did the same. And in we went. The hip-hop floor was the same, and we soon forgot our discomfort as we danced and enjoyed ourselves.

At some point I became separated from my friends and a tall attractive Black woman sidled over to me. "Hey. You wanna dance?"

I was flustered. "Er, I'm not gay!"

"Really." She looked me up and down, assessing me slowly.

With my baggy jeans and tee, my sneakers, and my shaved head with blond dreads poking out of the top like a pineapple, I could understand her confusion. I tried to clarify. "Yeah, we all dress like this in England!"

"Oh, that's why you speak funny!" She laughed.

I was indignant. "No, *you* speak funny!" I countered. "I'm from England, and we're speaking *English*!"

She laughed again and offered to buy me a drink, and I wandered over to the bar with her, enjoying her company and the lighthearted banter. We chatted and laughed for a while, then all of a sudden she stopped talking, looked at me for an uncomfortably long time, and said, "Come with me." I was intrigued so I followed her through the crowd. Before I knew it, we were in the ladies' bathroom. I assumed she just wanted company while she went for a pee. She couldn't be inviting me to listen to her take a dump, surely. A cubicle opened up, and she walked towards it, turned back to me, and said, "Come on!" *Huh?* I followed her into the cubicle. She shut the door behind us, pushed me up against the wall, and kissed me passionately. *Holy shit.* I felt an excitement I had never felt with any of the guys I'd been with, and I was terrified. I was too shocked to kiss her back, but she was unperturbed. Eventually, she pulled back. "You liked that, huh?" I just stared, dumbfounded. "Honey, you're a lesbian. You just don't know it yet!" And with that, she took a pen and scrap of paper out of her purse, scribbled a number, squeezed it into my hand, and walked out of the cubicle.

I stumbled back through the club, found my friends, and never mentioned what had transpired. I was scared, confused, and turned on at the same time. Several times in the middle of the night over the last days of our trip, I sneaked away from my friends to find a pay phone to call her. I left messages, but she never called me back, and I never saw her again.

When we got back to England, I put that first lesbian experience out of my mind and threw myself back into straight life. I didn't hate men, so surely I could forget what happened, live a regular life, work, meet a man, get married, have some kids. I wanted to be normal. I was finally at a place in my life where I had good friends, who thought I was cool and funny, who really liked me. I'd finally left those awkward, unpopular years behind, so the last thing I wanted to do was risk being alienated again.

You never know when a chicken sweats because of their feathers.

The Fridge attracted an eclectic mix of people, but I'd only ever met one person who might have understood my dilemma, although we'd fallen out, so that door was closed.

For over a year I'd seen this handsome guy on the dance floor at The Fridge and marveled at his skills. These were the days when dances like the Running Man, the Roger Rabbit, and spins and splits ruled the dance floor, and every week was like a dance competition. And I am extremely competitive. I'd spend the previous weeks scanning MTV videos for the latest moves so I could show them off that weekend. On the dance floor, I'd slowly weave my way to the vicinity of the best dancers and dance my ass off in their periphery until they acknowledged my prowess. That is how a lot of my friendships back then were made. This dude caught my attention because he usually came to the club alone but seemed to know everyone. He would spend the entire night dancing by himself, occasionally stopping to sip from a single glass of water.

He was an enigma. And boy could he dance. I was determined we would be friends. A couple of my crew had also expressed their attraction to him, so I'd be killing two birds with one stone. My normal tactic of dancing in his general vicinity hadn't worked, as he always seemed to be dancing in his own music video in his mind. It was frustrating.

Eventually I approached one of the girls I'd seen him occasionally greet. "Yo, your mate is a really good dancer. Where's he from?"

"Which mate?" she responded.

"The guy with the red shirt."

"Oh, him?" She smiled slowly with a glint in her eyes.

"I don't fancy him, I just like his dancing!"

"Yeah, sure. Lemme introduce you!"

Cool. We waded through the crowd, and she tapped him on the shoulder.

"Gina, this is Sharon. Sharon, this is Gina."

Huh? Sharon?

Although Sharon was a name historically used for both genders, in the UK this hadn't been the case. I knew a lot of Sharons, and none of them were male. This was why her friend had smiled like that. *The bitch.* I tried to hide my shock while Sharon's friend grinned beside me. I made some small talk, complimented Sharon on her dancing, then I rushed back to tell my friends of my discovery. "That boy is a girl!"

I'd never met anyone like Sharon. She wasn't just a tomboy like me. No matter how rough-and-tumble I was, there was no hiding the fact that I was female, and I was never in any doubt that I was. I wanted the same freedoms that boys had, but I didn't want to *be* a boy. Sharon was different.

Most of us dressed similarly in those days, so it wasn't the clothing that caused people to misgender her. She wore the same high-top fades that the guys were rocking. She carried herself in the same way that the guys did. She had no discernible female features, no breasts, no curves. Her face was that of a very cute young guy. Her physicality was on a level with the guys. There was absolutely no giveaway that she was in fact female. I didn't know at the time, because that knowledge was not readily available, but Sharon may have been trans.

I didn't care. She was a great dancer, and we were going to be friends. I introduced her to my crew, and we all began hanging out. I learned a lot about Sharon through observing her. Most people who knew her accepted her for who she was. She was just Sharon, who looked like a boy. Others who didn't know her just assumed she was a cute guy. Until I dragged her into my friend group, she had pretty much been a loner, just drifting through, dancing, then leaving. The reason why she sipped on just one glass of water all night at the club was because she never went to the bathroom. As in *never*. She didn't feel comfortable using either gender of bathroom.

On one occasion we were having a conversation as we walked through the club. She was so engrossed that she hadn't realized I was walking towards the ladies' bathroom. We stepped in, and she stopped dead in her tracks as she realized where we were. All the girls in there stopped and stared at her. Sharon turned and rushed out like she had been chased. That was the only time in over a year of being friends with her that I saw her enter a public toilet. We became close, but we never discussed sexuality. We swapped records, we went to the movies, we danced at the club, and she even came and hung at the house a few times, obviously when I knew my mum was at work.

Looking back, she may have been attracted to me. There

were times when she'd throw her arm around my shoulder as we walked, knowing that no one would bat an eyelid, as we looked like a regular girlfriend-boyfriend combo. But I was in such deep denial about my inclinations then that I saw nothing in it. I was convinced of our platonic friendship.

Sharon lived in South London with her Jamaican mother, who's opinion on her masculine-presenting daughter I never knew. I only met her once, and at that time she was attempting to smash my house up.

I'm not sure when I started to feel resentful towards Sharon, but over a period of time I began to feel used by her. I was the only one in my group of friends with a car, and when we were going out, I would often drive to pick them all up at their homes or very close by. I'd also drop them all off individually afterwards, only once in a while asking for gas money. Whenever it was that asking time, Sharon would slip out of the car and make a run for it. The first few times, I let it slide, but as time went on, my other friends began to tire of her failure to contribute, and when I finally told her she'd have to, she pulled one pound out of her pocket. I'd been picking her up and dropping her off for a year at that point. She was taking the piss. The next time we were all going out, I told her my car was full.

She still made it to the club, but when she saw me, she ignored me. Over the next few weeks, she kept blanking me in the club, so I assumed our friendship was now over. I asked her to return a large batch of records I'd lent her a few weeks earlier. She didn't. I asked again. I sent one of my friends, Maggie, as a mediator to meet her and collect my stuff. Maggie returned with just two records. At the time I had a large vinyl collection of all the big rap records of the era—Sweet Tee, Big Daddy Kane, Biz Markie, Public Enemy, Pete Rock and C. L. Smooth, Chubb Rock, Queen

Latifah. I'd lent Sharon almost my entire collection for her to put on tape. That's what we did in the '80s and '90s. Either we recorded stuff off the radio, hoping the DJ didn't talk too much through it, or one of the crew would buy the record and the rest of us copied it onto tape. I'd lent Sharon forty records. She'd returned two and was refusing to return my calls. I was furious.

Two weeks later, Maggie and I drove to Sharon's house. I told Maggie to wait in the car while I knocked on the door. A Jamaican man in his fifties opened. Presumably her mum's partner.

"Hi. Is Sharon in?"

"She's upstairs. Sharon!"

I didn't wait for her to come all the way down but walked into the house and met her at the bottom of her stairs. With barely any acknowledgment, she turned and headed back up to her bedroom as I followed. Once we got in the room and closed the door, I wasted no time getting to the point. "Where the fuck are the rest of my records?"

"I gave them to Maggie." I wanted to punch her right then, but I struggled to control myself. I hadn't written down all the albums and singles I'd lent her, but I reeled off at least eight of them that we both knew she hadn't returned. I watched the realization dawn on her, that my memory was better than she'd hoped, then saw her face harden. "I don't know what you're talking about. You ain't getting those records back, so come out of my house."

I completely lost my temper and launched at her. The fight didn't last long before I felt myself being grabbed from behind and pushed facedown on her bed. The man had obviously heard the commotion and ran upstairs to Sharon's defense. He held both my arms behind my back while pushing on the back of my head and forcing it into one of the bed pillows. Sharon at this point was punching me in the head as I lay immobilized, struggling to breathe. I began to panic, as I was running out of breath and was beginning to black out.

Suddenly I heard "Get off her!" And banging and crashing noises. Maggie, God bless her, had run into the house and to my rescue. I found myself free and able to breathe again, as Maggie had pulled the man off me. I staggered toward Sharon, but Maggie pulled me out of the room and dragged me down the stairs and out of the house. Sharon followed, screaming obscenities, as the man slammed the front door behind us. I was apoplectic with rage. I ran back and karate kicked the door several times, smashing one of the windowpanes and bowing the doorframe. I wasn't getting those records back, so I was going to make her pay in other ways. Maggie dragged me back to the car, and we screeched away.

Two nights later there was a loud bang at the front door and several long incessant rings of the doorbell. "Ah-ah, who is that?" Mum rarely had visitors at the house, and all her kids were home, apart from Taiwo, who had long flown the coop.

"I'll go check." I walked to the front door, and through the frosted glass, I saw two people. One, a slim Black woman I hadn't seen before, but the other, standing behind her, I immediately recognized as Sharon. *Shit.* I turned and walked back the way I'd come. Sharon's mum began hammering on the door.

Mum came out of the front room. "What is going on?"

"It's a girl I had a fight with. She's turned up with her mum. Don't let them in!"

"So I will leave them out there until somebody calls the police? Don't be stupid. I will talk to her, mother to mother," my mum said and went to open the door.

"But they're Jamaican!" I implored. At that point I was willing to use anything to stop what was about to happen, even defunct prejudices.

Mum opened the door, and Sharon and her mother stepped in. Sharon's mum was a petite woman. She was dwarfed by Sharon, but in height only. The woman was furious, and her body thrummed like a tightly strung guitar. I marveled at how a woman with no car had been able to hold on to that angry energy for the hour and a half journey it must have taken on public transport to get to us.

In contrast, Sharon stood behind her, with her head down, looking decidedly meek. Not the screaming, hitting banshee she'd been just forty-eight hours previously.

"Your daughter came to my house, attacked my daughter, and smashed up my property!"

"Did your daughter tell you that she stole *my* property?" I began but was swiftly shut up by my mother's hand across my chest, pushing me backwards.

"Let her speak."

Sharon's mum went into a long rant about my lawlessness while my mum stood patiently letting her get it all out. I itched to intervene, but not enough to openly defy my mum, even if this woman was only telling half the story.

When she had finished, my mum apologized on my behalf and tried to reason with her. The whole time, Sharon hadn't said a word.

"Well, my property is damaged, so I'm going to damage yours!" *Huh? What?*

We were all standing in the front hallway at that point, and the only available item for damaging was our house phone. In the olden days, before landlines became a relic, most households kept the family phone somewhere central, so everybody could hear it. Usually in the lounge, kitchen, or front hallway. These were the gargantuan plastic rotary phones that took pride of place in the home, usually next to the Yellow Pages, and displayed on some kind of decorative side table.

Ours was in the hallway, and Sharon's mum focused on that as an outlet for her wrath. She grabbed our phone and threw it to the floor. I instinctively stepped forward to stop her, but again Mum barred me with her arm, as if to say, *"Let her get it out of her system."* Sharon's mum began jumping up and down on the phone and kicking it.

They obviously didn't have a landline at home, as anybody who had one would have known that these phones were absolute bricks. They were mainly thick plastic, and the mechanics were well protected within that shell. They were virtually indestructible. This poor woman jumped up and down, trying to break the telecommunications equivalent of a boulder. If this wasn't such a fraught situation, I would have laughed my ass off. But I didn't. We stood and watched. The only sound was Sharon's mum huffing and puffing with the effort. She picked up the phone again and smashed it into the floor. Nothing. The phone landed undamaged. Mocking. Her anger grew with her humiliation. She began kicking the door nearest to her, which happened to be the door to my brothers' bedroom. It was closed and made of sturdy wood, and it barely budged with this woman's onslaught. This was becoming really embarrassing. She then tried to pick up the phone to use to smash the door.

This was when finally Mum said, "Okay, enough. You can go now."

Mum moved like a ninja. In one move, she had the front door open, had Sharon's mum by the scruff of the neck, as she screamed and cursed at us, and was throwing her out onto the street. I stepped forward, just in case Sharon tried to defend her mother, but she didn't. She walked out after her, without so much as a peep. Mum slammed the door shut, and it was only then that Sharon suddenly found her voice. She joined her mother in screaming abuse from the street, then ran at our door, kicking it. Luckily, it was made from much better wood than hers, but she succeeded in ripping off the letter-box cover.

Mum calmly picked up the phone, put it back on the side table, and went back into the front room, but not before turning to me. "You will replace that letter box, and any other damage done to this house, you will pay for it." The phone rang about ten minutes later. It was a wrong number. The phone worked perfectly.

I never saw Sharon again after that. She kept away from the club, and I heard rumors of her moving away and living life as a man, where nobody knew her. Despite the loss of my vinyl collection, and her attempt to murder me, I still wish her well.

If you think you have someone eating out of your hands, best count your fingers.

Early on, I realized that I seemed to attract two types of suitors. One type was the guy who saw my fierce independence and my lack of emotion as a challenge and wanted to tame me like a wild beast. Those relationships ended up being a battle of wills, and eventually I'd tire of being told I wasn't feminine enough. I'd just stop answering their calls and disappear from their lives. This is now called "ghosting." It took a lot more effort to complete a ghosting with just landlines. It meant getting someone to answer the phone for you, never answering the phone again, or changing your number, which back then involved money and paperwork. One such guy, Frances—who, as well as constantly comparing me to his exes, had a horrible habit of blatantly staring at other girls when I was with him—was still upset with me several years later when I bumped into him unexpectedly. " 'I'll see you around'?"

he spat. Apparently, that had been the last thing I'd said to him before not seeing him around ever again.

The other type of guy I attracted liked strong, dominating women. My masculine energy was very alluring to these types, as I wasn't prone to playing games, and I had no problem bossing them around. This would start off as fun for me, having a guy who basically did whatever I wanted, but soon I would become bored, and then unreasonably demanding, just to see how much I could get away with. I'd eventually drive him away or revert to my tried-and-true ghosting method.

Steven belonged to this second group. I met him while collecting my car from the repair shop when I was around twenty-two. He was tall, dark, muscular, and very chatty. He made me laugh, and I found his confidence attractive. When he asked for my number, I told him to give me his, as I was still living at home, and I was keeping my dating life as far away from my mother's consciousness as possible. At the time we began seeing each other, I was building elevators for Otis, and he repaired train lines, and we were both intrigued by each other's jobs. We spent a lot of time watching movies, listening to music, and making out in his bedroom in the house he still shared with his Jamaican mother, as he insisted he was saving money to buy his own house. He was a massive Funkadelic fan and introduced me to the sounds of George Clinton.

Steven and I lasted around five months before things ended with me driving him away with my excessive demands. There was at that time an epidemic of people breaking into cars to steal car stereos, so stereos had been invented that you could pull out and carry around like a briefcase. Your stereo couldn't get stolen from your car now, but it could get stolen from anywhere else, because you tended to put it down places because it looked ridiculous and was heavy as hell. They soon invented the more convenient face-off stereo, where the front clipped off and could be carried in a much smaller, less cumbersome case, which fit in a pocket or purse. It was significantly more expensive than the other type. For my birthday, Steven bought me the briefcase type. I told him to take that bullshit back and get me the better one. He did. We had been dating less than two months at that point, and I became brattier as the relationship developed. We were doomed. I did like him a lot, though, and he was the one I selected to take my virginity at the grand old age of twenty-two. He was patient, sweet, and gentle. But I still left that experience thinking, *What is all the fuss about?* And I largely felt this way with subsequent men I had sex with. I didn't have that aha moment till the first time I slept with a woman. But I did make sure to give the penis several opportunities to change my thinking.

14

Smooth Seas Do Not
Make Skillful Sailors

When I started out performing on the Black comedy circuit in the mid-1990s, the majority of the comedians had a Caribbean background, and many of their jokes poked fun at Africans. The stereotypes of us varied. There were the guileless fools, constantly being outwitted by Tarzan. There were the poor, hungry children on TV, looking sadly into the camera, while flies landed on their eyelids, and a soothing white voice asked for donations. There was the swag-less unfashionable African man trying to win the affections of much more desirable Caribbean women with corny lines while wearing crocodile-skin shoes, with no socks, and pants too short, revealing his ashy ankles. Then the favorite comedy go-to was the officious jobsworth, always upholding petty rules to the detriment of humanity, and common sense. That character was usually a parking attendant who would stick a ticket on your car right in front of you while shouting in the most obnoxiously loud, usually Nigerian, accent: "My friend, you cannot park here!" I'd sit in the audience and wonder, *Where are the African comics rebutting this crap? Where are the jokes pertaining to Caribbean stereotypes?* One Nigerian comedian, Toju, was working on the scene before I came out, but he was also an extremely talented impersonator and leaned towards that in his act. I decided I was going to be the Nigerian crusader.

I wrote a ton of jokes about my Nigerian heritage, how proud I was of all my names, even if I could barely pronounce them. I also aimed most of my Caribbean jokes at the Jamaicans. Mainly because they were the most vocal and boastful of all the islanders at any show, and just as the Nigerian accent was the go-to African voice, the Jamaican accent was the go-to Caribbean accent. Even non-Jamaican Caribbeans would default to it. One of my earlier routines was about how easy it was to create a Jamaican curse word—all you had to do was add "clart" to the end of it: "bomboclart," "raasclart," "pussyclart." I then took random words from the English language and added "clart" to them, to great comedic effect. "Washer-dryer-clart! Table-clart!" As I said, it was my early work, but it was a crowd-pleaser.

Another routine was about how my mother didn't understand Jamaican slang, and that she misunderstood the word *punani*, the Jamaican word for "vagina," thinking it was some kind of tropical fruit, saying things like "I would really like to taste some of this *punani*!" This joke and various other routines of mine ended up being stolen by a Canadian comedian, Russell Peters, who used to visit the UK to perform, and we ended up on a few shows together. Unbeknownst to me, he had cherry-picked my best bits to take back to Canada, turning my Nigerian mum into his Indian father, going on to use these and several more jokes stolen from other comics in his specials, becoming famous from material he never wrote. I confronted him later, after being accused by his fans of stealing *his* material. He apologized, promised to pay me, then reneged, ignoring me, and continued to use my material, only admitting the theft publicly during an interview twenty years later.

But I digress.

My fledgling comedy career was going very well, and after six months I decided to put off going back to work as an engineer for the foreseeable future. I was going to throw everything I had at this new vocation. I had been a good engineer, but I was never going to be the best engineer, and I felt that I could really be great at this comedy thing, judging by how well I was doing, and by how much I had fallen in love with the whole process of creating and taking it straight to the stage. The immediacy and freedom of it was intoxicating.

I decided early that if I was going to make this my new career, I had to broaden my audience by encompassing shows on the white circuit. Although shows on the Black comedy circuit paid well, with opportunities to play shows at large theaters in front of appreciative and lively Black crowds in pretty much all the major cities in the country, there was an even larger and more vast network of comedy clubs and pubs on the mainstream, or white, circuit, with opportunities to work more often. On the whole, these paid less, as people tended to go to those places regardless of who was on, whereas the Black shows were built around the people who were performing, so they were more of an event. With the Black events, I could work maybe a show every ten days to two weeks, but on the white circuit I could work every night. I wanted to get as much experience as I could, and also earn more money, so I took every show offered and pestered bookers to audition me for their spots. I would go anywhere in the country, often driving 150 miles to audition for a club, then drive back the same night, taking naps in lay-bys on the way home, as I didn't have money for hotels. I loved every minute of it.

Competitions were a way to gain exposure, and the most prestigious of those was the Hackney Empire's New Act of the Year Showcase for emerging comedians and variety acts. The Hackney Empire, a big, old vaudeville theater in London, had previously been a music hall, hosting performances by the likes of Charlie Chaplin, Stan Laurel of Laurel and Hardy, and Julie Andrews. The New Act of the Year Showcase always sold out and was attended by a who's who of industry executives looking for the next comedy star. I entered the competition in 1996 and came in second—a very respectable performance, especially as I was the only person of color in that competition, and probably in that entire fifteen-hundred-seat theater.

Although I didn't win the showcase, there had been TV scouts in the audience, and I was selected to perform on a talent show called . . . wait for it . . . *The Big Big Talent Show*, hosted by Jonathan Ross, a hugely popular talk-show host, kind of the UK's version of Jay Leno. It was based on a nationwide search for the next big talent and was aired on one of the biggest TV networks in England. *Oh my days!* I had been doing comedy for less than a year, and I already had a gig on TV. I was gonna be a star!

I couldn't wait to tell my mum that I hadn't been crazy to leave a good job as an engineer to become what she called a talking clown, and that I was about to be a millionaire TV entertainer. Up to that point, I had never invited her to any of my performances, due to her disapproval, but now she was finally going to see me in my element, in my first TV appearance. With Jonathan Ross, no less!

The day I informed my mum of my impending big break, she was reasonably impressed, but her fear of me embarrassing her live on TV took precedent. "This is a competition. I do not want to come there to watch you be eliminated from the first round. I will come when you get through to the final." I wasn't surprised or disappointed. I just had to be the best.

For my first performance on the show, I was asked to invite a friend or member of my family to come on and be interviewed by Jonathan Ross. The TV executives loved the story of my engineering roots, and so I invited Salim, my old Otis partner. He would sit on the couch, have a short entertaining chat with Jonathan, then Jonathan would throw to me, standing by my mic at another part of the stage, and I would do my five-minute set. Unfortunately, I was so preoccupied with my first TV set that I didn't have time to prep Salim for *his* first and only TV gig, or even check that he was a suitable representative of my brand. To this day I don't know whether Salim was harboring bitterness towards me for not being the assistant that he'd expected when I was assigned to him or he just froze in front of the cameras on this *live* taping, but after Jonathan Ross introduced Salim and asked him, "So what are your best memories of Gina while she was working with you?" Salim blurted out, "She would never clean the pit!" Jonathan, like 99.999 percent of the watching population, had no idea what Salim was talking about, that he was referring to the times we argued about who should clean out the bottom of the elevator shaft, so he asked, "Wouldn't clean the pit?" And Salim's response was "Yeah. She wouldn't clean it!" I stood frozen, watching this debacle unfold. Luckily Jonathan was an experienced talk-show host. He made a quick joke, tapped Salim on the knee, and introduced me. I collected myself and delivered my set. Despite Salim's epic fumble, my set was well received, and the TV audience voted me through to the final. I didn't invite Salim back.

Later my mum berated me about having Salim on, and reiterated how glad she was that she had not been there to witness this embarrassment live, but true to her word, she was in the audience for the final. She attended with a bunch of her Nigerian friends, all dressed in their best embroidered finery and most sparkly gold trinkets. Just as Jonathan was about to introduce me, he noticed Mum in the crowd. I mean, she wasn't hard to spot in this mainstream TV audience. It was literally white people, white people, white people, and then a bank of what looked like African royalty.

"Is that your mum?" Jonathan Ross asked me. Yup. "Gina's amazing-looking mum, everybody!"

My mum didn't need any further encouragement. She stood up with her arms outstretched and basked in the applause, as if she had been my number one comedy fan from day one. *"Yes, I am the one. I am the mother of the clown. She is here because of me!"*

I smiled inwardly.

I didn't win the final, losing to a young ventriloquist, Paul Zerdin, who went on to win *America's Got Talent* over twenty-four years later. Such is the hustle. I didn't mind. There was no money prize that I missed out on, just a trophy, and besides, a more important victory had been won. Mum had finally acknowledged my new career. From that day, she never again asked me when I was going back to my proper job. I had been validated by Television.

15

It Is When There Is a Stampede that a Person with Big Buttocks Knows that He Carries a Load

I t didn't take long to realize that the comedy scene in England was very segregated. White comics didn't feel the need to perform for Black audiences, as white people were the majority in the entertainment field, live and on television, in front of and behind the cameras, and therefore they had no incentive to broaden their viewpoint to include an audience they didn't have to care about, much less cater to.

White talent scouts never looked for talent outside their middle-class white comedy enclaves, so TV was mainly middle-class white guys espousing. Even white working-class comics felt shut out after their 1970s heyday, when most UK stand-up talent on television was sourced from working-class clubs and music halls, where the poorer white entertainers resided. It wasn't very surprising that most Black comics felt marginalized by mainstream TV and so only did Black shows. Their material was relatable to

Black audiences and bonded them in recognition of their shared experiences of being Black in Britain. The Black comics who had been successful during the 1970s had done self-deprecating humor that belittled them before white audiences, like talking about moving next door to them to lower their house values, talking about being lazy, and generally enforcing stereotypes. Basically, the UK version of the Uncle Tom/Stepin Fetchit characters of old American movies. The only Black comics doing white shows in the 1990s were Lenny Henry and Felix Dexter.

Lenny Henry started his career as a teenager working in men's clubs in the 1970s and became the only high-profile Black comedian in the country for decades that was truly accepted into the hierarchy. He did some questionable stuff when he was younger, like performing on *The Black and White Minstrel Show*, a variety show that ran on the BBC for nearly twenty years, on which the performers wore blackface and depicted Black people as buffoons. That made many Black people highly disdainful of Lenny. But to be fair, you didn't really have much of a choice in those days if you were a Black comic trying to achieve some success. Lenny Henry later became an outspoken critic on the lack of diversity in British TV and film.

Felix Dexter was a talented stand-up and actor who more successfully traversed the lines between Black and white circuits, having created several memorable characters on the UK's one Black sketch show on TV, *The Real McCoy*, therefore becoming famous in the Black community while still performing at mainstream comedy clubs among the royalty of white British comics. He never quite reached the success he deserved, as there seemed to be only room for one Black comedic star, and Lenny Henry was it. In fact, in one of my stand-up routine's I enthused that the TV industry had a nightclub "one in, one out" policy, and in order for any other Black comics to get a look in, we had to wait for Lenny Henry to die.

The Real McCoy featured mainly Black and Asian actors at a time when Black faces on comedy shows—or any other show, for that matter—were rare, unless a mugger, drug dealer, or prostitute was needed. All the players on the show became stars within the Black community, selling out theaters to predominantly Black audiences. There was a lot more money in the Black circuit then, which is why a lot of Black comedians never really felt a need to make that jump to white audiences. The attitude was *Why am I going to do this white comedy club for twenty bucks when I'm getting three hundred to do this Black show?* Obviously, there was a specific audience that came out to see them. When you watched comedy on TV or went to mainstream comedy clubs you never really heard comedians talk about their experiences as Black, Africans, or Caribbeans living in England or about their parents coming from a different place. The Black circuit filled that void.

The final season of *The Real McCoy* in 1995 featured up-and-coming stand-ups from the Black circuit. Scouts from the show were out hunting. I had become one of the hottest young comics on the circuit at that time, alongside people like Toju, the aforementioned Nigerian comic and impressionist; Slim, a talented comic of Jamaican heritage; and Richard Blackwood, a good-looking guy whose comedic style was modeled on the American *Def Comedy Jam* comics of the '90s.

I was killing stages all over at that point and being booked regularly. I happily continued to carve out a niche for myself within the Black comedy community as the outspoken African among a sea of Caribbeans, and it was a successful strategy. The instant TV stardom I'd envisaged after getting to the finals on *The Big*

Big Talent Show had not materialized, so I had simply returned to the white circuit and continued to appear at the clubs, gaining more experience.

There was already talk that I had been selected for a guest appearance on *The Real McCoy*, and I believed I was a shoo-in for that gig. Unfortunately, I still had an engineer mindset: you're supposed to get the right qualifications to get the right job, then do good work to get the promotion. It hadn't worked that well for me with Otis, but I still believed in the formula. I still had faith in the system of merit. In showbiz, however, I soon found out there was no such system. You may be the funniest, but you can still be passed over for your look, your voice, your age, your background, your size—*anything*.

After destroying a showcase that had taken place in a comedy room I was running at the time, and had hosted, that TV opportunity was given to another comic, who had a similar style to Dawn French, a very popular white comedian at the time who was married to Lenny Henry, so her style and material differed greatly from all the other Black comics. I was so cocky-confident that I would get the gig that I'd approached the producer of the show to ask what date I would be needed, and when she paused, gulped, and then informed me that they had passed on me, for about two seconds I'd smiled, thinking she was joking, before the horrible realization set in. I was absolutely devastated.

Looking back, I can see why they went for that comic instead of me. She was unlike any of the other Black comics working at the time. She had material that didn't reference her Blackness at all but instead erred towards a straight observational style. She used none of the tools we used. No Jamaican or African accents or overt physicality. No recognizable references that induced an almost Pavlovian response with Black people. In fact, if you had closed your eyes, you would have been hard-pressed to discern her race, and yet she was still funny to us, and that made her unique on the Black comedy scene. This knowledge made the rejection no less painful. I had been given an important lesson.

I say "given," not "learned," as over the course of my career I've suffered the same disbelief and disappointment again and again. The *Groundhog Day* of disappointments, if you will. I wanted my reach and success to be unlimited, and I was super competitive, so I actively pursued all avenues of stand-up. I straddled both Black and white comedy scenes by performing different sets for each type of audience. My more generic, observational stuff, I did for the white people, and my unapologetically Nigerian stuff, for the Black audiences. This all changed when a white Welsh agent—whom I was trying to persuade to take me as his client, having seen me at the white clubs—followed me one evening to a Black show. After my performance, he shouted, "Why are you saving all your best stuff for the Blacks and giving us whiteys the diluted shit stuff?" Best piece of advice I'd ever been given in my career. I had internalized the whole "White audiences won't connect with Black experiences" narrative.

From that day on I was authentically me in front of *all* audiences—well, semi-authentic, as it would be another fifteen years before I would acknowledge my sexuality onstage. My material about my Nigerian heritage worked just as well, if not better, in front of white crowds, as the characters were funny, and it also gave them a new insight into the immigrant experience. I was represented by that Welsh agent for the next ten years.

I was starting to earn a living from comedy. Not a great living, but enough to get by, while enjoying what I did, though I still bought the *Evening Standard* every Thursday to keep an eye on available engineering jobs, just in case the bottom fell out of this comedy career thing.

Greenwich in southeast London is very gentrified now, with

its trendy restaurants, cinemas, and museums, but in the '90s, it was a rough, working-class, racist part of town that Black people were often advised not to venture near after dark. Unfortunately, Greenwich was also home to a comedy club, Up the Creek, that was a rite of passage for any comedian who wanted to make it as a professional. I wanted to play there. The club owner, Malcolm Hardee, was a maverick. A character. A legend. And a crazy drunkard. There are so many stories about him. There's this urban folktale of the time when he was at a comedy and music festival—and he painted his dick and balls in fluorescent paint that was visible only under ultraviolet lighting. His wife later walked into the tent, and UV lights lit up a fluorescent ring around her mouth. Malcolm was always playing pranks like that.

He, along with two others, was known for the "Greatest Show on Legs" act—they would get onstage completely naked but holding balloons that they would move around in ways so that their genitalia were always hidden.

The audience at Up the Creek was famous for being rough. Comedians were advised to not attempt to audition for a paid spot at that club till they had at least two years under their belt, and to still prepare for the worst. If that audience didn't like a comedian, they wouldn't boo, like a regular rough audience; they'd give the comedian a long, hard stare, then begin calling, "Malcolm! Malcolm!" They'd just shout his name until Malcolm returned to the stage, usually from the pub next door, and abused the hapless comedian as he or she left. "Well, he was fucking shit!" or something equally humiliating. Then the crowd would shout, "Malcolm, show us your balls!" Malcolm had the most hideous testicles I have ever seen. They were unusually long, wrinkly, and disgusting. He'd open his fly and he'd take out one of his balls, and the crowd would go absolutely crazy. That was how rough that club was. And that's the club I wanted to perform in. I figured if I could handle this difficult of an audience, it would only make me stronger as a performer.

Veronica and I had been traveling around together auditioning for clubs since we'd come out of the comedy workshop, and I persuaded her to accompany me to Up the Creek. She was understandably concerned. "You sure you wanna do this?" she asked, surveying the room of shaved heads and blond perms. "Yup. If I can get this crowd, I can get anybody!"

As I looked into the crowd, I spotted a face I recognized immediately: Timothy. The guy who had made my life at Otis a living hell with his constant racist abuse. He was there with a group of friends, and I began to reconsider my decision. What if he started booing the moment I walked on? What if this room of white people decided to teach me a lesson for straying into their hallowed club? What if I just wasn't funny to them?

I turned to Veronica. "See that dude? That's Timothy! The guy who used to call me nigger at work every day. This gig might go tits up. If it does, I'll meet you in the alley out back, and we'll sprint to the car. If it doesn't, I want you to watch him and his friends and describe every fucking facial expression to me afterwards!"

"The next person coming to the stage is a girl. She might be good. She might be shit. It's Gina . . . !" That was Malcolm's standard introduction. I walked up onstage and launched into my set with as much confidence as I could muster. Lo and behold, the audience began laughing and enjoying me. Timothy sat in almost the center of the room, only three rows from the front of the stage, so he was clearly visible to me as I performed. I looked straight at him but feigned a lack of recognition, as I didn't think I would be able to adequately handle any kind of heckling from him or his friends. I just wanted to get this set done and get off.

Thankfully, Timothy's friends laughed heartily with me, while his head spun. He stared at me as if he'd seen a ghost, then stared back at his friends, then stared back at me. This continued for the entirety of my set. After that set, I did that thing where you replay an event in your head with all the things you would have done or said differently, had you thought of them. In my new scenario, I would have humiliated him in front of the whole club, and he would have been forced out into the street with the sounds of jeering from his own community ringing in his ears. But it wasn't to be. I was a new comedian and didn't have the confidence or experience to disembowel this man in a club full of his peers. Plus we were two Black women in a room of white people, not far from where the infamous murder of Stephen Lawrence had taken place. So I just did my set and took solace in the fact that he saw me successfully slay the room. I've never seen Timothy since. Lucky him.

I left the stage to enthusiastic cheers and applause. "She was pretty good, wasn't she?" Malcolm asked the crowd. The crowd cheered in the affirmative. "Should I give her a paid spot?" Again, positive applause. That's how I ended up getting paid gigs at arguably the toughest club in London within a year of starting stand-up.

Up the Creek was also one of the first places where I died onstage. I was overconfident with my previous win there and was sure it was going to be a repeat kill. I learned that night that no two audiences are the same. That night they just stared at me. I couldn't believe it. The same jokes I'd used to great effect just a few weeks before. I was never a person who overstayed their welcome, so I got my ass off the stage before they started calling for Malcolm. I drew a coffin in my notebook that evening.

A guy came up to me after that set. "You know what?" he started. "You'd be funny if you stopped talking about all the

African Black stuff." He then offered me a hit of cocaine. I declined. Coke, in my mind, from there on out has always been synonymous with failure.

But I still kept going back to Up the Creek. It toughened me up a lot, and although Malcolm passed a few years ago, it's still one of my favorite clubs to play to this day.

I took shows wherever I could. Travel was a large part of the job, and I loved it. I sometimes drove, but I also enjoyed long train journeys all over the country to all the places I'd never been allowed to go on school trips. I did shows in pubs and village halls. I did birthdays, hen parties, nightclubs where the mic was attached to the DJ booth and the cable was so short that I couldn't stray more than three feet from the DJ. I even did strip shows. One particular show I did was for a bunch of rabid women who'd booked their local town hall for a girls' night out. They'd also booked two male strippers. My job was to host the event and tell jokes between the two acts. I remember I drove two hours each way for a payday of £100 which was a lot of money for a night's work at the beginning of my career. I threw myself into the show, and at the end of the evening, the male strippers and I took a bow together onstage. I was in the center, holding a large penis in each hand. The job had a lot of variety!

Eventually I started to get booked for shows out of the country. There is a large expatriate community all over the world, made up of teachers, financiers, doctors, and anybody else who emigrated to foreign lands for work or play. A few smart people among them set up music and comedy nights, and they'd fly in entertainment from the UK for Brits missing entertainment from home—there was a huge market for it. My new career took me to places such as the Netherlands, Spain, Hong Kong, and Singapore, and I worked on adding as many stamps to my passport as I could. This was a dream come true. I'd always wanted to see the world, and now I was being paid to do it. Nuts! I loved meeting different people and exploring different cultures and food.

There was the time I did shows in Indonesia for a British guy, Eamonn, who went from being a firefighter in the UK to working as a well-paid marketing consultant in Indonesia. He put on comedy shows just for the fun and joy of it and brought me out several times to Jakarta, the smoky, dirty capital of the country, and also the beach resorts of Bali.

I enjoyed going to Asia, but I encountered overt racism at the airports, constantly being singled out for drug searches. It got to a point where I'd have to factor in extra travel time for "traveling while Black." While in Indonesia, I met a friend of Eamonn's, another wealthy white man, who owned a small hotel on Gili Trawangan, one of the islands off the northwest coast of Lombok, Indonesia. He asked if I wanted to come and perform at his place. As payment, he'd let me stay at his hotel for a week. This island was tiny—so small that they had no petrol-driven vehicles anywhere on the island. People got around by foot, bike, or horse cart. It was an island frequented by divers, as the water was so clear. I took a forty-five-minute boat ride there from Bali and did the first-ever stand-up show in Gili Trawangan for around seventy divers and instructors, on a makeshift stage fifty feet from the sea. My opening joke was about how I'd once done a scuba dive in Mexico, where because my swimming lessons had ended at eight years old, I'd ended up sinking to the bottom of the sea and doing more of a scuba walk along the seabed. That was one of my favorite shows of my career, and it ended with a standing ovation, and many offers for free diving lessons. I called my best friend, Lila, in London. Lila, an accountant, loved to travel with me on my world tours and later became my tour manager. I told her to get a last-minute flight out to meet me, which she did, and we spent a week eating fresh fish caught by the local fishermen and sunbathing. This was the best job in the world!

Another of my favorite places to perform was Kuala Lumpur. Our first experience of Malaysia, a mainly Muslim country in Southeast Asia, did not start off well. Lila and I had just arrived from Singapore, where I'd done several shows in various clubs and bars in the previous weeks. Singapore and Malaysia are neighboring countries, with Singapore being the wealthier of the two. A favored joke among comedians in Singapore was that Malaysians were lazy, weed-smoking criminals. This theme came up a lot in shows I did in the weeks I was there. I remember Lila and me marveling at how Malaysians were stereotyped in the same way Black people were, and how racist we thought it was. The night we arrived in Kuala Lumpur, we went through more "random" drug searches at this airport, then checked into our hotel and went out for dinner nearby. As we walked back to the hotel, a moped rode up alongside us, and the rider grabbed the bag I was carrying, with my phone, camera, and credit cards, and sped off into the night. Lila, who had been a high school champion sprinter, threw off her flip-flops and chased him barefoot down the street, but he was gone. We reported the robbery to the local police, who told us this was a regular phenomenon, and we went back to our hotel, furious but unhurt. Luckily, the moment I had checked into the hotel, I had put my passport and the majority of my cash into the hotel safe before I went out, so though I was inconvenienced by the robbery, my trip wasn't ruined. I had a show the next day in a sold-out four-thousand-seat theater, hosted by one of Malaysia's most famous comics, Harith Iskander. I was informed that most of the audience would be Malaysian, not the British, Australian, and American expats I'd been used to performing to. This was going to be different. I walked onstage and began talking about how I'd just done shows for their rival country, Singapore, and how they'd been calling Malaysians criminals and thieves. I then followed with: "I thought that was unfair and racist, but within four hours of landing, I was robbed, you thieving motherfuckers!" It was a risk, but it paid off. It got a huge laugh, and I went on to tell the story of my robbery, peppered with a few Malay cuss words I'd gotten Harith to teach me before I went on. It was one of the best shows I'd ever done in my life, and to this day.

16

Warm Water Never Forgets that It Was Once Cold

Nigerians often don't believe I'm Nigerian. They never have. I seem to not tick the boxes that deem me Nigerian enough. Whenever I announce my Nigerian heritage, suspicion and questions always follow.

"You are Nigerian?"

"Yep, that's what I said."

"You?"

"Yes, me. Well, my parents."

"Your parents. The two of them?"

"Yes."

"The mother *and* the father?"

"Yes."

"The man *and* the woman?"

"Yes."

"The sperm *and* the egg?"

"Jesus Christ."

In a way, I get it. I was born in England. I have a distinctly Cockney accent. I don't speak any Nigerian languages. Nope. None. Not my fault. My mum wanted us to be British. The mistake that a lot of African immigrant parents make when they have their children in another country is that they are so keen for their children to assimilate, they often prioritize the native language over their own, and my mum was no different. She wanted us to have all the opportunities that being British would afford us. My mum was well educated, and she had traveled extensively within Nigeria, as the daughter of a wealthy businessman. She could speak her own language, Edo, plus she could speak several other Nigerian languages, including Yoruba and Hausa. She never taught us any of them. As a kid, I was jealous of the Indian, Pakistani, and Greek Cypriot kids whose parents had taught them the language of their respective motherlands. When those kids wanted to have secret conversations among themselves, they'd often switch from English and leave the rest of us baffled. This made them no less English. They could easily switch back and forth from broad London accents. None of the African kids at my school seemed to have this skill.

Mum would often proclaim, "Yes, I want my children to be English!" And then she'd do her impression of the English accent that sounded like a cross between a seal and a ventriloquist dummy with its jaw unhinged. Even Nigerians in Nigeria sometimes insisted their children speak English, as it was considered a sign of higher education and class. My first cousin, Dorothy, was born in England but lived in Nigeria for eight years with her siblings and father. When she returned to London, she had a strong Nigerian accent, but she could not speak a word of Edo, our mother tongue. Her father had kept his children separated from Nigerian children so that they would not forget the Queen's English.

In our household in England, everything else about our upbringing was very Nigerian. We ate mainly Nigerian food, from jollof rice to pounded yam to ogbono soup, and everything in between. We dressed in Nigerian finery for weddings, parties, and social events. To all intents and purposes, we were Nigerian children. But when the adults spoke among themselves, we didn't understand them. Taiwo, my older sister, spoke some Yoruba from her eight years spent in Nigeria, but the rest of us, clueless. We were part of the "lost generation"—a generation of children born outside Nigeria, with no real ties to our home. We had lost our language and our customs, and had been assimilated into the more permissive society that was destroying our morals.

Mum always used Nigeria as a threat. If we didn't behave, we risked being sent home. Taiwo had not had good experiences there, so Nigeria was the bogeyman of destinations. There were many stories of bad kids being sent back to Nigeria when the parents became exasperated with their bad behavior. A lot of them never came back, or if they did, several years later, they were . . . different.

In Nigeria, they were subjected to a different level of discipline. The beatings my mum gave us paled next to what they did to unruly kids in Nigeria. Teachers at school were allowed to kick your ass, then you went home and got double whooped. One day they'd be rebellious, unruly children in England, then the next day they'd be gone. We'd see them return a few years later, having had the attitude beaten out of them. They'd have a Nigerian accent, and they'd be quieter and more respectful of their elders. Like they'd been replaced with a Stepford version of themselves. We knew a few kids that had happened to. The Nigerian boot camp worked for most of them. But not all.

One boy my brothers and I had known as children was Yomi. We'd all gone to school together. He was what you'd call a challenging kid. To us, he was just bad. From an early age he was constantly getting into trouble at school, talking back to teachers, stealing, and just generally uncontrollable. I never liked him. I had my naughty days, but there was always something off and a little not-fun dangerous about him. He never knew when to stop, and even as an eight-year-old, I was wary of being dragged into his orbit. His parents' constant beatings just didn't work on him, and as he got older, his digressions became more serious.

If there's one thing Nigerian parents are afraid of, it's their child bringing the police to their home, and therefore shame on their family name. Especially after they had made sacrifices to give their children all these opportunities and had tried to differentiate themselves from the Caribbean community, which they believed was more prone to criminal activity.

After one too many school suspensions, when Yomi was twelve, his parents told him to pack a case, as they were going "on holiday." They took him to Nigeria and came back without him. We didn't see him again till he was sixteen. When he returned he was even more off. Yes, he now had the Nigerian accent, but something seemed to have snapped in his head. I'm not sure whether the abuse he suffered there broke him even further or he'd spent six years biding his time before he came back to England to wreak revenge on his parents, but wreak he did. I never went near him again, but I heard from my brothers that he went completely off the rails. He became involved in all sorts of criminal activity, from robberies to assault. He was stabbed to death in a drug deal gone wrong at twenty-three.

When I was around fourteen, it seemed that Mum became embarrassed that we couldn't speak our mother tongue. She began berating us for having no culture and then began trying to teach us, but what would have been absorbed by us as babies wasn't going in now that we were teenagers.

"Sit down. I'm going to teach you my language!"

"Sorry, Mum, it's too late. I'm learning French now. *Bonsoir, Maman!*" Being the child of African immigrants had made me no friends at school, so I wanted no part of it.

Later, around the time I joined the Nation of Islam and began to take pride in my heritage, I decided I did want to learn to speak my mother tongue. I found an evening class that taught Yoruba. Yoruba is not my mother's language, but the Yoruba tribe is one of the largest in Nigeria, and therefore one of the most commonly spoken languages, and that was the only course in any Nigerian language available at that time. It would do. I turned up for my first class, excited to meet other young Nigerians in the same boat, looking to rediscover their culture. I was the only Black student. The class was full of what you'd call white hipsters, who stared at me as I walked in, no doubt wondering why their teacher had gone to sit at the back of the class. At least the real teacher was an actual Nigerian man. Mr. Adelogun and I bonded, and just by virtue of me having grown up listening to the Nigerian accent and inflections, I was able to pick up the basics quite quickly and became his best student. To be fair, the bar was set quite low. As in underground. That course ran for a year, then started again the following year from scratch. No advancement. I was disappointed.

My Yoruba skills ended at me being able to say hi to my mum, ask her how she was, and tell her my age—that was about it. But I was determined to take my new three sentences to Nigeria. I wanted to see where I came from. I felt like an outsider most of the time in England. I didn't fit in with white people, and I didn't fit in with the majority of Caribbean Black people. I wanted to go and find my people, and see the country of my parents' birth.

Considering Mum had spent my whole childhood threatening

to send me back, she wasn't too keen. "Don't go there. They will kill you!" Presumably because of my outspoken ways, and not my gayness, which she didn't know about yet. To many Nigerians in Nigeria, I'm one of the "lost generation"—born in England and supposedly far removed from my culture. There's this idea that the streets of London are paved with gold and opportunity, and that we have it much better than those who stay in Nigeria. So there is a certain amount of resentment and envy aimed at us. I found this out the hard way.

People's responses are different depending on where you tell them you're traveling. When I told people I was going to New York, their excitement was palpable: "Oh, bring me back a Statue of Liberty!" "Send me a postcard!" (This was the early '90s.) But a few years later, when I told these same people I was going to Nigeria, crickets. I'd heard a lot of stories about lawlessness and corruption in Nigeria, mainly from other Nigerians, but having learned about the true scourge of colonialism from the Nation of Islam, I was suspicious of what I saw as bad propaganda and brainwashing. I wanted to see for myself.

I planned a trip back with my friend Yetunde. Yetunde was a British-born Nigerian like myself, but she had lived a number of years in Nigeria and so spoke Yoruba fluently. I'd introduced her to my mum, and she had prostrated before my mum in the Nigerian show of respect when you greet your elders. Mum liked her immediately and then felt better about entrusting her with my safety in Nigeria, even though I was twenty-six at the time! We flew Virgin Atlantic to Nigeria and landed safely at the Lagos airport. We went through immigration with no major issues and collected our suitcases, but there was one more hurdle to cross. A line of customs officers waited behind tables on the way to the exit. I'd heard about the corruption at Lagos airport. Apparently these officers, to supplement their earnings, would stop foreign-looking travelers and make a show of searching their bags, expecting you to slip them twenty dollars or more to bribe your way out. *I am Nigerian!* I thought. *My parents were born here, and I will not be bribing my way out of this airport!*

Yetunde and I were separated. Yetunde went first, greeting the officers in Yoruba, therefore flagging her status as a Nigerian. She passed through without incident. I was up next. "*E kaale*, sir!" I wished the officer staring at me as I approached a good evening in my best Nigerian accent. He took one look at me and beckoned me to his table for a bag search. *Shit.*

"Open your case. Open. Your. Case."

I opened my case. He dug through the contents, which contained nothing useful to him. I'd made sure that I'd brought nothing valuable on this trip, just in case. After rummaging around for a couple of minutes, he looked up at me with a sly smile.

"Do you have anything for me?" I knew exactly what he was expecting, but I played dumb.

"Excuse me?"

"Do you have something for me?"

"What would I have?"

"Something!" He was becoming exasperated at my stupidity, but I was going to play this till the end. I wasn't about to be shafted out of money like some foreigner. I was Nigerian!

"Did you not bring anything for me?"

"I don't understand," I said. "I don't know you." I stared into his eyes, unblinking. For a long time.

Eventually he pointed with his lips towards the exit. "Go." He muttered something under his breath, probably calling me a fool, but I was out and scot-free.

We got into a taxi and headed to the Sheraton Lagos Hotel. I let

Yetunde do all the talking. My year of basic Yoruba training had done nothing to increase my Yoruba status.

Lagos is a vast metropolitan mix of slums, crowded streets, and traffic jams. It is densely populated with people who travel from all over Africa to try to make it in what is arguably the commercial heart of Nigeria. If the word "hustle" were a city, Lagos would be it. From the moment we left the airport to the moment we finally entered our hotel room, we ran a gamut of hawkers selling everything from drinks to fruit to cell phones to clothing to fire extinguishers. After we passed that particular extinguisher salesperson, I began to wonder if I'd made a mistake, not buying one, as our taxi driver drove like he'd stolen his car, and I became worried we would crash. If we were consumed by a ball of flames, my last thought would be of the fire extinguisher I could have purchased two miles back. The sheer population in Lagos meant that freeways were rarely ever free. We sat in traffic jams for the entire drive, and spent the whole time fending off relentless sales pitches from street entrepreneurs.

Huge, gleaming skyscrapers and apartment buildings stood alongside tin-roofed shacks. I saw many houses with makeshift signs pinned to the walls that said, THIS HOUSE IS NOT FOR SALE. Apparently in Lagos, home of the original Nigerian internet scam, people had been known to sell homes that didn't belong to them. Criminal, but very enterprising.

I couldn't wait to get out to explore. Our first taxi ride from our hotel into the city taught me a lesson in being a tourist in Nigeria. I was excited, wanting to record everything I could on my camcorder for posterity. As we drove, I put my camera out of the window to shoot the scenery.

"What are you doing? Put that away!" Yetunde hissed.

I didn't understand the urgency in her voice. "What are you on about?"

"The camera, you fool. This isn't Amsterdam. Put it down!"

Before I could even get out my rebuttal, I felt a tug. Someone was trying to pull my camera out of my hand, but luckily the camera strap was wound tightly around my wrist. Four young guys had appeared, jogging alongside the taxi as it slowed down in traffic, and they were trying to rob me, inside the moving vehicle.

"You cannot film here unless you pay," one of them announced.

"Piss off!" I struggled to keep ahold of my camera as Yetunde leaned over and tried to wind up the car window, all while the taxi crept along at five miles an hour.

"You pay or give us the camera!"

"Not giving you shit! Drive, taxi!"

"The light is red." The taxi driver pointed at the stoplight up ahead.

Yetunde shouted at him in Yoruba, and the driver swerved out of our lane, clipping the car in front, and jumped the red light, leaving the boys behind.

"I told you to put that damn camera away, you stupid cow!"

That was my first encounter with what are known in Nigeria as "area boys"—gangs of youngsters who roam the streets of Lagos extorting money from passersby, traders, drivers in traffic jams, drivers parking their cars, charging them a fee to watch their cars, whether they want the service or not. This was our first day in Nigeria. It was turning out to be a pretty exciting holiday. I don't have a single picture or video from that trip, as that camera never left the hotel room again, until we were heading to the airport for the flight home.

Yetunde had a bunch of friends in Nigeria, from her school days and her frequent travels back and forth. One night we were invited to dinner by two of her male friends, at the restaurant in the hotel where we were staying. These guys had done well for themselves and had money. They dressed very fashionably and carried themselves with the confidence of men who had the world at their feet. During the course of the dinner, they began espousing their views of women. They opined that their money gave them the power to, in their own words, "fuck and dump, these gold-digging *asewos*, who smelled their expensive cologne and buzzed around them like flies on shit. My Yoruba was basic, but it took me a millisecond from the context of the conversation to work out that they were referring to all women as whores. Never one to not speak my mind, I asked what we were, then, seeing as they had come to take us to dinner and were presumably paying for the meal. They laughed derisively, one of them even telling me to be quiet and stop interrupting. I told him that I didn't know who he thought he was talking to, but I would speak whenever I damn well pleased, and then I stared at Yetunde. My friend who was usually outspoken and confident, who didn't suffer fools gladly and had a fiery temper, sat there passively, saying nothing and pretending to laugh at their jokes. I had had enough. I stood, threw down some money to pay for the food that I'd eaten, excused myself, and went back to the room. Yetunde was furious with me when she returned an hour later. "Why, did you do that?" she yelled. "That was rude and ungrateful! You offended them."

"Offended *them*? You expected me to sit there, smiling, while they discussed women in such a derogatory and disgusting manner? Hell no. I wasn't that desperate for jollof rice."

"You can't talk to men like that here. This is Nigeria . . ."

Having spent her formative years here, she had a better understanding of how patriarchal it was, and she was genuinely frightened that my outspokenness would get us into serious trouble. After I hadn't listened to her in the taxi and nearly got us robbed by area boys, I decided I'd bow to her superior knowledge and try to bite my lip around Nigerian men for the rest of the trip. But I am my mother's daughter. It was a struggle, and I bruised a few male egos in that two weeks.

Despite the inherited homophobia in Nigeria (I say "inherited" since it was thrust upon African cultures from the white Christian missionaries hundreds of years previously), there was a thriving underground gay scene in Lagos, found mainly in people's houses and a few private parties held in hotels and clubs. Before 2014, during a wave of increased religious fundamentalism, Nigeria introduced a slew of draconian laws making the already illegal homosexuality even *more* illegal, driving the scene even deeper underground, but those laws had been largely ignored, with gays operating within their own subculture, mostly closeted from work colleagues and family. I'd met Yetunde in the gay scene in London, and she had a girlfriend at the time we were traveling in Nigeria together, but she identified as bisexual. She had some lesbian friends in Nigeria, and one of them came by to have lunch with us at the hotel. As we ate and laughed, I wondered what her life could possibly be like as lesbian in a country that would jail her for her sexuality. Considering the risks she was taking, just by being who she was, she was pretty relaxed.

Tumi, an attractive, voluptuous, big-haired woman, waved her hand dismissively when I asked how she lived. "Ah-ah. You get married, you have some children, and then your family can get off your back, as you have fulfilled your womanly duties!"

And there I made a startling discovery. Many gays in Nigeria married each other to allay their families' suspicions, often producing children. They then either moved their true partners into the house or continued their lifestyles outside the family unit. It was pretty genius and worked out great if you were gay and wanted a family, but the lengths Nigerians had to go to, to hide their true selves made me grateful that, even though in England I was still very much hiding my sexuality from all but my closest friends, I had freedoms and could live without fear of arrest, having been born as one of the "lost generation."

Decapitation is not the antidote for a headache.

I loved the markets in Lagos. They reminded me of the ones my mum used to drag me to as a child, but on steroids. They were huge, extremely busy, full of color, vibrancy, and a cacophony of sounds. People sold everything from yams to fabrics to live chickens. I bought a lot of trinkets, but my main priority was to find Nollywood DVDs. "Nollywood" is the term used for the Nigerian film industry—a play on "Hollywood." A large number of straight-to-DVD movies were made in Nigeria, and my mum was a fan. She hadn't been back to Nigeria since she'd arrived in England all those years before, but she kept abreast of the changes in her homeland through her friends and family who still traveled back and through her consumption of Nigerian films and television. I wanted to buy a large number of the latest Nollywood movies to bring back to her in London.

We had been told there was a large DVD stall in one particular market, but we couldn't find it, so Yetunde approached a nearby female market stall seller and asked her in Yoruba where we could purchase them. The woman stared at her and didn't answer. Yetunde asked again. The woman again refused to answer. Yetunde began asking the woman angrily why she was refusing to speak to us. At this point, I knew something was up, but I wasn't sure what, as my elementary Yoruba was not up to the task. The woman suddenly screamed at the top of her voice at us: "Go back to America with your devil tattoos!"

At the time, I had only one tattoo on my shoulder—this was the early 2000s, and my addiction to ink hadn't begun and the full tattooed sleeves hadn't become popular yet. Afrobeats hadn't taken over the world yet either, but the younger generation of Nigerian artists who have since emerged, like Davido, Wizkid, Tekno, and Burna Boy, are in looks pretty much indistinguishable from African American rappers. To this woman, we looked like African Americans. And having been fed the imagery of African Americans as criminals, we were not worth her time, or her courtesy, even though Yetunde had spoken to her in fluent Yoruba.

Over the following days, I noticed that despite the fact that Yetunde spoke her language perfectly, Nigerians detected her British inflections and were quite disdainful towards her. I could almost understand their confusion when they came across me. I had no distinguishing features or mannerisms that singled me out as having any Nigerian roots, but her? This left me disappointed. What was the point of struggling to learn the language if I'd still be an outsider, laughed at and dismissed?

I resigned myself to just trying to enjoy my time there and soak up as many good experiences as I could. I had made no attempt to contact my father, who I believe lived in Benin City, around 150 miles east of Lagos. This was partly through loyalty to my mum, who throughout my childhood had drummed it into our heads that he had abandoned us. I was curious about the other half of my genetic makeup but not ready yet to explore it. I needed time to acclimate. But I had originally planned to make this exploratory trip, to dip my toe in, then return later and perhaps connect with family I'd never met, including my mother's still living siblings, as well as my father. After my experiences on that virgin voyage to Nigeria, I felt it was unlikely that I would return. The rejection from my people stung. I was a citizen of nowhere, accepted by no one.

I never went back to that Yoruba class.

Someone else's legs are no good to you when you are traveling.

The comedy scene in Nigeria is large and vibrant, with its own stars who sell out arenas all over Africa and the world. Bright "Basketmouth" Okpocha is one of them. I met him while performing in a comedy show on Long Island in New York. He was the MC of a long evening of singers, poets, dancers, speakers, and comedians. African shows tend to do that. They cram in every available artist within two hundred miles and let them do approximately an hour each onstage, so the show could be days long, after starting at least two hours after whatever time is advertised on the flyer. Whenever I'm booked on a show with more than two African performers, I insist I go on first, so that I'm still the same age by the time I get onstage. The audience for this show was a mix of Africans, varying from young college students to their parents to the odd child screeching in the background. Some of these community events are family affairs, and Africans tend to be quite religious and conservative, so for a comedian performing at these, it can be a minefield. I kept my set very "family"—as in jokes about my mum—and my twenty-minute set went well. Basketmouth approached me afterwards. He was very complimentary about my set and had recognized me from a comedic character I had done on British TV, which I had loaded onto YouTube, and it had gone viral. The character was called Mrs. Omokorede. She was a pushy

Nigerian mother who would stop at nothing to make sure her daughter became a doctor. Sound familiar? Basketmouth told me he was booking a show in Nigeria later that year and would love to have me on it. I gave him my number and the contact details of my UK agent, and then I demanded a large fee, to be delivered in cash up front, and first-class flights to and from London, with a confirmation of the ticket purchase, before I'd even consider stepping foot outside my house. The reasons for these demands were twofold. I had done several shows in the past for Nigerian promoters, and these were the only shows after which I'd had checks bounced on me or the promoters disappear without a trace. And after my less-than-successful first trip to Nigeria, I was in no hurry to go back. The plan was that my outlandish demands would put Basketmouth off, and I wouldn't have to go.

Around four weeks after our conversation, I received a call from my agent. "Erm, Gina, a Nigerian guy just turned up at the office with a bagful of money. He says you know what it's for."

Shit. I was going back to Nigeria.

On hearing of my impending journey, my mum said, "You are well known in Nigeria now. Your father is going to turn up. Mark my words."

Basketmouth booked me on Virgin Atlantic flights to and from London. The show was on a Saturday evening, so I would leave London late Friday night to land on the Saturday morning of the show, perform, then leave first thing Monday morning. In and out.

I got to Heathrow early, checked in my luggage, and was belted in my seat, ready to sleep on the plane in my first-class cocoon and wake up in Lagos. The flight was full of Nigerians returning home. Africans like to travel with a lot of luggage. *A lot.* I've seen Africans dragging suitcases bigger than they are, trying to claim them as carry-ons. A plane full of Africans meant there were going to be problems with fitting everybody's bags in the limited overhead spaces. We were the last flight of the night at 9:30 p.m., and the captain of the flight announced several times that people needed to stow their bags quickly so we could take off. Nigerians ignored him, as if he was an annoying, chatty bus driver. The captain became exasperated: "We have to begin taxiing shortly or we will not be allowed to take off this evening. Please put your bags in the overhead lockers and fasten your seat belts." Nigerians continued milling around like he hadn't even spoken. I began to worry. Were we about to get stuck on this runway? After yet another impassioned plea by the captain, we eventually began to taxi down the runway. *Phew*, I thought.

Before we could pick up enough speed to take off, the plane began to slow down, and then halt. "I'm sorry, ladies and gentlemen. We were two minutes past the final takeoff time, and we have been informed that we can no longer fly this evening. Hotels will be arranged for the night, and we will try to accommodate everyone on other flights tomorrow." *Shit*. Even getting out on the first flight in the morning, I would be landing over two hours after the show would have started. On top of that, I discovered that my luggage, with the outfit I would be wearing on the show, was not going to make it onto my new flight, so whatever I was wearing was about to become my show outfit. Usually when I traveled on a long flight I preferred sweatpants, a tee shirt, and no bra. Thankfully I had decided to dress reasonably well for this flight, in that I was wearing a decent pair of jeans and my breasts happened to be supported. I'd have to use hand soap to wash my underwear in the hotel bathroom, as I had no spares. (From that day onward, I never traveled without at least another two days of emergency clothing in my hand luggage.)

I managed to get the first flight out of London the following morning, and we landed in Lagos at 9 p.m. Basketmouth had arranged for me to be collected at the landing gate by two security guys, and they whisked me through the airport VIP style. Not a single attempted shakedown. I was put into a waiting car for the hour-long drive to Eko Hotels and Suites, where the show was taking place, and where I would be staying. The show had already begun, and I was literally going to collect my room key from the front desk, then go straight to the large conference room where the show was taking place and likely be onstage within minutes of my arrival. Fortunately Basketmouth had booked around seven thousand other comedians from all over, so I had a little time. The lobby of the hotel was teeming with Nigerians dressed in their finery, wandering in and out of the show. My two bodyguards led me towards the front desk to check in. As we neared the desk, a young man jumped in front of me and began snapping pictures. I knew my little video had gone viral in Nigeria, but paparazzi? During the check-in process, the woman behind the desk asked me, "Will you both be staying in the same room?" *Both?* I turned to see who she was referring to, and an old bespectacled man stood behind me, dressed in a long white robe, or agbada, with a burgundy and gold hat known as a fila on his head. I knew instantly that I was looking at my father. It was like looking into my brother Dele's face if he was seventy years old.

"My daughter," he said.

"Eh, hello. Hold on a sec." I turned back around and completed my check-in. I wasn't being rude or dismissive, but I was overwhelmed with everything that was happening. It was a mad dash from the airport to the venue, I was about to go onstage in an outfit I'd been wearing for twenty-four hours, to perform for an audience of people who were not likely to accept me, in front of a father I was seeing for the first time since I was three. The universe was really messing with me.

"My daughter! It is so wonderful to meet you. We came from very far. We have been waiting for you!"

"It is wonderful to meet you too, sir." I did a half-kneel in respect of my elder, and we exchanged quick pleasantries as my two bodyguards looked on, impatiently waiting to escort me backstage.

"Meet your brother Uyi and your sister Sandra!"

The young man who had been snapping pictures of me as I walked in hugged me tightly, then a fresh-faced young woman stepped forward. *Wow.*

"We have to go, madame," said one of the bodyguards.

I asked my father and new siblings if they were coming to the show. They had been waiting in the hotel lobby and hadn't purchased tickets. I arranged for them to be allowed into the theater, and promised I'd meet them afterwards to catch up. I was then led backstage.

The show was on, and the room was full, with around three thousand Nigerians. Backstage there were at least forty entertainers milling around. Basketmouth approached me. "You made it! Perfect! You'll be on next." On the stage at that moment was a young white British comedian Basketmouth had also flown in from London for the show. This guy had risen through the ranks of the Black British comedy scene rapidly. He obviously had been raised around, and now socialized with, mostly Black people, and his comedy reflected that. He was absolutely destroying, doing jokes in a Nigerian accent. The audience loved him. They were practically falling off their chairs laughing. "Oya! Look at this Oyinbo boy talking like us! Ha!" He left the stage in triumph, and Basketmouth brought me on next. His intro made a big deal of the Mrs. Omokorede sketch, which was what I was known for in Nigeria, and as I walked onstage I noticed the poster for the show with all the pictures of the performing comedians. Under my name was a picture of me as the character. If that was what they were expecting, they were about to be disappointed.

I opened with the story of my journey there, and how Nigerians' huge luggage had nearly made me miss my show. I received titters. I then announced that I'd just met my father. That got a big cheer, but then I tried to follow with a joke, kind of based on what I was feeling. "I hope he doesn't ask me for money." That didn't go down so well. I decided to stick to my original script and launched into my tried-and-true set that had always worked for Black and African audiences. I told stories about my Nigerian upbringing in London, funny stories about my mum, I basically did everything to ingratiate myself with this audience. *Look! I may look and sound different, but I'm Nigerian too!* My set received sporadic titters. I got the feeling that half the audience were looking at me like *Who is this imposter telling jokes about Nigerians?* I didn't get booed off, but I got nowhere near the reaction they had given the white comedian before me, and this made me inwardly furious. *You motherfuckers!* I thought. *This white boy gets up here, does a vocal version of blackface, and you're all laughing like fools, while I'm here, as an actual Nigerian, and you're looking at me, like I just farted in your face?*

I left the stage at the end of my set with a bad taste in my mouth, but I kept up a happy demeanor, because as every performer knows, you may consider a show a bad one, but it isn't always the perception of the audience, so why point out the negativity that they themselves might not have noticed? I had often come offstage unhappy with my performance, only to have ecstatic audience members tell me how great I was, so on this occasion, I kept my mouth shut and smiled through the rest of the evening, hoping that I'd gotten away with it.

Basketmouth brought the white comedian back to Nigeria several times after that show. He never booked me again.

By the time the show ended, it was very late, and so I mingled with my father for a short amount of time. We chatted, I marveled at how much the brother I had just met, Uyi, strongly resembled both our father and my brother Dele back in London. I wouldn't say I was excited to be meeting my father and new siblings, but I had an almost scientific interest in what was happening. I felt like someone watching this from outside my body, like an alien observer. I stared at the stranger who's sperm I was a product of and tried to summon up feelings. Nothing. I didn't have any. I felt emotionally detached. I harbored no bitterness towards him, although I had listened for years to my mum's anger at him for his abandonment, and I had spent my childhood wishing he would come back for us. I just found the whole thing strange. I acted in a similar way to when I am introduced to new people after shows. I was friendly, respectful, and polite, and I enjoyed them in the moment, but emotionally I was not particularly invested. I took ample videos and pictures on my phone, to record this moment for my brothers and myself for posterity, and also because despite my father being ecstatic at the possible chance of a reunion with all his lost children, I knew I was unlikely to ever see him again after this trip. I made an arrangement for them to come back to the hotel the following day, to spend some quality time together before my flight back to London.

At the restaurant of the hotel the next day, we all ate hearty Nigerian food, and I asked the questions that had plagued me since childhood, like why he'd abandoned us. My father insisted he hadn't, that he'd begged my mum to return to Nigeria with him. He produced a stack of browned letters he had written to us over the years that had been returned unopened. He even claimed that he had called our home several times to talk to Mum, but she had refused to engage with him, and that on one occasion her new husband (the step-bastard) had answered the phone and shouted at him to never call there again. The whole time I was thinking that I probably would have reacted the same way had my husband abandoned me in a foreign country with two toddlers and been forced to have a baby alone in a hospital with no familial support whatsoever. But I let him speak.

My father handed me several necklaces made from coral beads that he had saved for me, Sheyi, and Dele, and three small books that told the history of his family and our ancestors on his side of the family. He questioned me about my life and was proud of my engineering qualifications, as much as he was of my fame as a comedian. He wanted to know why I was not married with children, and I thought it best not to ruin this happy reunion with an admission of my ungodly gayness, especially as that would have reflected badly on Mum's parenting. *What a terrible mother! Look what happened. She refused to leave England to be with her husband, and now she has raised a devil-worshipping, carpet-munching lesbian!* I made excuses about being too busy for love and changed the subject.

My father then begged me to pull out my phone and call my brothers so he could talk to his sons. I wasn't about to do that. I had voluntarily made the trip to Nigeria by myself, knowing that I may meet him, but my brothers had had no choice in this, and I wasn't about to subject them to a cold call from a father they'd never known. I lied, telling him that my phone was unable to make international calls, and I promised that when I returned to London I would give his number to the boys for them to contact him. He seemed satisfied with that.

I asked him why he had never returned to England to see us.

He answered that he had been unable to get a visa to return. I was skeptical, as I had seen Mum's friends and family travel freely back and forth between London and Nigeria over the years with no issues, but I said nothing. I observed his relationship with his two younger children, Sandra and Uyi. They seemed to truly love and respect their father. I thought of my two brothers, who had been deprived of a positive male role model in their lives, and how these two had benefited from the love and support of their father while we, his first children, had been left to suffer at the hands of the step-bastard, who had slid into my broken-hearted mother's life after our father had chosen his career aspirations over his family. I wondered if these two had been allowed to have friends and go on school trips. I wondered what their school lives had been like. Must have been nice going to a school where everyone was Nigerian. I bet they'd never been called "bubu" or "booty scratcher." I wondered but never vocalized any of it. What was the point? I was a grown-up now. Too late for petty envy.

I let my father talk, which he did, a lot, and I tried to glean as much information as possible. What I found strange was that sitting there with his twenty-seven-year-old younger son and twenty-four-year-old daughter from a woman who wasn't my mum, he still kept referring to my mum as his wife. He even went as far as to say that the child she'd had with the step-bastard, Asi, he considered to be his daughter, as my mother had never divorced him. I said nothing. Just let him talk.

He then casually dropped a bombshell I didn't see coming. "You must come back here and go to Benin so you can meet your older brother!"

Sorry, what?

"Oh yes, my oldest son was born in 1965. He is an accountant."

"Did my mum know about your son?" I asked.

"Of course! I knew she had a daughter; she knew I had a son."

I was shocked. In all the stories she'd told us about our father, him having a child before they met had never been mentioned. In fact, Mum had always told me that I was the oldest Iyashere, my father's firstborn child, and for the very little it was worth, I'd always held on to that. Why she had lied to me my entire life, I had no idea. I'd had an older brother and never knew it—I could have so used that knowledge at school.

After several hours of eating and chatting, it was time for my father to leave. I walked them to the entrance of the hotel, and as we walked, my new younger sister, Sandra, sidled up to me. She stared down at my wrist, at the Cartier watch I had bought myself in celebration of shooting my first stand-up special and selling it to a cable network in the US.

"That's a nice watch. Maybe when you leave Nigeria, you will leave it behind." She smiled.

I bristled inwardly. I'd met her less than twenty hours earlier and already she was eyeing me as a cash cow. I was annoyed but not surprised. I definitely wasn't coming back.

We said our goodbyes. My father hugged me tight and begged me to tell his sons he wanted to meet them. I promised I would, knowing that the chances of them wanting to meet him were slim to none. He cried as he walked away. My eyes were dry. I was much more like my mum than my dad apparently.

. . .

When I returned to England, I questioned Mum about this older brother she'd failed to mention my entire life, and she did the equivalent of a shrug, as if it was a minor thing that had just slipped her mind, and she began questioning me. She wanted to know everything that had happened, but then she became angry that I had not berated him on her behalf. She saw it as disloyalty.

"Listen, Mum, you brought me up to respect my elders. I showed him his due respect as an elder and as my father. Would you have preferred me to be rude to him and cuss him out? No, because then it would have reflected badly on you. You wouldn't want Nigerians to think you had raised an animal."

"Hmm. Okay." My mum grudgingly conceded, because I was right. She stared long and hard at the pictures and videos of the husband she hadn't seen in thirty-five years. "He looks old," she said, and that was the end of the conversation.

I told my brothers about the books containing our dad's family history and gave them the coral beads he'd given me for them. "Here's the deal: he really wants to speak to you guys. The ball is in your court. Here's his number." As I had suspected, neither brother was interested. Dele refused to even watch the videos I'd taken or look at the pictures, as he saw it as a betrayal of Mum. Sheyi, on the other hand, watched them but confessed, "I don't want any contact with him. As a father myself, I will never understand how he just left. I don't give a shit how many letters he wrote—he should have got on a plane and come here. You could cut my arms and legs off—I would drag myself by my lips to see my kids. I could never respect a man who never fought hard enough to see his children."

In an attempt to appease my father when he had asked for my brothers' numbers, I had given him mine. My phone started blowing up regularly from the moment I landed back on British soil. He'd call repeatedly: "My sons, I want to speak to my sons. Why are my sons not calling me?" I didn't know what to say. I was slightly irritated that he seemed to place more importance on speaking to his male progeny, though I was not surprised, what with the patriarchy of Nigerian society, and what was I supposed to tell him, anyway? "Look, your sons want nothing to do with you." I didn't have the heart to do that to him, so I began avoiding his calls. Whenever I saw a Nigerian number come up on my phone, I'd cringe a little and let it ring through to voicemail. It didn't feel good.

A year went by, and I was at Sheyi's house when the phone rang with a Nigerian prefix. "This is our father. Do you want to talk to him?" Sheyi's curiosity got the better of him. "Fuck it, answer the phone." I answered and talked to our father for a little, apologizing and making excuses for my absence. He then began to lament again, "My sons, I want to talk to my sons."

"One of your sons is here." I passed the phone over to Sheyi, who proceeded to have a conversation with him. I could hear the excitement in my father's voice: "Oh my God, my son."

"Nice to hear your voice," my brother politely responded and spoke to him for a little while, making small talk about his job, his wife, his kids. When the conversation ended and my brother hung up, I asked, "Are you going to keep in contact with him?"

"Nope," Sheyi replied. "My curiosity is sated. I don't need a father now. I'm a grown man with kids of my own—it's too late. I've spoken to him. It was good. I'm glad I did that, but I don't need to do that again."

But my dad kept calling and calling. He'd gotten a taste of one of his sons, and he wanted more. Sheyi was no longer interested in contact, and Dele had shut down any talk of a reunion, so I went back to ignoring my father's calls, eventually changed my number, and put him out of my mind.

A few years later, my brother and sister in Nigeria contacted me via Facebook. "Our father is very sick and he keeps asking for you. You need to come back to Nigeria." *Your father is not my father*, I thought. *He never raised me.* I didn't respond to the message. I was not going back to Nigeria to stand by the bedside of a man I didn't know. The Facebook messages kept coming, though. "Your father is sick, your father is sick, come, come, come." I still didn't respond.

I said to Sheyi, "Our father's ill in Nigeria. I have a funny feeling he's not long for this world. So if you want—"

But Sheyi cut me off. "No. He was never our dad."

I made the mistake of not telling Dele. He was so adamant about not being in contact with our father the last time we had spoken about it, I didn't even bother to call him and let him know that he was sick. I should have told Dele and given him the choice, and I regret that.

A few weeks later I received a message: "Our father has died."

"I'm sorry for your loss," I wrote back.

I texted Sheyi, "Our father has died."

He called me back. "That's no fucking way to tell me!"

I then called Dele. He was furious that I hadn't told him about our father's illness.

"But you didn't want anything to do with him," I reminded him. "You didn't want to see any of the videos I had. You said you didn't want to hear a word about him!"

"Yeah, well I was just doing that because of Mum," he told me.

The Facebook messages about our father's funeral began coming. "Will you and your brothers be coming to Nigeria for the service?"

"Again, I am sorry for your loss. But he was your father. I am sure he was a wonderful man, but he did not raise us, and unfortunately we never knew him. You have our deepest condolences, but we will not be coming to Nigeria for the funeral."

I was of course sad when he died, but more for the opportunity he'd missed to know his own children, and grandchildren, in England.

When I told Mum that he'd passed away, she didn't say much. Despite what had transpired between them, I never doubted that my mum's love for my father had been real, which was why her anger at him all these years had never abated. He really broke her heart.

"I bet they will try to get you to go back there for the funeral," she said. "Don't go. You will end up paying for everything."

And that was the end of the conversation.

17

A Bird That Flies off
the Earth and Lands
on an Anthill Is Still
on the Ground

Within my first year of comedy, I secured a regular television gig. After receiving much criticism of their lack
of diversity, in 1996 the BBC decided to launch a block
of programming targeted towards an "ethnic" audience, with
mainly Black talent in front of as well as behind the camera.
This included a drama, a talk show, a music show, and a comedy
panel show, all in one homogenous lump, as obviously all Black
people like the same things. This block was called *The A Force*.
No idea why.

The comedy panel show, called *Blouse and Skirt*, was based on
a Jamaican exclamation in the vein of "Oh my God, Blouse and
Skirt!" It was basically a roundtable of four comics discussing
current events, but the budget was so low, we didn't have a table.
We perched on uncomfortable stools, taking questions from the
audience and riffing on topical issues, all while trying to hold our

stomachs in. As if to maximize failure potential, the shows were hardly promoted and relegated to stupid o'clock: the graveyard shift of the BBC programming schedule.

Before the show went into production, I was recruited as a stand-in to see how the show would look, but somehow I did well enough to be promoted to co-anchor alongside longtime comedian and actor Curtis Walker, who had found fame as a cast member on *The Real McCoy*. Having been part of the first wave of Black comedy stars, he was comedic royalty, and he was none too impressed with co-anchoring a show with a cocky, big-mouthed fledgling. He hated me instantly, which, looking back, may have been justified, but nevertheless, this very much spoiled for me the excitement of this big opportunity.

The first season of *Blouse and Skirt* was one of the most de-moralizing and loneliest times of my life. With such a low budget for the show, there were no writers, and since I had no experience in writing topical material for a TV show, having been in the busi-ness under a year, I crowbarred my stand-up material into my an-swers, therefore using up all my good bits and then finding myself frantically writing more stuff for my live appearances. I felt under a lot of pressure and had no support from fellow cast members or the producers of the show, who often laughed at Curtis's jokes during rehearsal, then were silent at mine, eroding my preshow confidence, but then the audiences would laugh at my jokes at the taping. I eventually trusted only the audience and stopped telling my jokes at rehearsal.

The show was shot in Manchester, a city some two hundred miles from London, so after every taping, I retired to my hotel room, alone and friendless.

Curtis and I eventually bonded, well into the second season, when he realized, behind my bluster and naked ambition, I was a decent person with a great work ethic. We're good friends now, and he confessed that he'd assumed I was somebody who would have killed her own grandmother to get ahead. We bonded on our mutual hatred of the executive producer of the show, who had disrespected us both in the most horrendous way. He had brought in two unknown comedians from the US to be on the show, assuming they were better by virtue of the fact that they were American. They weren't.

This executive producer also put the Americans in better hotels than the ones we were staying in, and wined and dined them at an expensive restaurant, while the two stars of his show ate KFC in their subpar hotel rooms. And if that wasn't humiliating enough, he decided on a whim to use the *entire last episode of the second season* as a stand-up special for one of the Americans. So instead of enjoying another episode of satirical humor from me, Curtis, and two guest comedians, from a show we had made hugely popular in the Black community, our audience was—out of the blue—subjected to a half hour of this comedian doing Stevie Wonder impressions and warbling in front of a piano.

Both Americans got on a plane the next day, never to be seen on our shores again.

I resolved that I'd rather go back to engineering with a bunch of Nazis before I worked with that producer ever again.

The third season of the show had a new, better production team, a different producer, and a slightly better budget. We got writers, clothing, and actual chairs—no more uncomfortable stools. Unfortunately, the BBC were unchanged in their lack of support for the show—it felt like they were just filling a quota for Black content, as our show was again aired on the graveyard shift, and to add salt to the wound, aired twice a week, as if to get the season over and done with as quickly as possible and get back to regular white TV. To add acid to the salt in the wound, our show was also on *at different times* every week, so our audience had no idea when to catch it. This was before DVRs. All we had were VCRs, which didn't have the capability to track random showtimes set by TV executives who didn't give a fuck. On the positive side, this show made me even more "Black famous."

My fast rise on the Black comedy circuit continued to rustle a lot of feathers. A lot of the older Black male comics were affronted by it and gossiped about me. This scared me because I was just starting to find my sexuality and wasn't ready to come out to myself yet, let alone to others, and I was trying to keep it quiet. Rumors spread about me, and whenever a new female comic came on the scene, the male comics attempted to turn us against each other. I wasn't sure why they did this. Was it a way of keeping their boys club intact and the women in their place, using divide-and-conquer tactics? Maybe. Or maybe they were just a bunch of schoolboys who'd never grown up and hated being outdone by girls.

Early in my career, before I discovered what they were doing, I momentarily fell for their tricks and allowed myself to be manipulated into a confrontation with another female comic. Helen was biracial—half English, half Nigerian. Tall, slim, attractive, and, by day, a trainee lawyer. She had arrived on the scene initially as the girlfriend of the pretty boy of the comedy circuit, Richard Blackwood, and all the other male comics were falling over themselves trying to get her attention. It was pathetic.

The other male comics spent months whispering in her ear about how she could topple me from my perceived throne, and how I was extremely competitive with other women, which was not true—I was competitive with *everyone*. They dropped nuggets of disparaging things I had supposedly said about her, even though I hadn't even met her yet. They then came to me with similar stories about Helen's disdain towards me. By the time we met during our first show together, there was no love lost between us. We were extremely frosty towards each other, each of us believing the other's behavior confirmed what we had been told by the men. At one point, as we sat backstage, I was talking to one of the other comedians, complaining about a promoter who had not paid me a fair rate for a show I'd done. Suddenly I heard Helen's voice: "If it wasn't enough money, you shouldn't have done the show." I was inwardly furious. She had been talking shit about me, someone she didn't even know, and now she had the balls to interrupt my conversation, which had nothing to do with her. Who the hell did she think she was? I decided to keep my distance from that moment on, because I knew my temper, and I didn't need the extra headache.

One day a couple of months later, a male comedian, Kwaku—a comedian of Caribbean descent who used a Ghanaian stage name—approached me: "I hear you're gay."

"Really? Who told you that?" I was in a relationship with a woman at the time, but like I said, I was not ready to come out.

"Helen."

I made the mistake of articulating my *Who the fuck does she think she is?* thoughts out loud, and I heard later he ran back to tell her like a high school gossip. Now, deep in my subconscious, I knew Helen was not the one who had started this rumor about me, as I'd already heard that the male comics had been gossiping about my sexuality way before she had come on the scene. But the combination of my terror of being outed and the memory of our first meeting made me more furious that she was participating.

A few weeks later, I was booked to do a big show with about five other comedians in Battersea Town Hall, in South London, a large venue, home to many live comedy shows and theater productions. Helen had not been booked to appear but was hanging out in the dressing room. I had a great show and hurried back to the dressing room to make notes, grade my performance, and go through my list of bullet points, highlighting the most successful routines. I found her sitting in my chair. Her feet up on the green-room counter, her shoes just inches from my open notebook, as if she were challenging me. "Yeah, bitch, what you gonna do?" Felicity Ethnic, who is a British comedian known for her Jamaican characters, was in the room, along with a few other comics.

"You're sitting in my spot, and that's my notebook."

Helen proceeded to get up. Very. Slowly. At that point I decided this was as good a time as any to get to the bottom of what was going on. "While you're here . . . we might as well talk about the fact that you've been talking about me behind my back." I invited her to follow me to the bathroom, as I didn't want anyone to be privy to this conversation. "Why are you talking shit about me?" I asked once we arrived. "I don't even know you like that, and I don't know what it is you have against me, but you need to stop this shit." Helen, who was taller than me, by a pretty margin, obviously felt threatened by my aggressive stance and squared up to me. At some point her hands came too close to my face and I just lost my temper. I grabbed her and began punching. Felicity Ethnic, on hearing the kerfuffle, ran into the bathroom, wrapped her arms around me, and dragged me out as I screamed like a banshee. A crowd of gawking comedians gathered.

News of the fight spread around the circuit like wildfire. Even though I was ashamed that, again, I had been unable to control my temper and had resorted to violence, I felt no need to apologize to Helen, as I still felt that she had brought this on herself by bad-mouthing me.

Weeks went by. I refused to talk about the incident, to not

further stoke the flames of gossip, which I knew the male comics were devouring like famished dogs. Comedians around the circuit kept asking, "What happened?" I replied, "None of your damn business."

I was still working on *Blouse and Skirt* at the time, and a few months later, Helen's name came up as a possible guest comic. The whole room went silent. They all slowly turned to look at me. The producer asked, "So, Gina, do you have a problem with us booking Helen?" Even back then, in my early twenties, I knew how to run my business. After learning to maintain a stoic exterior, I was not about to let these people know my personal feelings or let my feelings get in the way of work. And I was certainly not going to use this small amount of power for petty revenge.

I also wasn't going to be the one to stop another woman getting work, especially because by that point I'd had time to think about what had happened, and I'd come to the realization that the comedian Kwaku, who'd told me what Helen had supposedly said about me, had been partaking in some classic high school shit stirring, and that the male comics had caused all of this. I told the producers that I had absolutely no problem working with Helen.

Later, while we were all sequestered in the Manchester hotel to shoot the episode, I contacted her to apologize and get to the bottom of how this thing had started. "Listen, you know, we're about to be on TV together. I want us all to do well, and we need to talk about what happened. Here's my hotel room number. If you want, walk down the hall, come to my room, we'll sit down, break bread, and clear the air."

She agreed. She came to my room, and I told her the reason why I had been so bristly on our first meeting. We both agreed that we had been fed toxic information about each other and manipulated. She also explained to me how she had gotten into comedy.

Helen was highly educated—a lawyer, for crying out loud. She had started dating Richard, who was the hottest male comic of the time. One day he heard her doing her father's Nigerian accent in jest, and he encouraged her to get into comedy. He told her that there was a Nigerian girl (me) who had the whole circuit on lock with her African jokes. "You could do that." As if the accent was all there was to what I was doing. As if I needed to be taken down a peg or two. Egged on by her boyfriend, and eager to try out new experiences, she decided to try her hand at this comedy thing, although it had never been a passion for her. She was actually a pretty good comic, and we could have coexisted quite happily from the start had the men not played us against each other.

We decided that when she came on the show, we'd put on a united front. We ended the show standing together, united, our fists in the air, reminiscent of the Black Power movement, but this time we were in solidarity with each other as women. We wanted the male comics to see us and know that they couldn't mess with us anymore. There weren't many shows for Black comics, and we needed solidarity, not the crabs-in-a-barrel mentality—a mentality that has worked too long in dividing our communities throughout the world. Well, I wasn't having it.

Helen and I became friends after this. Our friendship outlasted both her relationship with Richard Blackwood and her comedy career. Law had always been her passion.

I had an epiphany after this episode. I resolved to no longer give a damn what other comics thought of me. I obviously scared them! No longer would I sit staring out a window, almost in tears, wondering why these guys were so horrible to me. Fuck 'em all. I wasn't here to make friends. I was going to be the best comedian I could possibly be, and they weren't gonna be able to do shit but watch me succeed and hate me for it. And I would relish that hatred like a fine wine. I'd lick it, swirl it around in my mouth, then spit that shit into a little gross cup. Yup, my attitude changed overnight, and it made me so much happier.

I was going to give these comics something to be truly threatened by, and I never felt so free.

Slander by the stream will be heard by the frogs.

It was around this time that I knew that I'd have to come out to my mum. I had already come out to my brothers, who had shown absolutely no surprise when I'd told them I had a girlfriend. (In fact, Dele had told me he'd already known because a lesbian friend of his had kept teasing him, saying that she'd seen me at various gay clubs.) My biggest fear of coming out to my mum was not my fear of her homophobia, although that was a big concern, but more her anger at me ruining her standing within the Nigerian community. Although not telling her, and her finding out through the grapevine would be much worse. My mother is an important member of the London Nigerian high society and the belle of the ball wherever she goes, so the last thing I wanted to do was subject her to the malicious gossiping of aunties. "Look at her. She left Nigeria and refused to return with her husband, and now she has no idea one of her children is a muff muncher!"

There was no way I was going to sit down and do the "Mum, I have to tell you something" thing. That was for sitcoms and after-school specials. It wasn't going to end in a hug and mutual declarations of love, so why put myself through that pain? At least I didn't live under her roof anymore, so there was no chance of her throwing me out. My plan was to have no plan, and just drop it on her when the moment was right.

One day, while on my weekly phone check-in with her, Mum

voiced her regular complaints about how she was falling behind her friends on the number-of-grandkids race, and how her two eldest daughters were of childbearing age but had so far failed her.

"When are you going to settle down?" she moaned. "You are a qualified engineer, you've had your fun with this clown business. When are you going to find a husband?"

"Never, Mum. I'm gay," I blurted out. Just like that.

The phone went silent for a moment. "You are what?"

"Gay. Lesbian. Don't like boys. I mean, you did tell me to stay away from them, and I suppose it stuck."

More silence. Then: "What is this gay thing? It does not exist in Nigeria."

"I assure you it does, Mum. It's been a while since you went there."

Another extended silence. Mum was genuinely taken aback by my confession, and speechless for probably the first time in both our lives. "My daughter is a gay clown."

"You could say that, yeah."

"Oh God. So you will never have children?" This was my mother's biggest fear. Having a daughter unwilling or unable to fulfill her womanly duties reflected badly on her. I truly believed that Mum didn't really care if I was a lesbian or a nun, as long as I procreated and increased her grandchild quota. She wouldn't have cared if I'd mated with a goat. She would have proudly presented her half-goat grandchild to her friends: "Look at his little hoofs!"

"No, Mum. Just because I'm gay, doesn't mean I won't have children."

"Hmm." Mum seemed satisfied. "Well, don't be running around telling people. I don't want this to get back to Nigeria."

And that was the end of the conversation. She made it clear

that she did not want to discuss it any further, and would only refer to my girlfriends as "your friends." No further acknowledgment. And you know what? I was more than happy with that. She knew who I was, and was still willing to be my mother. That was enough for me. I was not willing to try to force any more than that on her, and I didn't feel I was missing out on anything at all. Even if I had been straight and had boyfriends, she wasn't the kind of mum I could sit down and talk through my love problems with anyway. She wasn't the mum you brought your boyfriends or girlfriends home to, unless it was the one you were going to marry. She wasn't that mum you saw in the movies who hugged you, told you she loved you, and let you cry on her shoulder when you'd been dumped. As adults, my brothers and I kept our love lives completely separate. The whole point of leaving home was to live your lives in complete freedom, away from the judgment of your parents. We took that to heart.

From time to time Mum would grumble about my lesbianity, but I would shut her down easily. "But I'm Granny. I'm a reincarnation of your mother. Didn't she say she'd come back doing what she wanted and not be beholden to any man?"

Mum would just look at me. She couldn't argue with that.

18

Be a Mountain or
Lean on One

Being on *Blouse and Skirt* really helped cultivate a Black audience for me. I'd turn up for shows and people were coming to see me. I remember within my first year I was able to do my first hour set at a fancy arts center. It was a little room, a fifty-seat room, and it sold out. *Oh my God! Fifty people have paid money to come and hear me do my jokes for an hour!* I was so proud, as I'd been going for only eleven months.

The next several years I spent working as much as I could, traveling all over the UK and building my reputation brick by brick. I worked for a chain of comedy clubs called Jongleurs that had seventeen venues all over the country. There was lot of hatred for the Jongleurs brand, as they were seen as the McDonald's of comedy, with their penchant for selling large carafes of cheap beer and welcoming hen and stag parties; but they gave me a lot of work when nobody else would, and as far as I saw it, people were people. I never believed in any comedy snobbery. I worked sporadically for other London clubs, such as The Comedy Store, the aforementioned Up the Creek, and The Balham Banana, a magnificent club that took over two rooms of a large South London pub. I did all this while demanding higher fees as a celebrity. It was a weird double life, but I was making a comfortable living.

Being recognized by Black people on the street from my TV work while still living in a one-bedroom flat in Tottenham and driving a Honda CRX (did I mention I loved that car?) was odd, though.

I took every small TV gig I could. I did many appearances as the token Black on TV panel shows and many talking-head shows, such as *I Love the '70s*, *I Love the '80s*, I love anything you can make a cheap TV documentary about, punctuated by rent-a-celebs. As a Black female comic, these were some of the very few TV opportunities available. It was great exposure, but TV execs then used my ubiquitous talking-head appearances as an excuse to not book me to host shows, even though white male comics appeared just as often on these and suffered no such typecasting. Judging by my conversations with other comics since leaving the UK, the situation doesn't seem to have changed. Tokenism is still prevalent.

There used to be a variety show on TV called *Big Break*, hosted by Jim Davidson, in which he introduced stand-up comics to a larger audience. It was exactly the type of show on which I would have gotten mainstream exposure and paid well. My agent at the time told me they were booking and paying a thousand pounds. That was a shitload of money at the time—a thousand quid to go on and do a ten-minute set? This was at a time when I was earning twenty quid here, five quid there, a hundred quid here, so a thousand pounds was a lot of money.

But I had a problem with Jim Davidson. He's a British comic who was hugely famous in the '70s and '80s in England, in that super white-working-class-male era of British comedy that I mentioned earlier. A lot of the jokes were very racist, ableist, and homophobic. One of his most famous routines included a Caribbean character he named Chalky White, whom he portrayed with a bad West Indian accent, usually as lazy and abusing drugs. Although he vehemently denied that his act was racist, as time went on, the accusations continued to mount.

When I was a kid, Davidson had a massive audience for his stand-up on TV. But when I watched him, he always made me feel uncomfortable. Even though I was young, I thought it was obvious he was ridiculing this Black dude he was portraying in his Chalky White routine. Strangely, a lot of Black people laughed at those jokes—including my mum. This confused me as a kid, as I couldn't understand why my mum would laugh at a guy for blatantly mocking a Black man. But again, at the time, there were many prejudices Black people held against one another, and it wasn't unusual for someone, even a Black person, to buy into the stereotype of Caribbeans being inferior. I wasn't personally offended by his jokes, as my mum had always told me I'm African, not Caribbean, so I didn't think the jokes pertained to me. But this fact didn't make his jokes any less offensive; they were still based on humor that was anti-Black. At that age I couldn't articulate all of this, but I knew I didn't like this comedian, I didn't find him funny, and I didn't understand why other people did.

Jim Davidson's fame started to dwindle in the '90s, as more folks realized how racist his material was. A few years ago, he was challenged on the accusation that some of his material was racist. His response? "I don't know what Black people think. I have not met them all yet."[3] Although he no longer performs the Chalky White character—he claims it's because he doesn't hear the West Indian accent much anymore.

Accusations of his racism, homophobia, and anti-immigrant sentiment continue to follow him. In 2007, his appearance on

Hell's Kitchen left many accusing him of homophobia, as viewers had witnessed him bullying one of the contestants, who was openly gay. *The Telegraph* wrote of his 2014 Edinburgh Festival Fringe show, "the sight of a white person going for laughs by impersonating non-white ones is as depressingly retrograde as it is dull."[4] But at the beginning of my career, in the late '90s, Davidson was still clinging to his fame. The BBC still gave him work and a platform. The same BBC that had begrudgingly given us the graveyard shift for *The A Force.*

When my agent brought up a possible booking on *Big Break*, I couldn't bring myself to do it. I had just started to build my name, and I was very pro-Black and pro-Pride. I really wanted to go on the show because it was a massively high-profile gig, and the money was fantastic, but as a Black person, I couldn't stand on a stage with this guy because I knew it would be interpreted as me validating him. My agent was furious. He even threatened to dump me if I didn't do the show. But I held my ground. At that point I had already been on *Blouse and Skirt* and I had built up a really good following among the Black community. If I had gone on that show, my community would have looked at me as a sellout and a coconut. I knew that my childhood instinct had been correct, so I turned the show down.

There was a white male comic I was quite friendly with—a big, tall man with a shaved head. He looked like one of the East End skinheads who had chased me as a kid, but he always waxed lyrical about how left-wing he was, how progressive, that he was married to a Black woman, that he was working-class, an anti-racist, *a human rights crusader.* He always used to wear a badge of honor about how conscious he was. I believed him at the time. But then he did the show with Jim Davidson and I lost all respect for him.

About three months later, I bumped into this same comic in the green room of the Battersea Jongleurs club, and being young, dumb, and very open about my feelings, I blurted out, "You're a fucking hypocrite." I said it in front of other comics, so that obviously made him feel even worse.

"What do you mean?"

"You always go on about how principled you are, but you forgot those lofty ideals for a grand."

He became very upset, and his wife tried to defend him. "No, he never even spoke to Jim Davidson. He stayed in his dressing room until it was time for him to come out and record his segment."

"Yeah, he stayed in his dressing room, but we're not seeing that. We're seeing him shaking hands with this prick on TV, so I don't wanna hear any more of his views on racism and social justice."

This comedian has hated me ever since.

He wasn't the only comic I felt had sold out. A couple of Black comics also did the show. I couldn't hate on them as much, as I knew how difficult it was for a Black comedian to get a break, and for some, ambition trumped integrity.

Later in my career, I'd often get booked for a TV show called *Mock the Week*, which was similar to *Blouse and Skirt* except it was made for white people, and therefore had a much bigger budget and a better, regular time slot. I filled their token spot. I did about eight episodes, and at the time, I held the record for the most frequently booked female and Black guest. I felt like they kept using me as an example when complaints were lodged that they didn't have enough women or ethnic minorities. I remember a meeting I had once with an executive at Channel 4, one of the biggest British channels. The woman said to me, "We already have a Black comedian on the network. Yes, we already have Richard

Blackwood." She actually said that to my face, which confirmed to me that there was a quota. As time went on, I realized that I was never going to get to host the show, or anything like it, although I was consistently good. Other (white, male) comics, like Russell Howard, could go on and sell stadiums based on his TV work, but there just didn't seem to be the same opportunities for Black comedians.

Basically, the TV industry in England is run by white, middle-class men. They tend to book people that look and sound like them, whom they can relate to. You switch on the TV and that's all you see. Call it racism, call it nepotism. It all leads to the same thing: a dearth of Black faces in positions of decision-making and power, which in turn becomes a dearth in front of the screen. I didn't complain, though. I just kept on doing what I was doing, cultivating an audience of people who wanted to see me and hoping that eventually that audience would become so huge the industry decision-makers couldn't ignore me anymore.

For a while I tried to fit into what I thought they wanted. I tried to tone down my Blackness on TV shows. I tried to avoid controversy, present an "Oh look—happy, shiny Gina" vibe. I couldn't keep it up, as it just wasn't me. I couldn't change my voice enough, or my mannerisms. I knew they wanted their Black comics to be safe and nonthreatening. I was often compared unfavorably to other Black female comics who presented more feminine and therefore were more palatable.

There is a vast gamut of white comedians, ranging from the super offensive to the surreal to the buffoonish, and everything in between. In the UK, one Black comedian on TV has to represent us all. Stephen K. Amos was on the scene a long, long time before he got his break on TV. He did one show that didn't quite work out, and the failure was used as an excuse not to book other Black comics. The networks would never have said, "Oh, this white guy's show didn't work out—that's it, we can't use any more white guys." But when it came to Black comedians, we were all tarnished with the same brush. Stephen K was perfect. He's very middle class, well spoken, not too offensive, gay, and therefore nonthreatening. Basically, he ticked all the boxes. Yet they still treated him like a pariah when his one show didn't work out.

When it came to my own career, there were those who said, "She has a chip on her shoulder. Maybe she's not getting the opportunities because she's not funny!" But it was not just me. It's the way Black comedians are perceived. I worked my ass off, I was funny—consistently funny—and I went on all the shows that kept using me again and again. I knew I was doing something right. But I was not getting the opportunities comics like Michael McIntyre and Jimmy Carr were getting. I did shows with Michael McIntyre—I used to headline and he was the opening act. But I still couldn't host my own show. Time and time again, I had to learn that in showbiz, it doesn't really matter how hard you work or how talented you are. If your face doesn't fit, if you don't have the right look or the right sound, then forget it.

I still nursed dreams of moving to America and making it big there. I knew racism was just as prevalent in the US, and there was probably also a glass ceiling there for Black talent, but I figured I'd at least be a millionaire by the time I hit it, and I could cry in my piles of money. If England was not going to recognize me, I could fulfill my childhood dream of living in California and making it big. But I decided I'd give everything I've got in the UK first before giving up.

My agent at the time encouraged me to take whatever little gigs I could get with the BBC, with the idea that the next opportunity would be for my own show. He kept telling me that I was next in line, that if I did this, did that, played the game, appeared in all the shows they wanted me to appear in, played second fiddle to whoever they wanted me to play second fiddle to, that when the time came I'd get my own show.

In 2001, the BBC launched their first digital channel, BBC Choice, which later became BBC3. To fill an eight-week gap in their schedule, they hired a bunch of comics and performers, giving each one a nightly talk show for one week, as a kind of audition, with a plan to award the best one a permanent slot. I was the only Black comedian picked for this talk-show experiment.

I'd been waiting for an opportunity like this my entire career, and I put everything into it. I worked around the clock. I made sure they employed Black writers, so we all could get a stab at some mainstream success (including my ex-nemesis, and now good friend, Curtis Walker). Whatever times the writers came in, I was right there with them. I took stuff home and wrote, I'd travel anywhere and everywhere to film skits, and I bent over backwards to be the easiest of easygoing.

We wrote a great show with sketches, one of which included me playing my own mother, harassing my guests in the green room before they then came out to be interviewed by me. I would then play back the video of the harassment to much amusement. My show had quite a few celebrity guests, including Jonathan Ross, who had been a fan of mine since Mum and I had appeared on *The Big Big Talent Show* years previously.

My show was so popular that the line for our live audiences would snake around the BBC building, and when my week was up, they called me back to do another week to fill another shortfall in the schedule, as my ratings were the highest out of all the other performers.

I was ecstatic, believing I was on my way to my own late-night talk show—my dream since I'd started doing comedy six years before. I had won! I temporarily forgot that showbiz isn't built on fairness. When it came time for them to hand me my show, as had been promised to the winner of this challenge, they changed the parameters and gave the show to a young white actor, Ralf Little, who was on a hugely successful sitcom called *The Royle Family*, a gig he had landed straight out of school. He had absolutely no comedy, interviewing, or hosting chops whatsoever, and he had pulled in a fraction of the viewing audience I had, but he was, as said by a random executive at the TV station, "more recognizable, and fits the demographic we are aiming for."

That show lasted one season.

I never got to host another talk show, but I watched as some of the ideas I'd pioneered on my show were used on other people's. With that promise broken by the BBC, I was left, once again, heartbroken and disappointed.

A few years later, I was approached by producers working with *The Lenny Henry Show* and asked if I'd like to write sketches for his new show. Lenny Henry had seen me on one of my many short TV appearances and thought I'd be a great addition to his show. I made it clear to them from the start that I was a performer, that I didn't want to write for other people. I was only interested in creating characters if I would get to play them.

I was asked to write some material they would take a look at, and they would take it from there. That's when I created Mrs. Omokorede, the pushy Nigerian mother whose daughter was going to be a doctor at any cost (sound familiar?), and Tanya, the fast-talking street girl who's catchphrase was "I don't think so!" I sent them in, and they loved them. By that point, they had also recruited Ninia Benjamin, Tameka Empson, and Jocelyn Jee Esien, the cast of 3 *Non-Blondes*, a British hidden-camera comedy created by Gary Reich—the same man behind the hidden-camera career of Sacha Baron Cohen, of Ali G and Borat fame. The trio would do pranks, like visiting a hotel and pretending they were African royalty, and the joke would be in the hidden cameras. Lenny wanted to recruit younger comedians to make his show a little bit more relevant and cool.

But they were actors, not writers. Lenny and his team needed material that these women could perform. On a phone call with one of the producers a couple of days after I had sent in my characters, they just dropped a bombshell on me. "Oh yes, we love these sketches that you've written. We're thinking you can play the Nigerian mother and then we'll take Tanya and give it to Tameka. You can still write the sketches and we'll pay you for writing them, but Tameka will be Tanya."

"Oh, okay," I said. "Let me think about it." I put the phone down. And then proceeded to destroy my living room. *Fuck, fuck, fuck!* I screamed and threw things around the room for about ten minutes to expel my fury. This shit was not about to happen to me again. They had promised me that I could play whatever character I created, and here was the BBC again trying to move the goalposts and scupper yet another opportunity for me to get on. Nope. Not this time. I calmly called them back. "I've thought about it. I'm sorry, but I created both of these characters, so nobody gets to play them but me." If I lost the opportunity to be on the show, then so be it. Nobody was creating anything for me, and yet I had now created something for myself, and they wanted to take it and give it to someone else. I told them that I was good with whatever decision they made, but I wasn't giving up my characters. They were mine. They called me the next day and agreed to let me play my own characters. Thank God, because the Nigerian Mum was very well received, but Tanya was the standout of the show.

Tanya did so well that she was on the show every week. She became insanely popular and catapulted me to mainstream fame in the UK. Tanya came before *Little Britain*'s Vicky Pollard and before Catherine Tate's "Am I bovvered" Lauren. It was because of Tanya that I was able to do my first string of UK national tours. I started to sell out large theaters, and my audience became decidedly more mixed. I kept my Black audience but added a mainstream white audience to the mix. I went from comedy clubs to theaters because of *The Lenny Henry Show*. People would yell out at me in the street, "I don't think so!"

Can you imagine if I'd given that character to somebody else? If I'd decided to continue playing the game that I was always destined to lose? Then someone else would have reaped all the benefits of my work, and I may never have reached the next level of my career.

I used some of the money I made from my UK tour to buy my first-ever brand-new car, a Mercedes-Benz SLK roadster. I went to the Mercedes showroom and picked exactly how I wanted my car to look, and in three months, I had it, an electric-blue, hardtop convertible with cream leather interior and a walnut dashboard. I loved it.

19

A Flea Can Trouble a Lion More Than a Lion Can Trouble a Flea

t was at this time I began being stopped by the police at least three times a week. The pattern was always the same: the police followed me for a distance, hoping to find something wrong or to scare me into making a driving error. If that didn't work, they'd pull me over anyway, just to ensure I indeed owned the car. Once, I was driving with my mum and I could see them following us. So I just pulled over and made sure that I was curbside so that when the police drove by they would see this older Nigerian woman sitting in the car too. They were constantly stopping me and checking my paperwork. The harassment never ended. It got to a point where I decided that the next time they tried to pull me over, I wasn't stopping.

A few days after I made that decision, the police began following me again—this time in an unmarked van. There must've been maybe five or six officers inside. *Oh, for fuck's sake. Here we go.*

I was on my way to the hairdresser's, driving from North London to East London. I was on the North Circular Road, which is kind of like a freeway inside London. My windows were rolled up. I had my baseball cap to the back, hip-hop playing. I knew that all they saw was the baseball cap and a Black face inside an expensive Mercedes, which to them was enough to warrant harassment.

They drove behind me and flashed their lights, indicating that they wanted me to pull over. I didn't speed up so as not to turn this into a car chase, but I ignored them. I carried on driving at the same speed, like a regular person driving a car they had indeed paid for, and had committed no crime. The van sped up alongside me, and from my peripheral, I could see them gesticulating for me to pull over. I kept looking straight ahead and carried on driving. I just wanted to get to my hair appointment.

They continued to follow me, wildly weaving in and out behind, flashing their lights and tailgating me. I continued to ignore them, keeping a steady speed. Once I got off the North Circular Road and into a more densely populated residential area, I pulled over outside a council estate in East London, in Leyton. The police jumped out of the van and ran towards me, flinging open my car door and dragging me out. They immediately started to search my car, looking for contraband.

"There's nothing in there. You pulled me over for no reason, so give me my ticket and let me go about my business."

"Nope, we're arresting you for failing to stop."

What? This was unheard of. Failing to stop usually comes with another offense. Failing to stop while being in possession of a class A drug or failing to stop and possession of a gun or failing to stop because you're running away from a robbery. You don't just arrest somebody for failing to stop if there is no crime to go with it. But they put me in handcuffs, threw me in the van, and left my Mercedes there, open, with my purse on the seat.

"Can I at least get my stuff?"

"No." They deliberately wanted to leave my car open so that it would get broken into. They wanted to mess with me as much as they could, hoping that when I returned, I'd find my purse gone and a trashed car.

"Oh my God, oh my God, is that Gina Yashere? Is that Gina Yashere being arrested?" It was a group of young boys who had recognized me from TV.

"Dudes! Watch my car! Don't let anyone break into it!" I shouted as they bundled me into the van.

The police took me away to a police station miles away from where my car was left. They put me in a cell for no reason; I'd committed no crime. It was a completely pointless arrest. I should have just been given a ticket. After about four hours, they let me go, with a form to fill out to pay a fine, or if I believed that I committed no crime, to go to court. They threw me out of the station late at night, in the middle of nowhere. I had no money because everything was in the car.

"How am I supposed to get home?" I asked them.

"We don't care. Off you go." They had deliberately stranded me.

I walked till I came across a minicab company. I told the available driver that if he took me to my car, I'd have the money to pay him, plus a considerable tip. He drove me to my untouched car. I paid him and I drove home.

I was so angry. I could have paid the small fine and that would have been the end of it, but I decided I was going to take a stand against the relentless police harassment I'd suffered for driving while Black. *I'm taking these fuckers to court.* I knew it was going to be a complete waste of money, but there needed to be some kind of pushback for what they had done to me that day.

When you go to court, you don't know when your case will be called, so you have to be there first thing in the morning and hope your case is called early. I knew these five police officers, who wanted to be out on the street and doing more exciting stuff, like harassing more Black people, would be furious that they had to sit in a waiting room for who knows how many hours for this minor case. I'd even hired an expensive lawyer to interrogate them on the stand. Total waste of money, but these cops had to at least be made to think that there may be consequences for harassing innocent Black people in their cars. Even if those consequences amounted to nothing more than sitting in a magnolia-colored waiting room, drinking tea and eating stale biscuits out of a vending machine. We were there from about nine thirty in the morning, and our case didn't get tried until about three that afternoon. They had to sit there all day. I sat with my lawyer in another room, down the hall from theirs. Every hour I would walk by their room: "You all right in there, lads? You all right? How's it going? Long day, innit? Are you bored? Yeah, that's how I felt when you had me in a cell for hours for nothing." We were finally called into court, and each of those police officers testified. I discovered in court that they hadn't even been on duty when they'd arrested me. They had been on their way to a training course, when they decided that I didn't deserve to be in that car. The first officer testified that I had driven erratically, which was bullshit. He said that I had been speeding. Again bullshit. He claimed that when they tried to pull me over I stuck my hand out the window and flipped them the finger and cursed them out. Lies. They all lied. When someone is arrested by the police, they are all supposed to write their statements separately from each other. But they all went up and told exactly the same story. Word. For. Word.

My lawyer got up and began to cross-examine them.

"So you say when you first saw Gina, her windows were up and the music was blaring?"

"Yes."

"So then when you pulled alongside her and told her to pull over, she immediately stuck her hand out of the window."

"Yes."

"Immediately?"

"Yes."

"Without taking time to open her window?"

Silence.

"So that means the window must've been closed when you pulled up alongside her, which means she couldn't have stuck her hand out the window to give you guys the finger. Otherwise you would have heard the glass smash and she would have said, 'Ouch!' as her elbow went through the window. So what you are saying is untrue, and furthermore you all said exactly the same thing in the statement." He went on to ask each officer if they'd written those statements independently of each other. They all swore an oath that they had. "It's funny how you all say that you wrote your statements independently yet all of you have the exact same spelling mistake on the name of the street that you pulled her over in." It was obvious that they'd all written their statements together. He blatantly showed them up to be liars in court.

I went on the stand and testified that I had not been speeding or doing anything that would have given them cause to pull me over. I also produced records of the sheer multitude of police stops I'd endured since purchasing the car. None resulting in a prosecution of any kind.

I admitted failing to stop. But only because I had committed no crime, and as far as I was concerned, I was being pursued by an unmarked van full of unidentified white dudes.

If I'd been found guilty and punished to the full extent of the law, it would have been a two-thousand-pound fine. They still found me guilty, but I was fined only a nominal fee of fifty pounds. It was their way of saying, "We know these police officers lied, and we know they harassed you, but we cannot be seen to rule against the police, so here is a small slap on the wrist." That was what was to be expected from the British justice system as a Black person. I was glad they hadn't fined me the entire amount. I had known I would lose against the police, but it had been just a matter of how badly I would. I took this as a small win.

My white lawyer was furious. "That paltry fine is obviously an admittance of your innocence! This is a travesty! I think we should appeal, and I'll represent you for free!" I'd already spent three thousand for this fun day in court, and I had planned to move on, but another free opportunity to punish these racist cops couldn't be passed up, so I agreed to apply for an appeal. But six months later, when the appeal came through, the lawyer was in the middle of another case and couldn't do it. He told me his colleague would take the case, but unfortunately not pro bono. Yeah, no thanks. I needed a cheaper form of activism. I paid my fifty-pound fine and walked away.

20

If You Are Building a House and a Nail Breaks, Do You Stop Building or Do You Change the Nail?

As time went on, I became more frustrated with my career in the UK. I felt like I'd hit the glass ceiling, and having been around for so long, I was being perceived as "old news." I was no longer the fresh Black talent that could be tokenized. I needed to have another plan and quick.

I loved traveling to the US every year on vacation, and whenever my best friend, Lila, and I would go, she knew I would find a comedy club somewhere to test my skills on a US audience, my plan to emigrate never far from my mind. Another avenue for getting noticed by the American comedy market was the Just for Laughs festival in Montreal, Canada. This is the largest comedy festival in the world, where comedians from all over are invited to perform, hoping to be snapped up for American superstardom. Shows vary from large star-studded televised galas to outdoor events to hole-in-the-wall comedy nights. It's an invite-only festival, and scouts from JFL scoured the world for talent, at showcases set up in comedy clubs in most major cities around the globe. There were many stories of comedians being given major development deals with TV networks to create their own sitcoms, just on the basis of a good set in Montreal. I was convinced that once they saw me, I'd be on a private jet to LA, eating caviar and crackers as soon as I walked off the stage. I just had to get to Montreal.

Though I had won places in the London showcases year after year, and had done well, I had never been picked to attend the festival. The last showcase I was scheduled to perform in—The Comedy Store in London—I had decided would be my final one. I was dejected by the yearly rejections and no longer wanted to humiliate myself in front of people who obviously didn't want me. I'd just have to get to America another way. I hit the stage at that final showcase with an attitude of no longer caring. I felt no nervousness. At that point I knew they were not going to pick me, just as they hadn't the previous four years, so I was just going to have some fun, tear this crowd up, and at least make it difficult for the people they *were* going to pick. I had a blinding set, and I was the only comic of all those who performed to be asked to attend the festival. Go figure. Turns out not giving a shit had freed up my performance. I was on my way. Managers, agents, and TV and film producers all came to Montreal looking for the next big thing. Maybe I'd be it. And even if I wasn't, Canada was just a hop, skip, and a jump from my dream destination: the US of A.

I ticked a lot of boxes in Montreal. Originally booked to appear at the Brits showcase (a show with all British comics), I was also able to perform on any type of ladies-night-style comedy bill as well as in Black (or, as they're called in North America, "urban") shows. *Uptown Comics* was the most popular urban show on the Just for Laughs calendar. This was the festival's version of an

American urban comedy night. It was all African American comics . . . and me. It was an eye-opener. I'd never heard the words "dick," "pussy," and "motherfucker" uttered so many times within an hour. Although all the shows I'd been performing in during the festival had had a majority white audience, this crowd was almost entirely Black, and they screamed with laughter. This night reminded me of the VHS tapes I'd watched of the iconic *Def Comedy Jam*, the stand-up show created by Russell Simmons, Stan Lathan, and Bob Sumner that had put urban comedy on the world map.

That night I was to perform with Patrice O'Neal, a hilarious comedian I'd met many times previously when he'd toured the UK, and Roz G, a comedian from New Jersey I'd never met before. When Roz G was introduced, the MC shouted, "You've seen her on *Last Comic Standing*!" *Hmm*. I took note of this. I went on later in the show and did well, despite my nervousness that this audience would expect more of what they'd seen earlier and might not be open to my stories about my Nigerian mother and my childhood dreams of being adopted by Mr. Drummond from *Diff'rent Strokes*. Later, I Googled *Last Comic Standing* and discovered that it was an American talent competition on NBC in the vein of *American Idol* but for stand-up comics. I called my agent that night. "Listen, there's a stand-up comedy competition in America, and I want to be the first British comic to be on it. Look into it. I'll fly myself out there to compete. Just get me an audition."

I enjoyed my first stint at the Just for Laughs festival, but nothing came of it for me. Disappointingly, there was no HBO development deal, no US agents falling over themselves to represent me. Nothing. I did shows, I was paid, I did some sightseeing, and I went home. Just another week in the life of a jobbing comic.

A few months later, while surfing through the preeminent social media site of the time, Myspace, I came across a page dedicated to the Bay Area Black Comedy Competition and Festival (BABCCF). It was founded in 1986 by Tony Spires. Previous contestants had included Jamie Foxx, Chris Tucker, and Nick Cannon. According to the Myspace page, it was the longest-running live showcase of urban comedians in the world, and it was currently accepting entrants for that year's competition. I was transfixed. I scoured the page, looking for any rules that would possibly exclude a foreign participant, and found none. The grand prize was a thousand dollars, which was less than half of what it would cost me for flights and accommodations in Oakland, California, where the competition took place, but I excitedly filled out an online application and paid my seventy-five-dollar application fee.

Competing in the BABCCF was about getting more exposure in the US and laying the groundwork to move there, although at the time I had no idea how I was going to do it. I was 100 percent confident I was not going to win, and I was pretty sure I wouldn't make it past the first round, but this was an experiment to see how my comedy would translate on the other side of the pond and whether I could straddle the lines successfully between Black and white comedy in America, as I had done in the UK.

Despite the fact that I was in the epicenter of a huge flare-up of symptoms of lupus, an illness I'd been diagnosed with a few years previous, having been accepted into the competition, I packed bags of painkillers and flew myself to Oakland. I didn't know anybody and had never worked with any of the comedians showcasing, but I had gone through all their Myspace profiles and confirmed that I was the only comedian from outside the US coming to compete. One particular comedian, Shea Suga, from Richmond, California, had messaged me on Myspace, having also done her due diligence. She had watched a few videos of my stand-up and told me how much she'd enjoyed my material and was looking forward to meeting me. When I arrived at the conference center where all the comics were meeting to sign in, I recognized her immediately from her picture, and we hugged like old friends. It was great to see a friendly face. She was from the area, so she gave me good tips on where to eat and what malls to shop at if I needed to get an outfit. Shea was also a hairdresser. She took one look at my "just come off a fifteen-hour flight and haven't been to the salon" head and commented, "Honey, we got to do something about your hair! Come, come . . ." She took me to the mall where she had a salon, relaxed my hair, then colored and cut it, making sure I looked my best even though we were competitors. "Oh, honey, you gotta be looking fly for this competition. This is Oakland. You can't be getting onstage looking all raggedy. They'll boo your ass off before you get to your first joke!" We are still friends to this day, and whenever I do shows in the Bay Area, I always get her to open for me.

The competition did not provide any travel expenses, so most comics were sofa surfing or staying in local motels. Coming from England, I had booked myself into the Oakland Marriott, as that was the only hotel name I recognized, and I wasn't about to stay in a dump. I had money, as I was making a great living from my UK comedy career, and this was going to be a fun exploration of the American urban comedy scene, as well as a great vacation. I'd never been to the Bay Area, always preferring New York or Miami, so I was looking forward to sightseeing between my performances. The Golden Gate Bridge, just half an hour away in San Francisco, was number one on my list.

My entire body was still inflamed and in pain from the lupus flare-up, so when the other comics were out socializing in the evenings, I remained in my hotel room, resting my swollen joints and writing my sets. I couldn't open with the regular material I used in the UK, as I was about to be performing in front of an audience that was not familiar with me. I needed to get in front of the confusion they would have the moment I opened my mouth, and have good jokes to explain my oddness.

On the day of the first heat of the competition, I sat at the back of the theater with Shea Suga and watched a steady stream of comics hit the stage with highly energetic sets, in the vein of the extremely popular '90s stand-up show *Def Comedy Jam*. There was a lot of material about sex, illustrated with act-outs, which included a lot of stool humping and pelvic thrusting. I was nervous but excited.

When it was my turn to hit the stage, I opened with an explanation of who I was. "Hi, everybody. My name's Gina. And yes, this is a British accent, and no, I'm not the butler from *Fresh Prince*. There are a lot of Black people in England. We are *everywhere*. We are just like you. We even get your TV shows and movies. The only thing is, we get them a little later. For instance, we just got *The Color Purple*."

This got a huge laugh, as this was 2006, and *The Color Purple* had been released in 1985. I then went into a routine about how furious I was at my mother for leaving Nigeria for England, that had she made the right choice, I would be living Missy Elliott's life. I'd also written a routine about the popular TV show *MTV Cribs*, in which cameras went into the homes of celebrities, the vast majority of them rappers, who then showed off their garish marble-encased mansions, their shark-size fish tanks filled with marine life they couldn't pronounce the names of, and their beds in the shape of a Lamborghini. My joke focused on the fact that these rappers were constantly espousing their street cred, how many times they'd been shot, and how "hood" they were, but in the next breath they'd say things like "I had these tiles brought in from Rome." The rappers always seemed to have a DVD collection that included *Scarface*. They idolized the Italian Mafia. I talked about how the Mafia did not reciprocate those feelings but in fact called Black people derogatory names like *mulignan*, which, not speaking their language, I assumed was Italian for Nigger. If they really wanted to continue worshipping people who hated us, they might as well keep next to the DVD collection a copy of the Nazi handbook *Mein Kampf*. It was controversial, but I got a great response. I pushed even further. I discussed the use of the word "nigga," which was not common among Black people in England at the time. (This has since changed with the sheer popularity of hip-hop with British Black youth, spawning our own version of it, grime music.) I talked about the fact that if I heard the N-word in England, it was invariably coming from a racist, and I knew what was expected. An ass whooping from me would ensue. I said I was confused by the n-i-g-g-a and n-i-g-g-e-r variations of the word. That I couldn't go to a KKK rally, and ask, "Sir, which version of the N-word are you calling me? Oh, *e-r*? Got it. Give me a head start, so I can run for my life!"

I received an ecstatic response from the crowd, and in that moment, I knew I could make it in America as a comedian. I had conquered a hard-core Black room in Oakland, California. I needed to figure out a plan to move here, stat!

Suddenly these American comedians who had been looking at me sideways like some weird oddity began speaking to me with a little respect, after realizing I was legitimate competition. Shea Suga was overjoyed for me. "Bitch, you murdered that motherfucker!"

The next day was the second round of heats, on which Shea Suga was performing with the likes of Baratunde Thurston (who went on to become a celebrated author, commentator, and producer). It was fun, having done my heat, to relax and enjoy the evening of comedy. Shea did very well, with her added cachet of being from nearby and being able to call out the local neighborhoods. One particular comic hit the stage and blew the room apart. He was a tornado of energy, with act-outs of the crackheads in his neighborhood of Harlem, New York, and hilariously crafted routines that had the crowd screaming. I knew instantly I was looking at the winner. He was the epitome of all the best aspects of *Def Comedy Jam*. His name was Smokey.

After both heats, the judges picked the comics who were to go through to the finals in a couple of months' time. I sincerely hoped I wouldn't make it. This had been a fun experiment that had gone very well, and no doubt I would make plans to return at some point to continue this exploration, but I was going back to London, then on to Australia for a month-long tour, to make some money, and it would be extremely expensive and extremely hard on my lupus-addled body to then return to Oakland to take part in a final I was absolutely positive that Smokey was going to win.

"The first comedian going through to the finals is . . . Gina Yashere!" *Shit*.

The other comics who made it through to the final were Vanessa Fraction, Drew Fraser, a comedian from Detroit called Coolaide (yep, that really was his chosen stage name), Retha Jones, and of course Smokey.

As comedians lined up to congratulate me, telling me how most of them had attended this competition three or four times and it was unheard of to get through to the final on your first try, I was frantically doing a pros-and-cons list in my head. Should I come for this final? Would it help cement a foothold in the US market? Who would be the judges? Was it worth putting more debt on my rapidly buckling credit card?

"Bitch, you coming back!" Shea shouted in my ear as she hugged me. "You can come stay with me!"

I found out that one of the judges of the final was Bob Sumner, who had co-created *Def Comedy Jam* alongside Stan Lathan and Russell Simmons. My plan was to be seen by him and become the first British comic to appear on that show. So it was settled. I was coming back.

21

Just Because a Man Is Short, It Does Not Make Him a Child

While doing shows in Sydney, Australia, I received a call from my agent, telling me that while I had been making enquiries to audition for the American stand-up competition, the producers of *Last Comic Standing* had decided that for season five they would widen the net and audition internationally. One of the producers, Page Hurwitz, who had previously seen me at The Comedy Store in London, had put my name forward. They were currently doing auditions in London, but I could do mine in Sydney, competing against the Australian comics for a spot on the show.

The stars were finally aligning.

I turned up at the Sydney Comedy Store one sunny afternoon for my audition. A long line of wannabe stars had camped out there overnight, but I, as a professional comedian, had an appointment, and I walked in ahead of the line. I did a forty-five-second set in front of the three comedian judges: Ant, Kathleen Madigan, and Alonzo Bodden, who had won a previous season of the show. The auditions and showcase were all being filmed for the show, and my previous experience of performing on television in the UK put me in good stead. The cameras did not faze me at all. I went up, did what I do, and was one of the comics picked to go through to the LA semifinals. I was ecstatic.

The rest of my Australia trip was a blur. From there I would fly back to Oakland for the final round of the Bay Area Black Comedy Competition and Festival. I decided that afterwards I would go to LA and spend a couple of weeks getting in as many rooms and clubs as I could find to hone my set for when I returned for *Last Comic Standing*. I was taking no chances. I needed to get through the semifinals of their competition too. The grand prize would be $250,000 and a development deal with NBC. And to develop a show in America, you had to live in America, which I'd been planning to do since I was a child.

The final of the BABCCF was held again at the Paramount Theater in Oakland. As I'd predicted, Smokey won the grand prize, and I was happy for him. I came in third, after Smokey and Drew Fraser. Not bad for a tourist! From there, I flew to LA, where I booked the cheapest room I could find at a Holiday Inn in Burbank, rented an old Honda Civic, and began nightly trips into LA to perform at any club that would have me. I'd become friendly with some of the LA-based comics I'd competed against in Oakland, so I followed them to their shows and got them to vouch for me and my funniness. Using this method, I was able to perform at The Improv comedy club on Melrose on the Monday evening urban night, as well as Mo' Better Mondays, hosted by comedian and actor DeRay Davis and promoted by a formidable former aeronautical engineer called Big Spike. Big Spike had been unsure of whether to let me on his stage, seeing as I was a foreigner he'd never heard of, but he gave me five minutes and was very supportive of me afterwards, telling me I could come back whenever I wanted. I was also able to perform at the iconic Comedy Store on Sunset Boulevard, again on their urban night, called Trippin' on Tuesdays, which at the time was hosted by the hilarious comedian and now in-demand executive producer Chris Spencer. I also got a set at the Laugh Factory's Chocolate Sundaes, another urban night. It proved a lot more difficult to get spots on the regular, "white" nights at these famous clubs, as the competition was much stiffer and these were considered the more prestigious nights, when Hollywood agents, casting directors, and bookers tended to come, so you needed a nod of approval from a much higher caliber of comedian to even get looked at. Even then, as a Black comic, you had to be a stand-out, hugely famous, or have a good agent to get the same stage time. Another way to get on was to fight seven thousand other comedians for a tryout spot, by lining up outside the Laugh Factory on a Sunday morning to sign a list to possibly get three minutes in an 8 p.m. audition show. I was not going to be in LA long enough to do that, and I felt with my experience in the game, I was not about to be camping with a bunch of office workers whose friends had told them they were funny. I figured if I did well enough on *Last Comic Standing*, those clubs would come calling anyway. So I concentrated on getting in all the rooms I was actively welcomed in during those two weeks—clubs, bars, outdoor patios of restaurants, anywhere I could perform in front of an American audience and hone my set. At the end of that fortnight, I felt ready for my upcoming big break.

A month later, I returned to Los Angeles for the *Last Comic Standing* semifinals. I flew there with comedians from London, Canada, and Australia. We were all booked into the Sheraton Universal, a hotel a stone's throw from Universal Studios. Meeting so many comedians from all over was exhilarating. We were all booked at local comedy clubs to warm up for our TV recording, so I got to watch and size up my competition. I put aside all my doubts about the fairness of these competitions and my previous mistreatment at the hands of this industry, and I prepared for the show that could change my life. This was it. I was about to make my debut on one of the biggest networks in the US. I was going to put my best foot forward and leave that stage with no regrets.

My previous foray into the US market had increased my confidence, and for me, it was just a case of which routine I wanted to pick that would be mainstream enough for network TV but different enough to make me stand out. I spent evenings in my hotel room piecing my jokes together like a jigsaw puzzle.

There were thirty-five comics performing in the semifinals. Three, including me, were Black women. Tracey Ashley, a hilarious comedian who'd traveled from Indiana, was experienced and, like me, had a meticulously thought-out set. Thea Vidale had already had quite some success as a comedian and actor, having been the first African American female comedian with her own show, the ABC sitcom *Thea*. She was hilarious and had toured the world as a sought-after comic. In fact, I'd met her at the Edinburgh Festival in Scotland at the beginning of my career and had gotten an autograph and a picture with her. I quietly wondered who had advised her to do this show, as it should have been way below her status, and I felt that doing this would be way better for the show's producers than it would be for her, but who was I to judge?

We three Black women sought each other out, bonded, broke bread together, but we *knew* what was up. Just ten comics would be picked to go through to the finals of the show, performing on national TV every week, before being whittled down to a final three, then the champion. We knew only one, if any, of those ten finalists was going to be a Black woman. Although we wished each other well, we discussed the fact that along with competing against the other thirty-two comics, we'd be specifically competing against one another for that single spot. Such was the plight of the Black female comic in this industry.

On the night of the show, the order we were to go onstage was random. Names were picked out of a bucket. The worst two spots to be in the running order were first and last. First because you were going on to a cold audience, and you would be the guinea pig to test what material they would respond to or not. Everyone could watch your set and adjust accordingly, therefore putting them at an advantage. Going last out of thirty-five comics, with the inherent stops and starts of TV production, meant you would be performing in front of a tired, laughed-out audience, and you would have been forced to sit through the performances of all the other comics, hoping none of them had jokes similar to yours, while you became increasingly nervous. Everyone hoped to be somewhere in the middle of the lineup. My name was pulled out first. *Uggh.*

Oh well, I reasoned. It was better than last. I'd get the audience and judges fresh, and be able to sit back and enjoy the show, obviously provided I'd had a good set; otherwise, I'd be watching jealously as everyone else went on and did better than me, while plastering on a fake smile for the cameras as my dreams died.

The show was filmed at the Alex Theatre in Glendale and was packed with members of the public, various agents, and industry bigwigs. The three judges were on elevated platforms in the middle of the audience, and they would be giving critiques after each performance. The show was hosted by Bill Bellamy, known for his longtime VJ work on MTV in the '90s as well as for his appearances on *Def Comedy Jam* and various other TV shows and movies.

All the semifinalists were corralled into a green room backstage where several camera operators would film us as we watched each performance on TV monitors and reacted to each comedian returning to the room after their set. It was a high-pressure environment. As I was going on first, I sat in a corner on my own, away from the other comics, going over my set and psyching myself up for the gig of my life.

You've got this. You're the best out here. You are ready. This is what you've worked for. All your wishes are about to come true, so go get that shit!

"Gina. Time to go!"

I was led to the side of the stage, where I was handed a mic, and a few seconds later, Bill Bellamy announced me, and I walked into my future.

My five-minute set was a blur, but I received a fantastic response from the audience. I'd killed going up first. I was happy with my set and knew that whatever happened, I couldn't have done a better job. I walked back into the green room to applause from my fellow comedians, then I sat back and watched the rest of the show.

Over two and a half hours later, it was time to announce the finalists. Several more cameras entered the green room to capture our reactions as the names were called. I sat with a purposefully neutral look on my face. I was like a swan. Above the water, serene. But underneath, legs flapping like crazy. My heart pumped in my ears, and I had to keep reminding myself not to hold my breath.

My name was the fourth announced. Some of the finalists pumped the air with their fists or shouted when their names were called. I put my face in my hands and thanked the heavens, then stood up to take my place onstage with the other finalists: Amy

Schumer, Matt Kirshen, Dante, Debra DiGiovanni, Jon Reep, Lavell Crawford, Doug Benson, Ralph Harris, and Gerry Dee.

I returned to London to prepare for my final trip back to LA for the next few weeks of filming. I found out a few days later that NBC would be providing us all with two-year work visas. Two. Years. I called one of NBC's lawyers facilitating the visas. "So this visa means I can live and work in the US for two years?" He replied yes. This was amazing. I'd finally made it! I was going to America, invited by a TV station.

Production of the TV show would take five weeks, and I'd be able to stay for an additional two years. I was determined to make the most of this opportunity. I'd bought a house just ten months before, and I had gutted it, taking out walls, rewiring, repainting, and built a new kitchen plus spent a fortune on landscaping. I'd hardly lived there, as I'd been traveling for work as much as I could to pay for all the renovations. I had a reasonably large mortgage on the house, and I decided that dealing with renting it out and managing it while also trying to start a new life abroad would be too stressful. I wanted to concentrate on this new chapter without looking backwards. I still had my first flat in Wood Green, purchased at the beginning of my career, which was rented on a long-term contract, so I'd still be keeping a foothold in the London market. This house could go. Someone was going to appreciate how much work I'd done on it and pay me top dollar. And the profit I made would go towards setting up my living arrangements in LA after the competition. I loved this house, but I loved my American dream much more. I put it on the market three days after returning from the semifinals.

When I announced to all my friends and family that I was moving to America, they thought I was crazy. "You only have a two-year visa!" "You can't live there forever!" The way I saw it, I had two years to work that visa into a green card and then finally into a US citizenship. I was confident I could do it. My plan was to win *Last Comic Standing*, use the $250,000 prize money to buy a lovely apartment in LA, then tour the US, going on to TV stardom.

I threw a big going-away party with my friends and family at the house, then began giving away and selling most of my belongings. My large collection of sneakers were grabbed up enthusiastically by my friends. I sold jewelry and clothes, and I gave bags of stuff away to charity. I left my best friend and unofficial tour manager, Lila, in charge of managing the sale of the house, as it wouldn't be complete by the time I left for LA, so she would be my point person. I would not have been able to do this without her. As a qualified accountant, she was also able to help me manage my finances and keep me afloat as I embarked on this new adventure.

Mum was not happy that I was leaving. All she knew of America was what she had seen on TV and in the movies. I was too old to be adopted into the Cosby family, therefore my only other option was to become a member of a gang in *Boyz n the Hood*. She was worried for my safety. She struggled with the idea that I had no plans to come back to the UK to live. I assured her I'd be visiting frequently, but I was to become the first and probably only child of hers to emigrate. Deep down, she had known this was coming. I had been open about my dreams of leaving England behind. I had never truly belonged here.

On the day I left England for good, Lila drove me to the airport. I had said all my goodbyes to my London friends. Some of them had cried as they waved me off. I shed no tears. I was too excited for this new journey that I'd been waiting to embark on all my life, and I couldn't get on a plane fast enough. England would always be there. It was in my blood.

I had boiled down my entire life into two suitcases. I brought enough outfits for the next few weeks of television. I had my Apple desktop wrapped in towels on one case, and I wore all the jewelry I had left on my body. That was all I needed. The most precious thing I had was my British passport, stamped with the US visa, which was the key to my new future. I hugged Lila tight and walked towards it.

As I boarded the plane to my new destiny, I smiled, recalling the last thing my mum had said to me when I'd gone to wish her farewell. "I always knew you were the crazy one. Just remember you have an elderly mother back here. Take care of yourself, and do not give me a heart attack."

Epilogue

'Ve never read an epilogue in my life. Who wants to read more book after they've read the book?

So I'm just gonna say goodbye, I hope you enjoyed my story. In fact, I hope enough of you enjoyed it so much that there is a demand to hear the next chapter of my story. So much more to tell! If not, it was a fun ride while it lasted. Peace.

Acknowledgments

I suppose this part of the book is where I thank all the people who made this memoir possible. In that case I have to start with my mother. Mum. Mumzie Wumzie, as I call her. This book is an ode to her work ethic, her tenacity, her strength of character, her stubbornness, her refusal to be held back. All things I've learned or inherited from her.

No, I did not enjoy her obsessive overprotectiveness as a child, but I now have a puppy and live in constant fear of her being run over by a car, or being eaten by coyotes, and I am tempted to have her tethered to my hip at all times. So although I don't have kids, I now kind of understand my mother's fear. And as my mumz would say, "Look how you turned out!"

Love you, Mumz. And yes, I know you like me too!

Lila Rowe. My best friend in the world. My confidante. My travel buddy. My unofficial accountant, tour manager, adviser. I really couldn't have done any of this without you holding me down. I can't thank you enough.

Edwin, my younger brother, the anchor of our family, and my other adviser. The person I call when I know I'm messing up, to shout some sense into me.

Jodi Lieberman. My ride-or-die US manager who took me on when no one else was interested, and who pestered American comedy clubs to book me, pretended to be my agent, and basically did all the jobs because you believe in my talent. We made it, Jodi!!

Brett Vincent. My UK manager. Another real one. I love how

you don't take no for an answer and hustle on my behalf. We are quite the team!

Conan Smith. My US agent. I walked into a meeting with you and told you that I probably wouldn't attend 98 percent of the auditions you sent me on, and you understood my brand immediately, when no other agent got it.

Nina Rose, the love of my life. The world we've built together adds a cherry on the cake of life.

Robert Guinsler, my literary agent who commandeered me out of the blue with the offer to write this book. Thank you for dragging me out of my comfort zone.

Tracy Sherrod. Thanks for saying yes and bearing with this first-time author.

Sam Srinivisan, my PR guru. Thanks for dragging people to listen to me talk!

Notes

1. Mawuna Koutonin, "Story of Cities #5: Benin City, the Mighty Medieval Capital Now Lost Without Trace," *The Guardian*, March 18, 2016, https://www.theguardian.com/cities/2016/mar/18/story-of-cities-5-benin-city-edo-nigeria-mighty-medieval-capital-lost-without-trace.

2. Dalya Alberge, "British Museum Is World's Largest Receiver of Stolen Goods, Says QC," *The Guardian*, November 4, 2019, https://www.theguardian.com/world/2019/nov/04/british-museum-is-worlds-largest-receiver-of-stolen-goods-says-qc.

3. Aime Grant Cumberbatch, "Jim Davidson's Discussion of 'Racist' Chalky White Act 'Causes Audience Members to Walk Out' of His Piers Morgan's Life Stories Interview," *Evening Standard*, March 9, 2018, https://www.standard.co.uk/culture/tvfilm/jim-davidson-s-discussion-of-racist-chalky-white-act-causes-audience-members-to-walk-out-of-his-piers-morgan-s-life-stories-interview-a3786331.html.

4. Mark Monahan, "Edinburgh Festival 2014: Jim Davidson—No Further Action, Assembly Rainy Hall, Review: 'Too Little, Too Late,'" *The Telegraph*, August 6, 2014, https://www.telegraph.co.uk/culture/theatre/edinburgh-festival/11016954/Edinburgh-Festival-2014-Jim-Davidson-No-Further-Action-Assembly-Rainy-Hall-review-too-little-too-late.html.